ALL THE SUNDAYS
YET TO COME

ALL THE SUNDAYS
YET TO COME

A SKATER'S JOURNEY

Kathryn Bertine

Little, Brown and Company
Boston   New York   London

First Edition

All the characters depicted in this book are indeed very real people. However, some names have been changed, deliberately misspelled, or artistically embellished to suit my fancy and/or protect people's privacy.

Lyrics from "The Promised Land" by Bruce Springsteen. Copyright © 1978 Bruce Springsteen. All rights reserved. Reprinted by permission.

From The Collected Poems of Langston Hughes by Langston Hughes, copyright © 1994 by The Estate of Langston Hughes. Used by permission of Alfred A. Knopf, a division of Random House, Inc.

Library of Congress Cataloging-in-Publication Data

Bertine, Kathryn.
    All the Sundays yet to come : a skater's journey / by Kathryn Bertine. — 1st ed.
    p. cm.
    ISBN 0-316-09901-5
    1. Bertine, Kathryn, 1975– 2. Skaters — United States — Biography. 3. Women skaters — United States — Biography. 4. Skating — United States. I. Title.

GV850.B47A3 2003
796.91'2'092—dc21
[B]   2003053244

10 9 8 7 6 5 4 3 2

Q-MART

Design by Meryl Sussman Levavi / Digitext

Printed in the United States of America

For Murray's

There's a dark cloud rising from the desert floor
I packed my bags and I'm heading straight into the storm
Gonna be a twister to blow everything down
That ain't got the faith to stand its ground
Blow away the dreams that tear you apart
Blow away the dreams that break your heart
Blow away the lies that leave you nothing but lost and brokenhearted . . .

—Bruce Springsteen, "The Promised Land"

Contents

Preface

No, I cannot do a triple axel. Sorry. Nor have I ever "tried out" for the Olympics. My face will never be on a Wheaties box unless I fall down in the cereal aisle. My talents have not been captured on *ABC's Wide World of Sports,* except for the time I was eating an ice cream cone at the Meadowlands while seated directly behind the New Jersey Devils' manager during his on-camera interview, my fifteen minutes of fame covered in breakaway chocolate sprinkles. But no triple axel. Only two women in the world (Japan's Midori Ito and our very own Tonya Harding) have ever landed that jump in competition,* and if I had been one of them, you would be reading a very different book right now.

And if you are new to the sport of figure skating, permit me to quickly clarify that there are no Olympic tryouts, per se. Instead, a vast series of progressive sectional competitions filters through the thousands of talented athletes. Eventually the best compete in a national championship, from which every four years the top three men, three women, two pairs, and two ice dance teams get to go to the Big O. Of the roughly 250,000

---

*In October 2002 two more women joined the elusive triple axel club: Yukari Nakano of Japan and Ludmilla Nelidina of Russia.

members of the United States Figure Skating Association, fourteen skaters make the twice-a-decade games. I was one of the other 249,986.

The popularity of figure skating has snowballed since that cold winter day in 1994 when Tonya Harding's unruly bench warmers used Nancy Kerrigan's knee for batting practice. Bad for the cartilage but good for the ratings: Pandora's box was opened and skating's dark side was revealed, letting loose a swarm of frenzied media. But before skaters reach the level of knee bashings, French judges, multiple gold medal ceremonies, and media blitz, the sport is surprisingly simple. Practice. Compete. Learn. Grow. Yet there is much to be told and little to be found about the skaters who fall into the great chasm separating beginners and Olympians. What has slipped through the cracks are the stories of those who strive for greatness but, for whatever reason, do not quite make it to the elusive top.

As a figure skater I have fallen on my derriere hundreds of times in front of friends, family, coaches, crowds, judges, no one at all, and the lone, complacent Zamboni driver. Yes, I enjoy wearing spandex, though I am not sure why. Maybe it is because this funny material is what so many of my memories come dressed in. I was a competitive figure skater, a good one. Maybe even a great one, depending on the generosity of your perception or the deterioration of your vision. I was good enough to make it into the highest rank of amateur figure skating: Senior Ladies. I competed vigorously, but not in the competitions that had "World Championships" in their titles or television cameras hovering over the boards. Just regular rectangular rinks and Dad-with-camcorder crowds.

I had the skills to turn professional and skate with two and a half prestigious ice shows all before my twenty-third birthday, yet I did not possess what one might call Olympic-caliber jumping abilities. Actually, my jumping talent was top-notch, it was the landing part that eluded me beyond the triple toe loop.

Yet this book is not a tale of what might have been, but a recollection of what actually was: an account of dedication and commitment to athletics, of achieving a sense of self through sport. My journey through figure skating taught me about setting goals and chasing dreams, as I eventually learned that all aspirations should be one-half iron will and one-half flexible spandex.

For every Tiger Woods, there is a cub of a golfer swinging away, for every Lance Armstrong, a kid whose pink Huffy just had the training wheels taken off. Where will they go? What is their greatness? I am hoping that this book reaches far beyond the topic of figure skating, as I wrote this not only for skaters but also for the broader spectrum of athletes, fans, couch potatoes, go-getters, doubters, dreamers, feasters, fasters, conformists, individualists, and memoir junkies everywhere. But, of course, I have an ulterior motive. Part of this book is for those who remember their own athletic prowess with a mix of nostalgia and the bittersweet nagging of the "if onlys." If only I had practiced harder, started earlier, thought tougher, stayed stronger . . . what could I have been? I hope that remembering the initial love of sport and the thrill of competition will come back to erase such doubts and serve as a reminder of athleticism's true gifts and glory.

Thanks for reading,
Kathryn Bertine

ALL THE SUNDAYS
YET TO COME

Chapter One

·ᴧᴧ·

The Trailer

The skaters called the dressing room "the trailer." That is basically what it was — a long skinny passageway, forty feet in length and only five feet across, something like the dimensions of a supermarket aisle. The trailer was a beast of mobile metal that rolled all around South America with the rest of Hollywood on Ice but always ended up in the same place, stage left of an ice rink's backstage. About as homey as a turn-of-the-century tenement, the trailer was an ill-lit, dingy tunnel that reeked with the unique stench of professional figure skating: a bouquet of overflowery antiperspirant, industrial-strength eco-terrorism hairspray, and the pungent aroma of showgirls who forgot their deodorant.

The Russians in the cast seemed to prefer antiperspirant to deodorant, or at least were unaware that the two could and should be used in combination. Most of the male skaters just didn't care. Some women cared but refused to admit that any tangy redolence came from *their* bodies. Blame fell on the wardrobe. With cheap containers of body perfume purchased from the local *farmacia,* the Russians sprayed not themselves but their show costumes with malodorous scents that could cripple an innocent bystander. By the grace of God, there was one odor we had become immune to: the undocumented birthplace of penicillin, the moldy innards of a well-worn figure skate. There was no smoking in the trailer, but the smell of cigarettes followed their addicts into the dressing room and wafted through the dead-end hallway, lingering for what seemed like forever.

Along the left side of the trailer ran a pipelike bar that was used to hang up the costumes. Everyone had his or her own personal section of the bar, on which we would hook our outfits chronologically according to how they'd be used in the show. The opening costume was first in line: a pink, purple, white, and gold ensemble that attached itself to a sheer, nude bodysuit that covered our womanhood with patches of diamondy sequins. They itched, but on the ice we smiled. In the trailer, we scratched. There was a feather headdress and a long violet sparkling skirt that was shed backstage in a "quick change" as we exited left of the curtain and ran behind the scenes to enter from the right for our next round of prancing. We tossed our sequin skirts to the dressing ladies, who quickly attached an even more revealing "curtain" of feather boas that dangled from a hook in our leotards right above our tailbones. As we swished and swayed with every step, the feathers tickled our thighs and our partially revealed buttocks through the holes of our fishnet stockings. The opening number had mediocre choreography and second-rate skating, but the costumes consumed the audience, and the whistles and catcalls seemed to satisfy management that all was well. Management never came back to the trailer.

The other garb on the rack was just as fantastic. Some costumes were typical skating dresses, all spandex and rhinestones, with little skirts that spun and leapt as our bodies did. The majority of outfits, however, made Hollywood on Ice seem more like Halloween on Ice. Each person in the twenty-two-member cast skated between six and seven numbers per show, and all the wiggling in and out of costumes every few minutes created a constant, schizophrenic pandemonium. With half-naked and half-costumed bodies strutting about at any given time, the trailer looked like the result of a merger between Disney and *Penthouse*.

Sandwiched between the opening costume and the finale bikini, there were a leather outfit for the *Flashdance* routine, a sequined half-tuxedo, half-hotpants getup for the Michael Jackson number, a cavegirl ensemble for the Flintstones section, a dark cloak and a glittery sea-horse costume for the Little Mermaid scene, and a brilliantly colored rag doll outfit for the Barbie skit. Foreign countries are oddly infatuated with both Michael Jackson and Barbie. Our Michael Jackson was a white, middle-aged blond Canadian named Lenny who sported feathered hair, a goatee, and a lower abdominal beer belly that even the loosest spandex could not forgive. The audience didn't seem to mind, and when the techno version of "Bad" came over the loudspeakers, the crowd cried, *"¡Baila, Miguel!"*

Beneath a long wig of white-blond hair, our lead Barbie was a short brunette Russian named Olga. For this number, the rest of the cast was divided into rag dolls and Barbie dolls. The rag dolls were supposedly sad because they were ugly. Wanting to be like the pretty and popular Barbie skaters, the frumpy dollies made a wish to the all-powerful fairy godmother rag doll and — voila! — instantly transformed into beautiful Barbies thanks to the magic of Velcro. The skit sent a debatable message of self-esteem to the young girls in the audience: if you pray hard enough and pull your clothes off at the right time, you too can have anything you desire.

I was one of the aesthetically challenged rag dolls, complete with wayward neon-green hair. When my yarn wig was not in use, it perched on top of the costume bar on a Styrofoam head so it would keep its glamorous pouf. The Styrofoam heads were perhaps the most interesting part of the trailer, at least in the beginning. The de*corp*itated Styrofoam silently stared down at us with a variety of inventive expressions. Bored skaters passed the time between shows by drawing on the heads. Some had wicked eyes, crossed eyes, eyebrows raised in shock or slanted in deceit, penciled-on jewelry or Magic Markered boogers. The showgirls drew lips that were full and colorful. Some puckered, some smiled, most frowned. The heads in the men's trailer sported wide, open, circular mouths and satisfied expressions. My hat perch was named Rick; it said so on the base of his neck, where he had been tattooed with a wide-tip black Sharpie. Rick had stunning eyelashes and seemed friendly enough but mostly kept to himself. A few people had turned the soft, vulnerable Styro-skulls into voodoo dolls, with straight pins and stitching needles impaling numerous orifices and perhaps the name of a former lover written in jagged lettering on the smooth expanse of white forehead or the crumbly stump of the neck. Estrella and Pegi, the women who worked at the seamstress table, would come in the trailer from time to time and ease the torment of the pin-poked heads, collecting the voodoo devices when sewing supplies were low.

Beneath the costumes ran a bench that housed individual drawers. These were for our skates and other personal items. Things left outside the drawers were either stolen or confiscated, and a fine was assessed to the skaters at fault for not picking up after themselves. Fines began at twenty-five dollars for a first offense, and the threat of them lurked everywhere. The most popular crimes a skater was convicted of were visible tan lines, sloppy makeup technique, leaving our trailer drawers open and trip-overable, and of course weight gain, whereby the fines increased if we did. The drawer at the far end of the trailer contained *la balanza,* which was pulled out every week for us to stand on and for management to assess who needed a "heavy" fine.

My drawer was filled with the usual clutter: extra skate laces, hair products, contact lens solution, a few old magazines in foreign languages, a Spanish dictionary, Walkman, books, gum, laxatives.[*] I kept stationery, too, and wrote letters home, enclosing South American postcards and photos. Russians borrowed envelopes from me but not writing paper. They addressed the front with the foreign characters of the Russian alphabet, wrote no return address, slipped in one hundred pesos, and sealed the envelope, pressing the adhesive edges until their fingers whitened.

The little children whose parents worked for the show would sometimes sneak into the trailer and stand on the row of drawers, hide behind our costumes, and jump out at us. Some of the skaters would get angry, but most pretended to be frightened, though we could see little knees poking through our feather boas and could hear giggles before we even entered the trailer. "*¡Ay, Dios mío! ¡Tengo miedo!*" we would cry, crossing our hands over our hearts, fainting with false fear into our rickety seats. Little Cathi would shriek with laughter, and her six-year-old cousin Stefanie would check my pulse, and proudly declare, "*Muerte. Muerte.*"

---

[*]For those of you with current eating disorders or the heartbreaking desire to start one up, I know what you're up to. I did the same thing, looking through books for tips on starvation. Beyond the basics you probably already know, you won't find any of my own personal tricks here. But if you choose to keep reading, I hope you'll find the little nubbin of digestible hope that I tried to hide somewhere in these pages.

*   *   *

There was a lot of nakedness in the trailer. Quick changes from costume to costume required hurried fingers to snap this and buckle that, while breasts and buttocks flew like wild animals released from confinement, bouncing around in bewilderment before they were caught and shoved back into sequined captivity. Boobs, butt cheeks, and bareness were the norm. No one cared, no one looked. Well, most people didn't. Modesty was abandoned at the flimsy brown curtain door where the stagehands dawdled to catch glimpses of the female silhouettes inside. I grew used to this fast, though in my tomboy youth it had been an insufferable ordeal if the subtle outline of my training bra announced its subterranean presence, giving gender to my otherwise unisex T-shirts. In Hollywood on Ice, half of the outfits *were* training bras.

We had even become accustomed to Pedro, the one male skater assigned to our dressing room. He sat at the end of the trailer and respectfully turned his back during our quick changes. Usually. He was not gay, as the majority of male show skaters are, and perhaps the reason he had no interest in the nakedness of our trailer was that he had slept with more than half the women in the cast. He had seen their tits and asses enough times that it was hardly a thrill in the dressing room. Neither Pedro nor I fit each other's criteria for sexual attraction. I was not often magnetized to men below my height, five-nine, and Pedro had a thing for petite Russian ladies, so that was that and fine by both of us. Yet it seemed odd to think of him as an object of desire for the fair-skinned, bottle-blond, cosmetically obsessed Russian skaters. He was a dark-skinned Chilean, about five-five, with teeth that mamboed around his mouth in various directions, a thick mound of black hair that looked wet but wasn't, and one crossed eye that appeared to want nothing more passionately than to be in the other socket.

We spent the majority of our time in the trailer on the nights that we had a performance, and we performed every night. Most nights we had two shows, and on the weekends we had three. The first curtain went up at seven-thirty and the ten o'clock show immediately followed. Having spent most of my life as an "early bird," it took my body quite some time to adapt to the night-owl culture of South America. Ten o'clock is when most Argentines eat dinner and begin their evening. To earn every penny of our $300 weekly salary, we had to be present for all sixteen shows. Arriving at the trailer at 6:30 P.M. and finally departing for the hotel at 1:30 in the morning, this worked out to about fifty-two hours of trailer time each week. When we actually had a moment to ourselves, there was always something going on in one of the two dressing rooms. The show itself was conducted and rehearsed in Spanish, and despite the language barriers, we came to understand one another's personalities quite easily through the cramped lifestyle of the tour and the endless hours. Rumors about who was sleeping with whom circulated in multilingual whispers, usually Spanish or Russian, and all one had to do was listen for the names. Blahblahblah Pedro Blahblahblah Bella . . . *y Olga también! Nyet?! ¡Sí!* I learned three Russian words on tour: *nyet, dosvidanya,* and *hooliganka.* Oddly enough, *no, hello,* and *you hooligan* seemed to suffice in answering just about anything the Russians asked me during my entire time with Hollywood on Ice.

Some skaters played cards or wrote letters home between shows. Others did sit-ups. Most smoked. I read—perhaps more than I had in college (where English had been my major). Hunting down bookstores in cities such as Mar del Plata or Santiago was simple, the classics racks were full of English translations. Nabokov, Lawrence, Stoker, Wells, Dickens, classic poetry, modern fiction, and the most indispensable reference, my Spanish verb dictionary, composed my traveling library. Felicia, my British roommate, brought a camera to the trailer and snuck a photo one night as I sat cross-legged on the folding chair, reading *Wuthering Heights.* I look studious. Serious, yet relaxed. There is a scholarly element about my posture. There is also a spiky-haired wig on my head. On my body, a skimpy, leather, punk rock outfit complete with metal studs and choker necklace. Suggestive fishnet stockings confine my neatly crossed legs and black thigh-high spandex boot covers. My face is painted to match my hoodlum demeanor; a rebellious eighties party girl in the *Flashdance* skating scene. My facial expression, however, is one you would observe on a graduate student immersed in her research. Around me the photograph reveals numerous half-naked women caught mid–quick change, as I sit and wait patiently for the musical cue that begins my upcoming number.

Most of the skaters were friendly with one another, which was a good thing because of the cramped quarters of the dressing room. No one was extremely fond of Pam, or more accurately, her role as the line captain. Pam was responsible for assessing fines and scheduling long, tedious rehearsals. In a variation of Snow White and the Seven Dwarfs, our trailer was a happy home to Ice Bitch and the Eleven Waifs. From the first little chair to the last, there was Pedro (Dopey), Jody (Happy), Felicia (Friendly), me (Sneezy, for I sat next to a Russian with a hairspray fetish), Bella (Aqua-Nety), Olga #4 (Chain-Smokey), Yulia (Purgey), Olga #1 (Just Plain Snotty), Ice Bitch, Krystal (Bipolary), Donna (Prim and Properly), and Sunny (Adultery). The trailer was also a classroom of sorts. We learned valuable lessons on the principles of ignoring and the art of nonconfrontation: Yield to the one with skates on. Emotions ran high, but I preferred that to the days when there were no emotions running at all, and everyone in the trailer silently wondered what the hell we were doing there in the first place.

Along the right side of the dressing room sat twelve flimsy folding chairs that faced the wall, where twelve cheap squares of mirrored glass were bolted beneath a row of finicky lightbulbs. Someone was always complaining because one or more of her flickering orbs was stolen while she was out on the ice performing a number. The shoddy, bargain-priced spheres burned out frequently, and the stage manager always had better things to do than replace them. Every burnout sparked a rash of thieving rearrangement, and the skater-vandal who thought she was being sly always looked suspicious when her mirror had six round illuminations and her neighbor was completely wattless. My chair was fourth from the door of the trailer, an easy-access pilfering location. The light-abducting Grinches never stole all the bulbs surrounding my mirror. It was never *that* dark. Just shadowed. Gloomy. Mood lighting, someone observed.

Before our mirrors, each of us had about a foot and a half of narrow shelf space where we set up our stage makeup. War paint was perhaps the more appropriate terminology. Thick tubes of tan concealer, face powder with the consistency of whole-wheat baking flour, red lipstick more effulgent than strawberry Kool-Aid, cheek blush the color of pure embarrassment, and eye-shadow palettes that illuminated our lids brighter than Vegas on a Saturday night were scattered beneath our mirrors like shiny plastic ammunition shells. Curled up in plastic cases, false eyelashes slept, awaiting application. It is not a natural feeling to have something the size of a prehistoric caterpillar glued to the delicate rim of a human eyelid. Out on the ice and under the brash lights, the giant lashes made our eyes look large and sensuous. Up close in the trailer under the whimpering lightbulbs, our eyes looked freakish and extraterrestrial.

At first, it took a while to get the hang of smearing on the war paint correctly, but after a few weeks of practice, my face went from tomboy to porn star in under sixty seconds flat. Some of the showgirls, however, arrived at the trailer an hour before curtain call to begin their beautification process, which was no more harried than the creation of the Sistine Chapel ceiling. They painted themselves with such accuracy and concentration that it was often sad to realize that no one in the audience would be able to see the intricate details of their labored artwork.

At the end of the show I chiseled off my makeup even more quickly than it was applied, first peeling off the mammoth lashes and tossing them back in their petri dish. Each night our mirrors offered us a before-and-after reflection of ourselves, whether we wanted to look or not. Plain girl . . . *Showgirl!* As time passed, I began to understand why some of the women never took their makeup off at all. It was easier to be one person than two.

Small reflections of personal sentiments were hung on our mirrors, mementos from our past presequined life that we taped in the corners or drew onto the glass with glitter pens and permanent markers. Some skaters stuck stickers that spelled out their names in bubbly letters or in clowns bent into alphabetical contortion. We spelled only our first names. No one knew anyone's last name, except some of the Olgas.

Olga was not one skater, but four. Half of the cast seemed to be named Olga, like Dr. Seuss's classic story of a woman who had twenty-four sons named Dave. The lengthy Russian surnames of the Olgas were eventually replaced with numbers: Olga #1, Olga #2 . . . A problem arose when the Olgas forgot their own numbers, and each claimed with Russian persnicketiness to be Olga #1, in which case we simply referred to them in the collective plural: the Olgai. The Olgas differed from one another—slightly. One was a rather nasty creature of mean disposition and dirty sexual habits; the second was a cold, miserable young woman who came to the trailer each night with a plethora of purpling bruises, courtesy of her boyfriend/fellow skater, Grígor; the third was a nice woman who had unnerving Silly Puttyesque flexibility; the final Olga, who got to be the pretty Barbie on the ice, was about as interesting as damp lint when removed from the Barbie costume trailer.

One Olga had Russian rock stars taped to her mirror. Donna adorned hers with Disney stickers and a faded Canadian flag. Yulia and Olga #4 had cut out stretching exercises from the fitness page of an Argentinean *Mademoiselle*. Sometimes Krystal had a wrinkled and creased photo of a boy in the corner of her mirror, sometimes not. One thing she never took down was a motivational quote, stuck to the upper-right-hand corner. *I AM NOT HUNGRY!!!* it lied, handwritten in voluptuous capitals.

On my mirror, I kept a picture of my college rowing team. The men liked to ask questions about the sleek yellow racing boat. The language barriers called for interesting analogies. How heavy? Like fifty pairs of skates, Nikolai. How long? Like trailer.

The women looked at the photograph more closely and took turns guessing which rower I was. There are nine of us in the boat, forever frozen in mid-race posture during a small regatta on Lake Moraine, three miles outside the campus of Colgate University. We had just passed our rival school, their bow barely noticeable in the right-hand corner of the frame. Our expressions are of pure determination, our muscles flexed in rigid lines of exertion. It is mid-April in upstate New York, a week before we would win the state title. There is snow falling in the picture. We are wearing tank tops.

"You?" an Olga asked, pointing to the woman in the five seat of the eight-oared shell. Five seat was part of the engine room of the boat, where the four most powerful women were assigned.

"Yes."

"Strong!" she said, then looked from the picture to my body sitting there on the trailer's folding chair. "Were strong."

"I was," I agreed, frustrated by the verb tense I had to choose.

Hollywood on Ice was not quite what I had envisioned as a little girl, dreaming of one day becoming a famous figure skater. I used to wave at the skaters in the Ice Capades, hoping only that they might wave back, not knowing that the future would bring a successful audition with the company. But in 1997 the Ice Capades changed ownership and closed suddenly, calling off my starting season, and with it a feature role. After a brief stint with Holiday on Ice's European Christmas tour that fall, I auditioned for Hollywood on Ice and a few months later found myself in South America, in the trailer. A professional figure skater by definition, a professional booty shaker in reality. Some skaters had been with Hollywood on Ice for years, and Lenny, the Michael Jackson impersonator, had kept his spot in the show for nearly two decades. Every skater had his story, and every one had his moments of meltdown. In some cases, hours. We learned to console or to turn the other cheek. All four of them, when necessary.

When a skater's yearlong contract with Hollywood on Ice was up, he either renewed it or cleaned out his spot in the trailer. Every once in a while, someone would "disappear" overnight, either fired, escaped, or pregnant, and the vacancy in the dressing room was quickly filled with a new skater, usually Russian because they were cheaper to hire, their visas less expensive. They picked at the sticker-lettered name that their predecessor had left on the mirror. No one left addresses or phone numbers, no one said, "See you next season." For most skaters, one season was enough.

Sometimes I wonder where the trailer is now and who is in my seat, fourth from the door. Does she have enough lightbulbs? What does she have clipped to her mirror? Is she hungry? How long has she been there, how long will she last, and does she ever wonder who was there before her? Is she the rag doll or the pretty Barbie? In a small enclosure, forty feet long and five feet across, there is little room for such thoughts. Only now, years removed from the trailer, can I begin to describe the world I saw cooped up inside that oblong box.

꙳

Chapter Two

Life Within the Electric Pet Fence

Twenty minutes north of New York City, the village of Bronxville sits among a handful of other little suburbs that knit together Westchester County, home to an abundance of BMW station wagons, pedigree golden retrievers, and purebred debutante socialites. I was born into a single-parent, only-child, family—except for the detail of my married parents and older brother. My family never really enjoyed that joke. Oh well. My father and I would form an unshakable bond through sports early on, Pete (my older brother) would dart in and out of my childhood, and my mother and I would fare well for the first nine or so years of our familial attachment.

On a spring Sunday morning in 1975, I slithered into the world by way of the maternity wing in Bronxville's Lawrence Hospital, just down the hall from where my father had been born thirty-nine years before. The date was clad in irony, as I was born on Mother's Day. Despite the calendar's promise of a close mother-daughter bond, time would fashion our personalities into polar opposites. I found happiness and inner ful-fillment in athletics and physical activity. My mother sought a higher truth in silk upholstery and color-coordinated dust ruffles. We were, to say the least, different.

Mom was a financially successful interior decorator who possessed a strong passion (which often crossed the boundaries of reality) for all things aesthetic. She fit snugly in to the eccentric role of an image-oriented, upper-middle-class dysfunctional-family-denying suburban wife and mother who greatly enjoyed her days within the perplexing microcosm of Bronxville. A figure-skating daughter fit perfectly within her definitions of glamour and image, and she sought credit whenever possible. I could never figure out if I was supposed to give it to her. On rare occasions, I received compliments from strangers on my skating-sculpted legs, and my mother enjoyed responding, "Thank you, she gets those from me. Those are my legs. Mine." If I tried to regain credit, it started an "I know you are but what am I?" banter that went in silly circles, leaving me half laughing and half in a temper tantrum.

"But, Mom, *I'm* the skater! They're *my* legs."

"But, dear, those are *my* genes."

Mom fell just on the far end of the quirky spectrum. A daughter talented enough to turn professional and join a prestigious ice show made her proud and happy, but more from the icon standpoint than from the hardworking, goal-accomplishing perspective. Sparkly diamonds, pink dresses — good! Strong muscles, sweaty armpits — bad! She kept inventory of my trophies and medals and enjoyed embellishing the stories of how I had obtained them. I once skated in two different competitions over one weekend. In one, I finished a very rewarding sixth place out of twenty or so of the best skaters in the Northeast. In the other, a rather participant-anemic meet, I came in first against myself. Later that day, I listened as my mother called the local paper to tell them all about my newest gold medal. At least my mother (and her genes) never took credit for the hardware. I always got to keep my medals. Mine.

"Oh, honey, she's just proud of you," other parents assured me, smiling, as I tried to hush my mother's impromptu recital of my private accomplishments, wailing loud pleas of *"Mooooooooooom"* until I was all voweled out. But her motherly pride was a tad off-kilter. It was a little tricky for me to figure out as a kid, but something in her tone and words went a little bit beyond the living-vicariously-through-your-child thing.

Although my skating fetish made a good conversation piece among her garden clubs and PTA meetings, my abilities were too often exaggerated to a level just beyond my actual talent. I tried to correct "the facts" whenever possible.

No, Mrs. Baldwin, I didn't land a triple axel . . . I tripped on an axel.

No, Mrs. Sweeney, the medal I won last week was actually plastic, not gold.

Yes, Mr. UPS Man, I am going to the Olympics. As a spectator.

My mother carried a plethora of glamorous, posed skating photos in her Louis Vuitton pocketbook and whipped them out before one of her clients or friends had a chance to finish the question "How is Ka—?" Not necessarily an atypical action for parents with young children, but when your child is twenty-five years old, it's a little too eager. Especially the near-deathly embarrassing showgirl snapshot from Hollywood on Ice, which I've removed from her wallet and cut up upon every visit home. The damn thing comes back like a bad spirit as I find myself perennially revived from the negative she secretly had made and keeps hidden in some undisclosed location.

From milkman to mayor, no Bronxvillian escaped the exposés of my personal accomplishments, broadcast live from the studios of WMOM. But this overload of verbal publicity was not the source of my true discomfort. What ate away at me was that my mother did not seem to understand the difference between what I did and who I was. Sure, she could rattle off lists of awards I had won, grades I had earned, or genes I possessed, but she never knew that my favorite color was light blue or that I thought Shel Silverstein was the coolest person ever or that at eight, I had a huge crush on the boy who lived next door and that I cried when he went off to prep school. She knew only the outer layer of my still-forming self, as if my shell of "little daughter" didn't seem to have a "little person" tucked inside.

As a child, I was vaguely aware of what my mother's occupation was all about, and her career was fascinating to me then. She was in charge of deciding how the inside of other people's houses should look. She said buy this and that and put it here and there, and people paid her for the arrangements she came up with. I remember trips to musty antique shops and enormous fabric warehouses brimming with bolts of material in every color, shape, and texture that the universe had to offer. I took phone messages for cuttings for approval, gave our address for fabric swatch deliveries, and was on a first-name basis with "FrankFromRegency," the upholsterer who called almost daily, talked fast, and requested to speak to Diane instead of asking if my mommy was home. He even entrusted me with long messages: I wrote with bold strokes that love seats were ready for pickup but that ottomans were on back order, due in three weeks.

Sometimes my mother took me antiquing with her. My job, as a little person with small limbs, was to sit in the rear of the station wagon and hold on to the massive structures from yesteryear that stuck out far beyond the capacity of the Buick Skylark. I was not a fan of antique shopping, never quite understanding why I wasn't allowed to sit in dilapidated chairs that looked as though everyone else had lounged in them, or touch books that a million other people had clearly been allowed to read, but I loved going along for pickups and deliveries. The trip from our home to the On Consignment antique store my mother frequented in Bronxville was no more than three minutes by car, but to a young furniture roper like myself, getting these stiff, four-legged mahogany beasts back safely to our garage was an ongoing adventure I took great pride in. An ancient cabinet jutting out the rear of a sagging white station wagon with ropes holding down one end while my hands grasped the other and my feet stuck out the window was the closest thing Bronxville ever saw to a rodeo. The flexibility I exercised to sedate the untamed furniture might have been an early sign that figure skating was right up my alley.

My father does not share my mother's passion for decorating to the same degree. If left alone to redesign the living room, my dad would replace the sofa with his rowing machine, flick the decorative brass trinkets off the antique bookshelf and fill it with historical nonfiction hardcovers, and then tack a few deer heads above the mantel in place of the pastoral watercolor. Just over six feet tall with graying brown hair that's hanging in there as best it can, the sinewy legs and shoulders of an athletic rower, and a kind face that looks at least ten years younger than his sixty-five, my father is a laid-back and easygoing person, bordering on shy at times, yet very firm in his beliefs and values. From his post-college navy days through his thirty-five-year law career, my father has been a man of principle. Hard work, he thinks, will open just about any door. *South Park,* he thinks, is one of the most entertaining television creations of all time.

My mother, who is long and lean with perennially tan skin, bright hair, and an always-painted face that also appears more youthful than its sixty years, is an intense lady. No one in my family has yet been able to pinpoint why or what she is so intense about, but nonetheless, she constantly exudes a strong passion for propriety at all times. A mix of the buttery afterglow of lightning and the striking eye-catching pallor of white neon, my mother's hair is a colorless blond with hints of a former yellow tucked into its past. What clues there are of the golden brown of her natural tresses have been left only in photographs from decades before I was born. Held in place by the chemical bonds of Miss Breck's hairspray, there is no movement to my mother's uniquely bouffant hair at any time. I have seen her exactly twice in my life with wet hair, each vision astonishing and beautiful. Her hair looked wonderful in its natural state, moving freely with the suggestion of curls taking shape as it dried in the sun. As for the rest of her look, she owns not one pair of blue jeans and would never consider wearing a shirt that went on overhead. Appearance, she believes, will open just about any door.

My parents' marriage seems an odd union to me, falling under the category of opposites attract or perhaps opposites ignore and accept each other, then silently wonder if they made the right choice. Their relationship always reminded me of twin-stick Popsicles, a forced conglomeration that seems like a good idea but looks a lot more natural when separated individually. Politically, my mother is the self-proclaimed Democrat who gives the glaring once-over to anyone on the streets of Bronxville who doesn't look as if he belongs there. My father is the staunch Republican who, upon seeing the minuscule tattoo on my foot, looked long and hard at the permanent ink and finally said, "Maybe I'll get one, too." Peter and I grew up as Republibrats and always went with the Perots and Naders just to disassociate from our parents every four years. I turned out to be a lean, flat-brown-haired, unmade-up, emotionally intense, outwardly laid-back, multiple-jeans-owning, hardworking generation Xer whom older people constantly ask, "And when do you graduate from high school, dear?"

Eleven years would pass before skating became the focus of my energies, and there are hundreds of photographs from my competition days in which podiums, ice rink lobbies, and snowy parking lots capture the background of my preteen days. Oddly enough, there are no baby pictures of me until the toddler years, thus creating plenty of opportunity for my older brother to deny my natural arrival into the Bertine family. Peter's stories of my true existence during those years of unphotographed babyhood include alien breeding, abandonment by a she-yeti in upstate New York, and my personal favorite, highly engineered robotics, whereby "if you press the freckle on your chin, you will deprogram and spontaneously combust. Give it a try!"

With almost seven years separating us, Pete and I each led only-child lives and rarely interacted for the first decade of my life. My brother was Santa Claus, the Easter bunny, the tooth fairy—something I believed in but rarely got to see in person, an entity of fascination whose constant absence made him all the more mystical and intriguing. Pete went off to numerous boarding schools and sampled a handful of colleges along the East Coast before settling on NYU, leaving me to figure out the perplexities of Bronxville and adolescence for myself.

My early childhood in Bronxville was a pretty darn pleasant decade. If I wanted a toy, someone bought it for me. I was driven to school in the silver BMW each morning, though the building was less than two hundred yards from my house. I charged books to my parents' account at Womrath's bookstore on a near-daily basis. "Spoiled" was not a concept I understood at the time; books and toys were things that I *needed*. Mom was busy, Dad was busy, Pete was busy. Books and toys were my busyness, and no one seemed to mind. I assumed all kids lived this way, going about their busy little lives, given whatever it was they believed they needed. New toys and personal attention felt like one and the same, and neither my parents nor I fully understood that what I liked better and remember more clearly than all the toys and books themselves was having my parents take me to the stores. There, I would seek out the longest checkout line to stand in, to make the experience last as long as possible.

Elementary school was a blur of self-discovery, in which two memories stand out above all others. In kindergarten my teacher, Mrs. Michael, put a little cutout photo of each student next to three blank lines, where we were supposed to inscribe what we wanted to be when we grew up. *I want to be a fix-it woman,* I wrote. Inspired by the fact that my bike chain had fallen off that day and I had figured out how to put it back on all by myself, I felt as though I had unlocked every secret of the universe. I didn't know what a fix-it woman was or what she did exactly, but I knew that I just had to be one. Complicated dirt bikes made all future problems seem easy to repair, and being a fix-it woman would keep me busy, busy, busy.

In the third grade I temporarily abandoned my fix-it dreams to raise a family. At the age of eight I became a mother for the ninth time. In 1983 the Cabbage Patch Kid craze hit the nation and while people waited on lists for months to "adopt" one of the smushy-body, hard-faced weirdo dolls, I signed up for as many as I could possibly get at every toy store in Westchester County. I built them an empire in my closet, with beds and clothes and plastic food, and played with my kids for years, long after the other girls my age got tired of them and the toy store shelves ran overstocked with the remnants of a passing fad. I did not tell anyone that I pretended the dolls were my true family or that my favorite made-up game was the Have-a-Chat circle, in which I sat them down on their square little butts and put plastic hamburgers in their lumpy laps, and we all told one another what we had done that day. Lonely for human, familial company but unsure of how to ask my parents for it, I found substitutes in Eddie, Jeffy, Gabby, Audrey, Kimmy, Maggie, Carrie, Sniffy, and Frizzy. When Hollywood on Ice cast me as a peculiar-looking misfit rag doll, I felt I had a solid understanding of how to portray the character. *Smile, wave, look thrilled to be a rag doll, and think about how much Icy Hot to smear in Barbie's bra later.*

Growing up in Bronxville was like being surrounded by an electric pet fence that emitted a low-frequency culture shock when you left its borders — it didn't hurt really, just left one a little stunned for a while, a little wary of where the doggy door to reality actually led. The Bronxville school system, where I spent kindergarten to twelfth grade, is one of the best in the nation, but like the town, it is about as diverse as a bag of flour. Seeing the same people day in and day out for eighteen years was strangely confusing, a sort of social incest that one could neither acknowledge nor deny, and escape was rare indeed. We didn't play dueling banjos porchside with one another, but the music that poured out from the CD players in our Beamers and Benzes all sounded relatively similar. My class had seventy-four students, roughly half of whom were female, and every other one named Katie, Kate, Kathryn, or another Ka-rivative. If I shared anything in common with the Olga contingency in the Hollywood on Ice trailer, it was the understanding of a need for distinction, even if only in name. At home I was Katie to my mother, Kay to my father, and Youlittleshit to Peter, which actually managed to sound endearing every now and then. But I hungered for all seven original letters of my name.

"We named you Kathryn on your birth certificate with the intention of calling you Katie," my mother not quite explained to me during one of my unheeded requests to go by Kathryn.

"Then can you change my real name to Katie and start calling me Kathryn?"

"Don't be ridiculous. Katie." Evidently I was very good at being ridiculous. Bronxville is not a place for ridiculousness.

Although my classmates and I grew up, no one was truly able to grow out in Bronxville. The boys who threw sand in kindergarten could never quite abandon their troublemaker reputations, and the kids who ate paste were just plain doomed unless they broke free and went to prep school somewhere in New England, daring to come back only if they had become inarguably hot in their later teenage years. The girls with pretty blond hair who took reservations for seating companions at lunchtime in elementary school had it made through high school, with senior prom dates lined up by the start of seventh grade.

At Bronxville High, I drifted somewhere between the categories, a social floater. I liked the kids with the wild reputations just as much as the kids who studied all weekend. I liked to read, but I wasn't a certifiable nerd. I had crushes on plenty of boys but was too petrified to show any feelings. I was good at sports, but no one really paid attention. I had no distinctive style that set me apart from anyone else; my clothes came from the Gap and J. Crew, and so did most everyone else's. For every ounce of coolness I tried to exude, even if it was just saying "hey" to an upperclassman, there was a dorky, weird, gangly, self-conscious, funny-lookin' loner at the gate of my brain who never failed to comment, *Dude . . . you're hopeless. You're the only one, too. Everyone else is com-*

pletely normal, super popular, really pretty, and they all laugh at you when you're not looking, so just take a seat there in your tapered jeans and Benetton sweater that the girl sitting next to you is also wearing even though she wore it last week and you thought you were safe till at least next Friday and be sure to look utterly bored in class and for God's sake, woman, don't you ever tell anyone that you actually like playing in the school band. Hopeless.

Bronxville was a tough place to be an individual; the teachers praised it, the local papers ran stories on personal successes and achievements, and the majority of parents gave their accolades, but peer support was almost nonexistent. When I did well at a competition and got my name in the paper, instead of getting proverbial pats on the back, it was not uncommon at lunchtime for me to find my manual transmission Jeep Wrangler broken into and wheeled out into the middle of the street, a $50 parking ticket under the windshield. When I started a club called Varsity Athletes Against Substance Abuse (three members total) to dissuade elementary-school skids from getting into drugs, my name was listed at least six times in the Personal Pet Peeves section of the yearbook. When I became captain of the cross-country team senior year and ordered a blue-and-gray leather varsity jacket, I found threats of having it slashed and burned written on loose-leaf and shoved in my pockets, the perpetrators angry that I, a girl, had dared to wear a "boy's" jacket. So much for school spirit.

What fueled many kids at Bronxville High wasn't always the desire to succeed or the love for a specific talent, but rather a fear of failure and a hunger to be distinguished from the norm in some way. From the ballerina who brought Slim-Fast shakes for lunch in sixth grade to the binge-drinking freshman headed to rehab before junior year, our private poverties each stemmed from the basic longing for personal attention. From hell-raiser to bookworm, all any of us kids in Bronxville really wanted was permission to be ourselves, a desire we kept hidden in the secret pockets of our matching L. L. Bean book bags.

Aesthetically there is no village quite as beautiful as Bronxville, with its million-dollar estates, Miracle-Gro gardens, and dainty shops that locals describe with that wonderfully snooty word, *quaint*. Yet there is an unspoken hollow beneath the wealthy exterior, a sadness for those who look close enough to see it, an emptiness in the heart of Bronxville's plenitude. From the outside, the town seems to provide any physical luxury its inhabitants could possibly want, but in all measures of emotion, I have never known a place with so many kids in need. Bronxville was a town where parents felt their children were safe and sheltered, where everyone was happy, and where other people's children were the ones with problems or difficulties, certainly not their own. The mentality among too many parents was that Bronxville's spotless image would act as the Great Nanny, keeping watch over their children. In reality, Bronxville was a place where all too often children had to raise themselves no matter how many parents were in the picture.

Later on, in college, I talked about Bronxville with Gary Ross, Colgate University's dean of admissions. As we spoke of the good, the bad, and the bizarre qualities of surviving the Westchester experience, Gary summed it all up by saying, "Bronxville is a tough place to grow up," thus marking the first and only time I have heard this sentence uttered without sarcasm. As I waited for the angelic backlighting and the halo to appear over Gary's head while he spoke without moving his lips, *I understand your pain, child. . . . Colgate is here to take it all away,* I finally realized that the location of my upbringing did not have to define who I was, though it took some time to get used to the idea. Like the trailer of Hollywood on Ice, Bronxville has a profound lingering effect on the psyche, but in most cases the scars aren't permanent. It's more like a mental paper cut, which can heal quickly when not constantly pried open to see if it is healing quickly.

Yet as my popularity began diminishing in high school, my skating started flourishing and my time at the rink erased most of the social hardships I'd endured in Bronxville. My goal of seeing the world, of stepping away from the only one I knew, seemed to have an indirect effect on my athletic dreams. Figure skating was my escape, the physical and psychological place I could go when I needed the embrace of acceptance and the comfort of something larger. In my case, an entire universe of acceptance came in the form of an empty sheet of ice that lay only a few miles away from the single-square-mile suburb of my childhood.

The one thing Bronxville did not have was a skating rink. That be-longed to Yonkers, the nemesis neighbor to B'ville ever since the day that sections of the towns began to share a zip code and caused certain prop-erty values in Bronxville to decrease. Peepul in Yahnkas tawked like dis, ya know, whereas the inhabitants of Braaawhnxville conversed like so, do we have a mutual understanding? I loved Yonkers. The name was fun to say, and it looked like a word that should be squiggled above the head of some flabbergasted cartoon character. *Yonk*-ers! *Yonk*-ers! That was enough for me.

I learned to skate before my memory understood that it should hang on to such valuable details. Supposedly I was four, and took to the ice like a human pendulum between my parents' legs until my own limbs figured out what to do on the slick surface of solid water. That happened rather quickly, though there was no *a-ah!* moment of greatness that any-one could see, no inkling that figure skating and its glittery facade would become a passion for the wobbly little beanpole with concave ankles and a strong disdain for feminine clothing. Skating was not something my diminutive mind considered a sport, it was just something to do, some-where to go, a form of entertainment second to watching Saturday morn-ing *Smurfs* or venturing to the local Baskin-Robbins for a mint chocolate chip clown cone.

What I remember most from those years of skating in the late sev-enties and early eighties are Monday afternoons when the Bronxville Elementary School reserved ice time at Murray's Skating Center in Yonkers, five miles away by car. For six years, I zoomed around the frozen oval, wearing Wrangler jeans and wool sweaters from the boys' department at Fierson's (Bronxville's only worthy clothing store among its numerous boutiques of dainty feminine elderly wear), watching the robot graphics on my Freezie Freakie gloves emerge when the tempera-ture dropped below fifty degrees. More interested in playing tag and crack-the-whip than attempting anything artistic, I jumped over cones, zigzagged between the indifferent teenage rink attendants, and stole the hats off fellow skaters' heads. In the lobby, we all drank hot chocolate, dipped into our Lik-a-Stik candy, gnawed on a freezer-burned Chipwich, or ordered ancient tile-shaped squares of frozen pizza, hoping not to irritate the old woman behind the counter, who gave us the evil eye if we decided we wanted a giant pretzel covered in an avalanche of salt boulders instead of the crusty pizza irreversibly rumbling through the roller grill. We ate, we spilled, we laughed, and then it was back to the ice for more practice at childhood. I lived for Mondays.

Sometime in the fifth grade, a few friends decided to take a group skating lesson during one of the routine Monday sessions. Reluctantly, I joined them, preparing to be utterly bored. I was, at first. The gentle forward and backward glides seemed easy compared with speedily chasing down the rink attendants. Swizzles and three turns came naturally, and the bunny hops and two-foot spins felt as though I had already learned them a long time ago, somewhere else, a place or time I couldn't remember. Not a past life per se, just a past Monday.

The instructor soon recommended I try private lessons. Ooooh. Private . . . that meant personal attention! That meant being the center of someone else's busyness. Pete went to private school, Mom and Dad had private discussions about lots of things, and now I could have my own private lessons, all revolving around me me me. Yeehaw! Sign me up! Oh, wait, just one thing I have to know right now. . . . *Do I have to wear those dumb skirt things?* I asked the teacher in my most serious voice. The woman smiled and said no. *Promise?* Yes. *Okay then . . . but no skirt, ever.* Dresses were absolutely out of the question.

As soon as I became aware of the concept of clothing somewhere around age three, dresses became the object of my disgust. They were too itchy and pretty and hard to run around in. The one exception was a denim skirt, which I agreed to wear as party clothing. With my mullet haircut, cowgirl skirt, red Keds, and designated dress blouse—a glittery, yellow Pac-Man T-shirt with my name ironed on the back in navy blue fuzzy letters—I was shamefully easy to pick out among my Mary Jane–wearing, frilly-dress-sporting, curling-iron-haired peers. When my interest in figure skating rolled around, my mother must have cried with relief, knowing that beads, jewels, and other shiny flecks of femininity would work their way into my wardrobe sooner or later, although neither of us imagined the amount of glitter that would envelop my body as a showgirl with Hollywood on Ice.

*   *   *

My first skating dress was a gift from my earliest teacher at Murray's rink, a basic-skills instructor named Joanne, who one day handed me the most horrific lump of bright green, scratchy, sequinless, wool/polyester fabric with a thin ribbon of gold trim around a hole that I assumed to be the neck. The shade of green fell somewhere between army and algae and the shape was something like a pillowcase with sleeves. The dress was from the early seventies and could have easily been the descendant of a couch slipcover from the previous decade or a former pair of van curtains. The garment lay heavy in my hands, the prickly material not much softer than a budding cactus.

"I want you to have this," Joanne said, relinquishing her dress with an inflection of warning, "but only if you'll wear it. It meant a lot to me." Why I took it at all I'm not sure, but it just seemed like the right thing to do and I was genuinely touched by the offering. Picking up Joanne's hint of nostalgia, I took the thing with oohs and ahhs and promised to keep it in good condition. Needless to say, it is still in very good condition. Hanging like a phantom of reminiscence in the depths of my closet next to my final competition dress of red velvet and sheer chiffon beaded with Austrian crystals, the ancient green frock has somehow eluded Goodwill and the Salvation Army. I never did wear it, and I never will, but giving it up does not seem like an option. I have come to understand that this is a bad pattern for any relationship, whether with cotton or human, but still it hangs unworn and unmovable from both my closet and my memory.

The first competition dress I ever wore was an off-the-rack, long-sleeved dark purple spandex outfit that wrinkled with bigness and was decorated with two thick, shimmery pink vertical stripes running down my nonexistent chest like a psychedelic interstate. This dress was re-placed the following year with a magenta outfit covered in sparkly rhine-stones and silver bugle beads, after I felt ready to make the commitment to sequins. There was even a tiny beaded star on the butt, a signature mark of the dressmaker, and I went around lifting the ruffly skirt and proudly mooning all my little Murray's friends and asking, "See my star? See my star? I am *SuperStarbutt!* Up, up, and away!"

For the one-minute-and-ten-second skating program I was able to pacify the tomboy within, deciding I could cope with the short-term commitment to spandex, especially if it was unique from all other dresses. Practice clothing, however, was another story. Two more years would pass before I converted to the religion of a skater's wardrobe: tights, skirts, and delicate gloves spared of snot-slicked, temperature-sensitive Go-Bots. Only after one coach refused to teach me until I wore the appropriate attire did I begin to take notice of my appearance. At the time, I didn't understand what the big deal was. I had on my favorite navy blue corduroys and my red-and-yellow horizontally striped wool sweater; my hair was in a failed ponytail clump; and my glasses, smudged from a hard day of fifth-grade life, were reinforced to my skull with a pair of fluorescent green Croakies.

"You have to wear tights," a coach named Tracy said, waving a hand toward the girls who skated by in their shiny leggings and matching skating skirts. I wanted to cry. Tomboys did not wear tights, and anything pink was a terrible, terrible thing. Tracy gave me one lesson, and later called my mother to say she was too overbooked with students to continue with me.

Murray's then closed for the summer, and in the fall of 1985, at eleven years old, I had a lesson with a woman named Linda. She didn't mind my sweatpants. She thought Freezie Freakies were cool but disliked the ones with My Little Pony on them, too. I forgave her for liking the color pink, and with that settled, Linda worked with me for the next decade. During that time I morphed slowly and eventually settled comfortably into spandex.

In time, Yonkers became more of a home to me than Bronxville. I joined the Yonkers Figure Skating Club and fell in love with the royal blue nylon-and-polyester silk-screened jacket with the white skating panda on the back, proudly wearing the flimsy fabric every chance I got. The jacket itself was about as heat-efficient as a plastic Baggie, but the sense of belonging to something greater than my preteen self generated enough warmth to overpower any winter weather. With twice-daily trips to Murray's and hours of interaction with kids from other towns, I entered a different world when I passed through the double glass doors (only one of which worked) of Murray's rink. Even at the age of eleven, I recognized that the world inside Murray's was not the same as the one I knew in Bronxville. Here, no one cared if a girl lacked the newest clothes or if her parents did not own a luxury automobile. All the teenagers at Murray's had big hair, ears pierced from lobe to cartilage, long iridescent fingernails, and gold chains that spelled out their names in loopy script punctuated with cubic zirconia.

Bronxville girls had neatly trimmed hair, single-hole lobes, French manicures, and gold necklaces passed down from pre-Mayflower days. Despite the loud makeup and megajewelry the Yonkers teens fancied, the kids at the rink didn't give a hooey about other people's appearance, and those who played nice and skated hard were liked by everyone.

Even better than the freedom to ignore appearances, Murray's gave me the one thing I was unable to find in Bronxville: an identity. The kids at the rink renamed me, tossing away Katie and replacing her with Skatie, knighting me into the realm of individuality that until then I had believed was unobtainable. With that nickname came the power to test out a new sense of self. Katie lived in Bronxville, but Skatie lived in Yonkers; and all that was lost in one village was found in the other: self-confidence, poise, the love of sport, and the power of mind and body. There were no other Skaties at the rink, just as there was no other Murray's in the world. Skatie could wear mismatched gloves without receiving funny looks or social ostracism, so that is exactly what I did, even if I actually had matching ones in my skate bag.

I spent five mornings a week, four evening sessions, and Saturday afternoons on the ice at Murray's. Patch, freestyle, ice dance, precision practice, public skating sessions. Skating was my first true love; it made me dizzy with emotions I could describe not through words but through movements, and it provided a base measure of happiness that called for all other life endeavors to measure up. Murray's set the bar quite high. Had I been allowed to set up a cot in the boiler room, I would have done so and moved in without hesitation. A stray cat named Skates made her home in the lost-and-found box filled with mittens and other misplaced warmness, and if she could do it, then so could I. I often fantasized about having the ice all to myself in the darkest hours of the night, skating whenever and wherever I pleased, carving my existence into the unmarked canvas of fresh ice, sleeping only while the Zamboni came out to renew my palette. The closest I came to moving in was arriving at 5:30 A.M. and sometimes leaving as late as 10:00 P.M., and still it seemed not to be enough.

꜅꜅꜅

Chapter Three

Murray's

The Edward J. Murray Memorial Skating Center lies directly off the New York State Thruway, southbound off exit 6E, in Yonkers, New York, just north of the Big Apple. With no visible signs or advertising, the bubble-shaped dome of the building is the only clue that this architectural mushroom houses an ice surface beneath its plastic bulge. The facility is typical of what most northeastern rinks built in or before the 1960s look like, with a round, bloated roof supported by a network of wooden poles and beams. Today, modern rinks resemble warehouses: square and squat with a flat roof, more efficient paneling, and often boasting multiple ice surfaces inside. Murray's was not one of these rinks. By physical standards, it was the trailer park of all skating architecture, with a disheveled paint job, splintery bleachers that knew few visitors, and a chain-link fence that sagged in boredom from its duties. But Murray's, like most other things in life, was not something to be judged from the outside no matter how rough its exterior appeared. Inside, the Yonkers Figure Skating Club made its home, and although outsiders usually considered the qualities of our facility outdated or oafish, these were the very points of character that we considered endearing and distinctive.

The roof covered only the top of the rink, enclosing the west end and curving down over the elongated north and south walls, still leaving about six feet of open air from the ground up. The east side of the rink was almost completely open, and the elements found their way onto the ice when the wind blew westward. Rain, sleet, snow, and hail would accumulate in the east end, but in the early hours of each new day so too would warmth and sunshine. The roof was made of a patchwork of semiopaque green plastic squares interspersed with sheets of metal and aluminum siding. There were makeshift skylights with the same transparency as wax paper. Between the rafters of the calico-pattern covering, fluorescent lights hung down on metal skewers. Usually they worked just fine, but there was always a wayward bulb blinking on and off to a fidgety frequency as if just trying to get a little attention.

When it rained, the giant awning leaked in numerous places, dripping onto the ice rings of yellowish rainwater that hardened into lumpy halos of gunk and remained there for as long as the inclement weather did. These obstacles caused some nasty skater spills from time to time, but most of the seasoned athletes knew exactly where the protuberances accumulated and formed a sense of radar, gracefully navigating their way around the miniature mounds of frozen runoff. Rain meant condensation, and condensation brought fog into the rink during the fall and spring seasons. The steamy vapor of warm bodies colliding with the cold, wet air made skating dangerous in such poor visibility, although we giggled at the fog's funhouse effect as it engulfed our practice sessions. Every ten minutes during a fog-laden session, all the skaters stopped what they were working on and headed into the middle of the ice, where we would all skate very fast in a circular pattern for three or four minutes. The speed of our collective motion created a powerful, fanlike vortex, which lifted the weather up into the heavens of the rink like a cloud we had the momentary ability to control. Slowly, the fog would fluff down again and blanket the ice, and we would repeat the pattern as many times as necessary — a small army of weather warriors dressed in bright spandex called to defend our frozen territory.

The fog and the ice doughnuts left by rainy weather were not as perilous as old, ingrained hockey ruts, which could take a skater down faster than an untied lace. Hollow furrows in the ice swooshed out by hockey players from previous practices often needed multiple Zamboni passes before they evened out. Murray's Zamboni was a one-trip kind of machine. The old blue clunker lumbered out a few times a day, whereas most modern rinks unleash their Zamboni every couple of hours to ensure that quality ice is frequently refreshed. For the most part, Murray's ice was smooth and fast and remarkably consistent, given all the factors of eastern meteorology that the poor old outdoorish rink had to endure.

As if the troublesome weather wasn't enough, there was the sun, which in the early-morning hours pounded its rays onto the easternmost edges of the ice. After a few minutes the rink became puddly in these areas, and falling here left skaters with their asses much soggier than their egos. We wasted no time taking off skates or changing tights; we simply skated wet-legged for the rest of the session and hoped our body temperature would rise before the chill set into our skin. Murray's skaters were tough athletes who learned fast that training there meant more than just adapting to the environment; you simply had to love the sport with every fiber in your body.

Leaves blew in during the fall, landing silently onto the ice and skittering across the oval surface with the breeze of our movement. Flower buds followed the same route in the spring months, as did snow during the winter. The snow was the most scenic seasonal effect, for it came through the rink on windy gusts and each flake sparkled in the light of the fluorescent lamps and cascaded down onto our hair and clothing, a fine dusting of confectioners' sugar. The snow melted into the hair of skaters who were working hard, the heat of our athletic bodies turning the flurries into warm trickles that ran through our hair and flew off our faces when we spun. For the skaters who slacked off and barely broke a sweat during a snowy practice, the weather branded their inaction by turning their hair crystalline white with a gentle frosting of winter.

What also flew into the open end of the rink, during every season, were birds—pigeons in particular—that were too dim-witted to fly south for the season and decided that the compressor's warm exhaust fans would suit their tropical needs just fine. Despite life-size plastic owl balloons that the management had attached to the ceiling beams at the end of the rink, the pigeons nested in a few choice rafters above the ice, sending down all sorts of refuse: yarn, twigs, an occasional egg, and, worst of all, feces. Pigeon poop was not an uncommon obstacle to skate through at Murray's rink, and although there was a metal scraper by the Zamboni door for us to use when birdie nature called, we rarely got to it fast enough. That stuff freezes quite quickly. I have not been able to find a metaphor for the sound of aviary waste splattering to the ice, and perhaps that is for the best. Skating at Murray's was as beautiful as it was difficult, but it was never less than character-building.

Inside the lobby there was a ticket booth, a skate rental counter, a snack bar with giant garage-door-size windows, a few restrooms, an office, and the reverberating furnace room with refrigeration compressors that thundered like locomotive engines and kept everything happily freezing. Six long, thick gray benches pockmarked with constellations of toe pick divots and heel punctures provided a place to sit while tying up skates, and trophy cases filled with hockey and figure skating awards gave the lobby a bit of decoration.

Rubber matting covered the lobby floor and led out to the ice arena and its modest surrounding bleachers. In certain places the mats ran askew and exposed patches of pavement that wreaked havoc upon the tender edges of a skater's expensive blades, calling for a trip to Mr. Kohler's, the much-loved skate sharpener whose seemingly simple job was in fact the cornerstone of every Murray's skater's world. We wore skate guards — or at least we were supposed to — long rubber runners that slipped over our blades and gave us the freedom to walk wherever we pleased. Except onto the ice. To see a skater take to the ice with the pair of forgotten guards still clinging to her blades is like watching a cartoon character try to outsmart a banana peel. My first experience with unremoved guards was at the age of eleven, though I escaped embarrassment because I was performing in Murray's annual ice show as Pinocchio, and my flailing limbs and questionable relationship with gravity looked quite in character.

One weekend a year, in mid-May, Murray's took on a whole new semblance as the annual skating show turned our beloved pigeon barn into a rink that would rival anything on Broadway. The parents created scenery and costumes that changed the little rink's homely interior into a Disneyesque setting. There were spotlights and flowers and crowds (heavily laden with relatives) that left no seat vacant, and we performed to the caliber of these grand surroundings. For nine months preceding the show, we skated with poor lighting, a leaky roof, and freezing temperatures, all the while dodging bird doo, but for that one weekend we shone like stars and our rink backed us all the way as Murray's became our Broadmoor, our Lake Placid, our Coliseum, our Madison Square Garden. We disbanded after the show, because Murray's closed for the summer and we scattered ourselves to different rinks.

When Murray's reopened in early October, we welcomed back those who had trained far away over the summer and watched with eager competitiveness to see who landed what new jumps, whose style had improved, whose bodies had grown up. There were four girls I saw on a regular early-morning basis: Michele, Vanessa, and two sisters, Carolina and Maritza, and all memories of Murray's and figure skating are infused with their faces and movements. Carolina was the most balletic, Vanessa was the goofball kid with wonderful showmanship, Michele was the workhorse with powerful jumps, and Maritza had all the aforementioned qualities and later found her way to a high level of pairs skating. Starting my lessons a few years after these girls entered into figure skating, I used their range of talents as goals to strive for on my way to an unforeseeable finish line, the way a competitive runner concentrates only on passing the woman in front of her, and then the next, and the next. Each skater was a rung in the ladder, a foothold on progress, a gauge of dedication on Murray's one-of-a-kind measurement system, and by age seventeen, I had worked my way to the top of Murray's talent pool. More than the skating itself, I loved my place within its social structure, because everything about life felt good at this rink.

My mother — who had very specific rules about leaving the house with her undone hair and rougeless face — was not one to rise before the sun, so my father woke me up in the mornings, every day, fifteen minutes before the clock reached five. The Hello Kitty alarm clock next to my bed worked just fine, with its red arm pointed just north of the five and its monotonous little bleeps of earliness playing backup to my father's perfect accuracy. I slept in only on Fridays, when the rink was booked for Pee-Wee hockey practice. For the five years before I was old enough to drive myself to Murray's, my father was the saint in chauffeur's clothing who dragged himself out of a warm bed to support his only daughter's cold obsession with figure skating.

My bedroom door would slowly creak open, until the wedge of

light from the hallway searched my walls and windows and eventually
settled its brightness on my bed.

"Kay . . . "

"I'm up. Yup. Okey-doke. Up."

Sometimes, in the winter months, I offered an arm into the darkness instead of verbally confirming my awakeness, and my father would
pull at the suspended limb until the rest of my body slithered out from
beneath the blankets. My mind wanted to skate, but my body temporarily revolted. These were the mornings of late December through mid-
February, when the temperature fell so low that my feet would freeze to
the point of numbness within their skating boots. When this occurred,
jumps were landed with luck, spins were executed by muscle memory,
and choreography looked a bit different as grace froze along with the
limbs that tried to dispense it.

In the few minutes that followed my initial waking process, I
played a game of sorts to help take my mind off the earliness of the day
and the low temperatures of the still-sleeping house. In the bathroom
across the hall, my father made his presence known by the sound of the
electric razor. Its echo buzzed into my room, and although I do not remember consciously deciding to do so, I began to race the razor. I would
attempt to dress—*underwear! three layers of tights (one nylon, one wool,
one spandex)! skating skirt! T-shirt! turtleneck! long-sleeved shirt! sweatshirt! sweatshirt! sweatshirt! ponytail!*—before the razor stopped its
song and dance and the prickly layer of morning stubble fell from my father's face.

I usually beat the old Norelco, which took about a minute to complete its course. It was only during a brief spell of puberty that I lost the
races, because of the new entanglement of hooks and straps that slowed
the dressing process when I had to add *bra!* My dad wore an old pair of
gray sweatpants and his favorite goofy, coffee-stained sweatshirt that I
bought him at a competition and that read, MY TRIP TO HAWAII, MY MER-
CEDES, MY VACATION, MY HOME, AND MY RETIREMENT ALL WENT TO BUY
ICE TIME!

My own washing up went quickly; a swift drag-over with the
toothbrush, a splash of cold water to the face, and the insertion of two

mutinous contact lenses that required more than a few blinks to evoke their powers at such an early hour. No morning shower; I did that at night and hoped the staying power of Ivory was indeed 99.44%.

Breakfast was quick, a bowl of cereal. Oatmeal maybe, if I had the luxury of waiting for the water to boil in those premicrowave days. A wrapped-up muffin to devour in the car was thrown into the skate bag, which was thrown over one shoulder. The other balanced a book bag. In my left hand were my school clothes, as I went right to class from the rink. My right hand was free to pet our devoted mutt Taffy and leave a Milk-Bone for her, and then pull the kitchen door shut at 5:00 A.M.

I have twice been struck in the head by the *New York Times,* my presence upsetting the newspaper's daily flight pattern to our stone porch. A faint apology would echo up from the dark driveway, where John the paper man laughed at his unintentionally accurate aim and then continued on his route.

The digital thermometer in my father's old silver BMW sent forth a *ding* if the outside temperature dropped below freezing. This was the bell of warning, the chord of winter, a most brutal sound at five in the morning. Sometimes the car "dinged" before we reached the end of the driveway, but in the dead of January the bell tolled as soon as the ignition engaged. My father would look at me and chortle, "Oooooh!" with an inflection that told me he was happy not to be the one in spandex as we watched the thermometer digits continue their cruel, flickery countdown to the actual temperature.

The sky would still be midnight black when we arrived at Murray's. Daylight was a good hour and a half away yet from its own practice schedule. The only car in the parking lot belonged to Jungle, the live-in rink attendant who oversaw the maintenance of the compressor valves and drove the Zamboni before the figure skating practices. Jungle was a nice man in his mid-thirties whose real name I never learned and who always came to unlock the rink's door when I whumped on it at 5:15 with mittened hands.

"Juuungle! Lemme in, please!" Inside the lobby, his reply came around the corner before he did. "I hear ya, I hear ya."

With an old ambulance stretcher for a bed set up in the boiler room and permanently grease-stained clothes, Jungle had the kind of thankless job that would have turned most people glum, irritable, and old before their time. Yet with half-closed eyes and a wild case of bed head, he never failed to open the door with a toothy grin and a comment slightly more creative than "good morning": "Sheesh, kid, never miss a day, do ya?"

My father waited in the car till Jungle appeared, then drove off. I'd shout a thank-you toward the car, not knowing then how much I would come to mean it in future years. The old car disappeared down the rink's steep driveway, alternating its path between the office in Bronxville (winter) and a boathouse in New Rochelle (spring), where my father had his own training schedule as a rower.

As I sat in the lobby and slipped my feet into my "patch" skates, my coach, Linda, would stroll in with a Styrofoam cup of Dunkin' Donuts tea in one hand and skates in the other. We laced up in silence, comfortable enough with each other's presence to know that early-morning stillness is a language we were both fluent in. Before getting onto the ice, I took the ten-dollar bill or check my father gave me every morning and put it into the open envelope on the office door, writing my name on the sign-in sheet below. In my near decade of mornings at the Murray Skating Center, there was never a discrepancy between the amount of cash in the envelope and the number of skaters on the ice. The price never increased above five dollars an hour, and theft never found its way into our ramshackle rink, which is a fact that not many other skating facilities can boast.

The first hour of practice belonged to figure skating's lesser-known side—"patch," or compulsory figures, where each skater has a 10-by-44-foot section (or patch) of ice on which to practice her circles. During evening sessions the ice was crowded and we rotated patches each week so that no one was stuck in the same place all year, but in the mornings we became creatures of habit, picking out patches safe from bird-crowded beams and claiming the space as our own through unspoken repetition. Odd-numbered patches ran along the right side of our rink, even on the left, and patches 4, 6, 7, and 9 were smack in the hub of

Grand Central Pigeon. Patch was a quiet hour, but at Murray's small outbursts of "Ewww!" and "Shit!" rang out with understandable cause. For an hour, Linda guided me through the set patterns of various figure eights with slow and careful attention to detail.

There were three different shapes and sizes within figures, and more than twenty patterns between the categories. Everything was performed forward and backward, right foot and left, using both the inside and outside edges of the blade. What looked easy from a distance was complicated up close. There were the common two-lobed circles, called eights, specific in measurement to the height of the skater performing them. There were three-lobed snowmanlike circles called serpentines and small, compact, quick-movement, miniature multilobed "loops," which were my own personal nemesis. The perfect circles were etched into the ice with a compasslike contraption called a scribe. The scribe had a nail in the tip, which shaved out a thin tracing of ice. It was moved by hand from the center of the circle and swung around until a complete circumference was carved. Over and over, I traced my figures into Murray's ice with slow and steady speed, as my quadriceps anchored all the physics of movement into precision and traceable strength.

Rockers and counters — quick turns of the foot and swift changes of edge — cut carroted indentations on the great lobes, while brackets added outie-shaped belly buttons at the tops and bottoms of the figures. Three turns took pie-slice-shaped bites at various places in the circle's crust. The push-offs at the center of the figure left great ruts of quickness and power, arching like comet tails that trailed behind us, our balance stemming from its curve. In figures we were surgeons of all things circular, knifing our blades into the skin of skating, operating on the particulars of balance to see if we could not perfect its hold.

I competed in events sanctioned by the United States Figure Skating Association (USFSA) and the Ice Skating Institute of America (ISIA), the two governing bodies of figure skating competitions (think major and minor leagues, respectively), and rose to the levels of Senior Ladies and Freestyle Nine before I turned eighteen. The freestyle tests I passed with ease and comfort, but figure tests gave me nerves that made me shake like Elvis on speed when I stepped out on the ice before the panel of stern-looking judges. The watchful eyes that I thrived on in competitions and exhibitions shot lasers at me during figure tests. Testing was difficult and expensive, often between eighty and one hundred dollars a try. Test sessions had to be reserved months in advance and, if failed, could not be retaken for at least thirty days. The body-wracking nerves turned my circular lobes into epileptic hexagons, the three tracings that were supposed to converge into one narrow line looked more like an unbraided mess of unerasable markings, and my free leg (the passive foot is required to stay off the ice at all times, punishable by immediate failure if it so much as grazes the ice) touched down more times than two Pop Warner teams in a scrimmage.

Although at first I abhorred the precise repetition of tracing, there was a reward in figures that provided a physical rush when all those practices finally paid off and I eventually executed the tests correctly (or the judges took an extreme measure of pity on me). The reward of consistency, of truly understanding how to do something so well that the task itself and the one performing it seem to become one and the same, is like no other sense of grace that a body can comprehend, feeling struggle blossom into second nature. Failing all those figure tests at first only made passing them that much better later on, the same way that even the most painful memories eventually stand to remind us of our deepest inner strength.

I traced these patterns for seven years, slowly advancing from the preliminary to the eighth test (nine levels in all). Yet when I found myself at the highest level of figures, the cusp of the gold medal test, skaters across the country received the bittersweet news that compulsories were to be abolished by the USFSA. The ice time allocated for figures was replaced with mere freestyle sessions or other delegated practices that were hardly conducive to scribes, circles, and the slow-moving procedures of patch. Though it might have taken me ten attempts to clear the final test, I'll never know and there will always be a slight ache of incompletion in my skating memories.

Figures were discontinued for a variety of reasons, ranging from poor media interest/coverage to allowing those skaters with better athletic and freestyle capabilities to advance without the discipline of figures to hold them back. Figures and freestyle skating were so different from each other that while some skaters excelled in both fields, few were able to master each with equal strength. Understanding the contrasts and similarities between figure and freestyle skating is like asking a hockey goalie to jump up and cover left wing for a period. All the dynamics are the same — ice, edgework, balance, control — but it is an entirely different feel and perspective. Even the blades vary; freestyle skates have gargantuan toe picks of crocodile-teeth proportion while figure blades have toe picks ferocious as a sea horse, as well as a precisely hollowed edge that allows for more concise turns.

The slow pace of figures meant that the cold found its way into all my layers within the first ten minutes at Murray's. In the lobby, the moment a skater opened one of the four chunky blue doors that led out to the ice, the morning air reached inside and with a tiny but distinctive grasp momentarily pulled the breath away from whoever dared venture out. We measured the morning's coldness by the skater's quick, hiccupy loss of oxygen. The louder the inhale, the more we layered. On top of the three tiers of spandex, I put on sweatpants and on top of that, my fluorescent rainbow-striped leg warmers that screamed with original 1980s style. My fuzzy red fleece and the nylon Murray's club jacket did their torso-warming duties while my leg-warmer-matching hat capped it all off. It was just that cold. There was even a nose warmer that my father purchased for me as a novelty gag: a small, green crocheted circle with a light blue pom-pom on the tip and two long strings that tied around the back of my head and looked completely ridiculous. I loved the thing. It actually warded off winter quite well, and if I wasn't wearing the nose mitt during figures, someone always asked to borrow it.

"Skatie, can I use your nose thingie?"

"Sure. Don't snot in it, 'kay?

"I'll try."

The cold hour of patch affected not only us, it bore its way into everything around us as well. I once knocked over Linda's large cup of tea and, expecting it to splash over my skates, jumped out of the way. But it landed with a frozen *kunk* on the ice, and splintered out a few shards of Earl Grey.

I welcomed anything that might momentarily distract me from patch. During those first few minutes when no one was on the ice with me, I performed a ritual that seemed far more productive than practicing my figures. Alongside the rink, enormous semis and tractor-trailers lumbered up and down I-87. Although their rumble was loud and distinguishable, I could see only the side view of their headlights as the trucks flew by. Wondering if, in the darkness of the morning, the truckers could see me—the sole inhabitant of a well-lit ice rink—I held my right arm in a ninety-degree angle and pumped my fist a few times towards the interstate, eagerly awaiting the responsive *whoooonk, whoooonk* of any eighteen-wheeler's belchy horn. About one in three attempts garnered an anonymous *whoooonk,* making me feel quite special for no apparent reason.

On the days when I had a test in first-period science or English class, I would hand Linda my self-made flash cards of vocab words and cell genetics. I executed backward outside edges and rocker turns while defining *magnanimous* mitochondria and *mellifluous* cytoplasm, and Linda corrected my posture and pointed out my grammatical and scientific errors. *Check your left arm back, lift the right hip, wait for the center, and no, Katie . . . van Leeuwenhoek invented the microscope, not Sonja Henie.* The quizzing simultaneously took my mind off the figures and made me concentrate harder, although I remained oblivious to the true education I was getting.

Michele, a skater four years my junior, was dedicated to her sport and showed up before dawn every day about the same time I arrived at Murray's. She took the patch of ice diagonally across from mine and we formed a bond from our peripheral vision. Circling our way around our figures, we interacted at the top of serpentine patterns, slapping high fives or pulling ponytails, whatever kept us human in this early-morning freezer of our dreams. Linda hovered over my tracings as Michele's coach, Robert, oversaw hers. Linda and I would smile, shake our heads, and roll our eyes every time the infectious laughter across the ice started up and echoed over to our side of the boards. Robert was a prankster, Michele was a little comedienne herself, and the two of them giggled through entire lessons, making everyone's morning a little less early and the sport itself a little more soulful. Then again, the earliness was not something that I ever really noticed.

Only in retrospect would I come to understand the impact of such a schedule, which gave me two extra hours of life every day. People—

usually nonathletes — would ask, "How could you get up so early, every day for so many years?" The usual response was "I dunno, I just do" because it sounded less impolite than answering, "How could you not?" I loved skating, skating was at 5:30; therefore, I came to love that hour. Michele understood this. Some mornings, in the dead of January, when the sun rose so late and the temperature was so low that tears formed in my eyes and froze in the corners, and all we knew for certain was that figures were hard, our feet were freezing, and the cold bore straight through our fifty-seven layers of spandex, all I had to do to keep from quitting was look over and see that Michele was there, too, unintentionally transforming figure skating from an individual endeavor to a team sport all in the yank of a ponytail and the echo of a laugh.

Here, in this shabby house of ice and pigeons, unlike my place in the community of my high school peers, I became popular. The beginner skaters wobbling around Murray's rink asked me how to do certain spins or jumps, and without hesitation I showed them anything they wanted to see. They watched me, just as I had gawked at the older skaters who had once seemed so much more accomplished than I could ever hope to be. I wanted to be graceful for them as much as I wanted it for myself. I was determined but realistic; the Olympics were not a likely aspiration. My skating ability was a talent, not a gift. But if being an Olympic contender felt anything like it did when a little kid tugged on my skirt and said, "You're good!" then Murray's made me a quiet champion of intangible standing.

My peers at Murray's and I represented a break from the norm for one another, a clue that the world had other people in it than just the ones we went to high school with. At school in Bronxville, the social pressures and competitiveness that infiltrated its academic structure tormented me. I could handle kids rolling my Jeep into the street, but by senior year things were getting a tad personal. I was definitely considered a bit of a weirdo. Okay, maybe it wasn't such a good idea to run for sophomore class president and deliver my prevote speech in rhyming couplets. Maybe in the mornings I could have been nicer when I asked the boys who did drugs in the girls' bathroom if they didn't mind stepping outside while I changed out of my skating tights. Maybe I could have shut my yapper every once in a while when the Spanish teacher asked if anyone wanted extra-credit work. Some things I clearly brought on myself. But a few incidents still got to me.

My remedial math class had a field day with my overachiever figure skating image and enjoyed a good teasing whether or not the teacher turned her back. *Class, if we multiply anything by zero, what do we get?* "The sum of Katie's friends?" was a popular hypothesis. *Mis amigos* in my advanced-placement Spanish class fancied using my name in fictitious derogatory sentences as they constructed future perfect verb tenses. *¡Ningun invitaremos Katarina a la baile!* No one will ask Katie to the prom! I looked toward the teacher, eyes hopeful with silent pleading. *Invitará, invitará,* she corrected.

When the mockery got really unbearable, sometimes the teachers intervened by giving me a mercy dismissal. Yet it seemed odd that I was the one who had to leave class instead of the perpetrators. Some teachers were fantastic, sensing when kids were hurting from the thorny social system. A kindhearted guidance counselor smiled and nodded in unquestioning support when I told her I would apply only to colleges that no other kids in my class were considering. Bronxville gave me more of an education than I was able to understand at the time: that being an individual can sometimes make for a lonely experience. But being part of the norm . . . I tried to believe that was even worse.

Murray's was a family; we marked not only holidays and competitions together but also individual achievements and personal tragedies. Murray's brought my first experiences with sweet sixteens, bat mitzvahs, weddings, and funerals—things that didn't happen much to teenagers in Bronxville. Far more impressed upon my memory than the landing of my first axel or competition medal is the face of a nine-year-old skater streaming with tears at her twelve-year-old brother's funeral. Robin's older brother Marc was always at the rink, part of a band of skater siblings who ran around the building making up games while their sisters skated.

When Robin came back to the rink a few days after the car accident that took her brother's life, Murray's was there for her the same as always, providing hopeful consistency in a time of unimaginable loss. We were just kids. None of us knew exactly what to say, so we just hugged her, skated around, and hugged her some more. At Murray's we knew about skating but we also knew that there was life beyond the bubble of the building. Literally, we saw the world outside of Murray's. Beyond the scuffed-up Plexiglas, past the dry-rot bleachers, through the chain-link fence and out into the open air of Murray's roofless, wall-less rink, we saw that life went on with or without skating.

Despite the abrasive weather and the second-rate facilities, no one ever quit skating at Murray's. Quitting, if I used the word, meant only that I wanted to go into the lobby and warm up for a few minutes. Sometimes kids reevaluated their dedication to skating and came to the rink less frequently, perhaps finding another extracurricular activity or skipping out on summer training, but no one ever truly quit. We couldn't . . . Murray's would not let us. It was as if Murray's became a part of every person in the Yonkers Figure Skating Club, an extension of ourselves, an unexorcisable spirit, an invisible cord bonding place to person. That rink was an entity in which each one of us could quietly confide our dreams, a frozen wishing well. Murray's was haunted, but not supernaturally. Just naturally. Every skater loved this icy residence and I believe that the old rink loved us right back. We could *feel* it. Even if we could feel nothing else — toes, fingers, face, or feet — we could feel the presence of Murray's affection when we were on the ice, and if we were far away, we could feel that it missed us and couldn't wait till we came home.

The second hour of morning practice began at 6:30. I returned to Murray's lobby to change into my freestyle skates. The sound of the hot-air hand dryer in the ladies' room hummed through the rink lobby during winter mornings. There was always a skater who dragged a chair into the tiny washroom area and sat down, elevating her legs. Shoving her feet into the hand-drying air blower, skin to hot metal, the frozen athlete would keep hitting the button, renewing the thirty seconds of warmth until all toes were wigglable. Taking off our skates, we stepped on one another's bare feet, trying to shock the blood vessels open and allow more flow to our ten tiny extremities that had begun to purple. A mitten was placed on the foot-in-waiting, while the opposite toes were lovingly stepped upon.

Back on the ice, we warmed up during freestyle. With quick, athletic movements we began to heat our bodies, following the logic of "the faster you move, the warmer you'll get." It was not uncommon to see layers of shirts adorn the side boards about fifteen minutes after a freestyle session began, sweatshirts hugging each other like phantoms trying to keep warm without their bodies. I followed a certain routine: skate forward around the perimeter of the rink for three minutes, then backward. Then attempt a few spins to warm up the legs, a couple of footwork patterns to ready the feet, a flurry of arm movements to leave no limb neglected. I did the jumps last, giving barely tepid muscles less of a chance of being pulled. First came the leaps I had already mastered, followed by the ones I struggled to call consistent, and then those that I could only dream of someday landing. Again and again I heaved my body into the air, gambling with gravity and poise, feeling my odds of remaining upright grow slowly from one morning practice to the next.

The sound system we used for playing our cassettes was a small black radio not much bigger than a Pop-Tart that we set on the barrier in front of the hockey booth, and through a hole cut in the booth's Plexiglas an extension cord ran into the overhead speaker outlet. Jungle flipped the power switch inside the lobby, and we had music every morning unless the weather had something to say about it. The plastic tape deck was winterly challenged and sometimes froze up so much that we could not get our tapes in or out until the box thawed later that afternoon, finally opening its cryogenic jaws with a slow, bored yawn. When one person's tape got stuck in the box, we listened to it all morning, temporarily adapting our programs to someone else's music. Freestyle programs composed of theater music, classical concertos, operatic arias, or snippets of Yanni reverberated from the tape deck, as did the music of our exhibition routines, usually inspired from whatever radio songs were currently popular and skatable. This was the dawn of pop music gushings and glam rock ballads, and there was not a female figure skater in the country who escaped the eighties without once skating to the latest drooly yearning of Debbie Gibson's "Lost in Your Eyes," Bette Midler's "Wind Beneath My Wings," Richard Marx's "Right Here Waiting," or the inevitable "Take My Breath Away" from the chick with the funky hair on the *Top Gun* soundtrack. Murray's fuzzy sound system had an eerie yet comforting way of making everything from Beethoven to Whitesnake sound remotely similar.

The little tape machine had an appetite for cassettes, eating technical programs and warm-up mixes and show routines like three-course meals of forbidden pleasure, and those tapes that escaped digestion were not safe from the dangers of falling between the broken side boards. A graveyard of lost music lay silent in the unreachable chasm between the hockey booth and the boards, the only chance of resurrection left to the masterful maneuvering of a hockey stick and a will of undying patience.

During freestyle practice, the sun began to poke its way up from Manhattan and into Murray's; I loved this time of day the best. I liked the way the sky looked with all those colors. Linda and I picked out streaks of sunlight and colorful clouds and remarked on what a pretty skating dress such a color would make. Most of my dresses ended up being warm shades of peach, pink, red, or yellow. I have seen other sunrises since Murray's, supposedly spectacular. I've watched that brilliant thing come up over the Andes, the rolling hills of Switzerland, the meadows and valleys of the northeastern United States, and the lip of the Grand Canyon. I even saw it peek through the world's most glamorous scaffolding, the Eiffel Tower. But never have I seen the sun rise so beautifully as when it ascended each morning above a little mound of landfill surrounded by a chain-link fence and a few dead trees in the eastern end of a parking lot adjacent to the New York State Thruway.

At the end of each practice, my father returned in his lawyer clothes and overcoat to catch the last few minutes of my training, hand me a Lipton's iced tea from Murray's fifty-cent soda machine, and tell me, "You looked great out there, honey."

"Thanks, Dad," I'd respond and, with a quick glance toward the pigeons, add, "Careful, you're standing under a very active rafter."

My father barely knew a bunny hop from a quadruple toe loop, but he always understood the smile that came forth from all the efforts in between. Even in the years after I got my driver's license and drove myself to Murray's in the mornings, my dad still came by every now and then at 6:30 just to watch, bring me a muffin and an iced tea, and stand a little too close to the overhead beams.

At 7:30 and not a second sooner, I reluctantly got off the ice after doing my five good-luck axels. Off came the skates and all those layers, toes were shoved into hand dryers, then on went the school clothes and bladeless shoes.

The life lessons learned at Murray's spanned so many years and covered so many topics that, from sunrises to cytoplasm, I am almost positive that no subject passed by untouched. The definitions to all those important words in an athlete's dictionary were learned under the roof of that old rink. Perseverance. Dedication. Pride. Pain. Strength. Stamina. Sweat. Power. Speed. Agility. Grace. Yes, I learned those things. But ask me what I *remember* and simpler concepts come to mind. Cold. Sunshine. Mittens with holes. Darkness. Snow. Music; there was always music. Friendships. Patch 14. Linda's voice and posture. Dad's freezing Beamer and the miserable but honest *ding* that gave sound to quiet coldness.

꙰

Chapter Four

Holiday on Ice—Entrance to the Raisin Stage

Before hopping on the trailer of Hollywood on Ice that rolled its way into my life, carting all the costumes and makeup and Olgai with it, there was the two-month precursor of skating tour life that came with experiencing Holiday on Ice.* The two shows were remarkably different in style and content. Hollywood's routines were mentally simple and technically made sense, whereas most of Holiday's were like performance-art exhibitions crafted by coked-out freak artists. The former had costumes crafted with prism-colored jewels and Day-Glo feathers in sultry, revealing arrangements, while the latter used frumpy, plucky feathers in a less-than-seductive tar-and-feather motif just this side of the colonial era. The cast for the most part was cut from the same cloth in both tours, consisting of former competitive skaters who had been in rinks so long that there was no magic or joy left in the act of skating. "Professional"

---

*And so we have entered a chapter with the possibly confusing comparisons of two similarly named ice shows: Holiday on Ice (my first minitour) and Hollywood on Ice (longer, hellish tour). To distinguish between them with ease, I have created helpful mnemonic devices for you to employ should you wish to do so. Holiday on Ice was the European tour that dressed me up like barnyard animals; hence it might help to remember "Holidays in Europe are rather fowl." Hollywood on Ice was the South American tour on which most of my time was spent in the icky cubicle, hence, "Holly would rather be anywhere but in the trailer."

had become more about earning a living than reaching an elite level of expertise.

I did not consider my expectations of professional skating to be of an unnaturally high standard. All I needed was the challenge of good skating. I was a relatively low-maintenance person; frills and benefits were unnecessary as long as there was solid ice, well-choreographed routines, and a packed audience. After talking with local veterans of the Ice Capades, I assumed I had a pretty good idea of what was to come in the world of pro skating. The show would be time-consuming and at times difficult to learn. There would be long rehearsals, late performances, and red-eye travel agendas to keep up with. Some hotels, like the skaters, would be nicer than others. My skating and my level of performance would improve. Weight would be an issue for some people, but not for me, everyone assured me. I was healthy and fit and looked like the basic all-American figure skater: strong legs, svelte torso, slender arms, expressive face, and a perky ponytail.

Homesickness might hit now and then, but I was never really the homesick type. Bronxville wasn't a place I longed for, and family life was better appreciated from a distance. Above all, I knew that I would love this experience of professional skating and speak of it proudly for years to come. Ten years had gone into the planning of this dream and the execution of this goal, and fresh out of college, I was ready to put it all into action. The bottom line was that I would have to practice hard and perform well, just as I had had to do for all those years to get to this level of athletic accomplishment. These were my expectations of the Ice Capades. But after the Ice Capades folded only days before I was supposed to join their tour, leaving me scrambling for another way to fulfill my professional dream, I simply carried these beliefs over into my prospects of Holiday on Ice and Hollywood on Ice. That was my first mistake.

Holiday on Ice brought more than enough personality clashes between some of the skaters and choreographers, but like most situations that leave one questioning one's beliefs and values, there was something to be learned from the time spent with the show. The first and foremost was the deception of titles—Holiday on Ice was about as festive as rain on Christmas, at least from the standpoint of the skater. Second, the axiom of not judging a book by its cover proves true for ice shows as well.

November is not the best month to sightsee in Europe, but in the fall of 1997 I was off to Switzerland for work, not vacation. Holiday on Ice's headquarters was located in Switzerland's capital, Bern, where the cast was to train for a month before heading to Paris to perform in Holiday on Ice's Christmas skating spectacular. I was twenty-two, just six months out of college. A woman named Christa, who was the director of casting, had hired me after viewing my audition video of two exhibition programs I performed during my senior year at Colgate. One was a sassy little tropical number with quick athletic jumps and a bare midriff, the other was a more reserved program that oozed the dramatic goo for which skating is notorious. The contrast of styles worked in my favor, and Christa telephoned with good news. She helped me make the arrangements over the phone, explaining that I was to pay my own way to Switzerland but that at the end of the Christmas show I would be assigned to one of Holiday on Ice's three worldwide tours in Europe, South Africa, or England. The remaining travel finances would then be in the hands of the company. The plane ticket seemed well worth the eventual benefits, and Holiday on Ice paid for the hotel room during our training and performances. On the morning of November 17, I flew to Switzerland, leaving the memory of the Ice Capades behind, ready to restart my dream of skating professionally.

Leaving home for the tour was a little different from leaving home for college. For one thing, I had no idea how long I'd be gone or what country I would be in come January. I couldn't drive back on the weekends, and there was little chance of having friends and family stop by to check in on me now and then. As far as I could tell, the whole setup was perfect. My parents, who remembered when Holiday used to tour the United States years ago, were thrilled that my goals were finally falling into place. In Europe, no less. There was no need to worry, it wasn't as if I was running off to some remote corner of South America with some skating company no one had ever heard of, touring villages that had never seen ice. What could possibly go wrong in nifty neutral Switzerland and super-chic France?

My father said, "Go get 'em, honey," my mother gave me a list of art museums to visit in Paris, my brother offered up a "Cool, fool!" and asked how long I'd been a figure skater, and off I went to skate my way into the world outside Bronxville.

Not speaking a word of German in either the French or Swiss dialect, I managed to get myself from the airport in Zurich to the Ambassador Hotel in Bern, two hours away by train, taxi, and lots of pointing and nodding. English was not spoken as commonly as in other foreign countries, and I did what I could not to further the stereotype of the linguistically ignorant Ugly American tourist. Christa had mentioned that I would be the only American on the Christmas tour.

"Ingrid likes rooming with Americans," Christa explained of my future roommate, with a snorty little laugh, dropping the unspoken hint that there were others who did not. All I knew of Ingrid was that she was a nineteen-year-old Belgian who had an older sister currently touring with one of Holiday's yearlong shows. Perfect, I thought, a roommate with some inside info on Holiday. Maybe Ingrid would know what I could do to better my chances of landing a permanent solo spot on tour. I looked forward to having a roommate as I thought back to my summer training days in Lake Placid boardinghouses, where the bond of skating and dedication to athleticism usually forged quick, solid friendships. Maybe Ingrid and I would become lifelong pals and look back on our skating past over the years, laughing about our touring experiences and pulling out the photo albums to show our children's children how talented we had been. *Kathryn, just look how high your jumps were! Why, Ingrid, you sure could hold that spin! Look at all those funny costumes the backup skaters wore!*

My roommate arrived at the hotel later that night, educating me to the fact that obnoxiousness was not strictly an American epidemic. So much for the lifelong friendships and family photo sharing. As I sat on the bed watching CNN and finishing off my dinner — a turkey sandwich with a small brownie—Ingrid burst through the door, spewing international expletives at her gigantic suitcase and its wayward wheel.

"Are you Kathryn?" she asked in her Belgian accent, adding, "How can you eat that stuff and still be so thin?" Ingrid would be the last person to use my name and the word *thin* in the same sentence for a very long time. My Belgian roommate was five-four with dark hair that fell just below her ears, beautiful clear skin, wide brown eyes, a slightly upturned nose, and the kind of pouty mouth that might have been absolutely gorgeous if she'd kept it shut once in a while.

Ingrid managed to stretch the two-month experience of Holiday on Ice into an epic test of patience beyond the norms of human psychological endurance, although I'm sure I did the same for her with my stubborn mannerisms and an attitude that became way too defensive during our daily show rehearsals.

That night, as Ingrid unpacked her unwieldy belongings and vast array of interesting opinions, I hoped my roommate was not a foreshadowing of the other skaters' personalities. On everything from education, which she considered unnecessary beyond beauty school (she had dropped out a few months ago), to skating, a subject in which she considered herself an expert, Ingrid had the answer, whether I had asked a question or not.

"If you ask me," Ingrid said, spreading cellulite cream over the tops of her thighs and the shanks of her buttocks and then sticking a cigarette in her mouth, "America is just too damn powerful for its own good."

Letting the former comment go, I spoke my first complete sentence of the night. "No way, Ingrid. Not in here."

After growing up in both the womb and the house of a chain-smoker, I had little tolerance for the habit. Reluctantly she obliged and went into the hallway while I dealt with the strange concept that there were figure skaters who smoked. The next day I found out that I was in the extreme minority of show skaters without black lungs. Only four out of the forty cast members didn't smoke, which was roughly the same percentage of those who could actually figure skate at a "professional" level.

Ingrid huffily came back to the square little room, and as we settled into our pink-and-brown single beds with the rather nuggety slab of pillow, my mind wandered to the events of the coming days and I dozed off somewhere in the middle of Ingrid's list of Bill Clinton's governmental and aesthetic problems.

"That man may have good hair, but he does not know what the hell he's doing with foreign policy. . . ."

That makes two of us, I thought as I drifted off to sleep.

The rink was just over three miles away from the hotel. Trolley cars and buses were the most feasible way to get there, but I opted for the hourlong walk through the city. From the hotel into the center of town past the pubs, department stores, and onion sellers' carts, Bern soon opened up to display a beautiful river with a backdrop of not-so-distant mountains twice as steep as Colorado's most jagged peaks. Past the river's bridge, the city funneled into a small town with rolling hills and sheep that followed me up the sidewalk, baaing along on their side of the fence. In the last mile before the rink another township sprouted up, and behind the gingerbread houses and small buildings was the warehouse of Endemol Entertainment, the corporate owners of Holiday on Ice. Endemol is the same company that produces the reality television show *Big Brother*, in which a cast of strangers are lumped into one house until sanity and ostracism pare them all down to one mental survivor. Endemol also produces *Fear Factor*, in which willing participants are coerced to eat goat testicles and jump off skyscrapers. Next season, they plan to launch *Big Holiday's Fear Factor on Ice*, in which one lucky contestant will be sent to Bohemia, locked in a freezer wearing a chicken suit, and fed nothing until she agrees that death by skyscraper might not be so bad. Stay tuned. Pass the testicles.

There was no "rink" in the cold brick warehouse, just a square of ice 40 by 60 feet, a fraction of Murray's standard 200-by-85-foot surface, sunk into the concrete floor in the rear wing of the building. On one end of the little rinklet was the costume storeroom. The other end housed the scenery shop, where whirring saws and sewing machines screeched in the background and echoed over the ice. A tiny door in the east wall opened up to let forth an itty-bitty Zamboni, no bigger than a doghouse, that made its rounds piloted by a grumpy, wrinkled man named Yoshi whose sullen posture and scrunched-up face made it clear that he'd rather be anywhere else.

There was a small coffee room where most skaters migrated to smoke between scenes. Above the coffee station was the sliver of window leading to the sound booth, which the choreographers waved at when they wanted the music cued. All we saw of the man who pressed PLAY and REWIND was a tuft of hair and a spot of scalp that darted in small horizontal movements. Overhead hung the heating system, a maze of inflatable, condom-colored pipelike balloons that drooped from the ceiling. It was rarely used. The cold was the worst part of the dismal building; only two skylights let in what little sun there was, and the brick walls did nothing to insulate us from the outside temperatures of a European winter. This warehouse was at best a concrete igloo, and none of us were dressed in the appropriate whale blubber.

On the first day of rehearsal David and Evelyn, the show's choreographers, introduced themselves and called us to gather around. David was a flamboyant English man of fifty whose genuine passion for skating could be seen in his facial expressions. His face was as busy as he was, zipping candidly in every direction. Skating was still a big old bowl of cherries for David, and he clearly loved his job. He smiled when he spoke and was happy to converse with the skaters when they had questions or concerns. His eyes lit up and his limbs gesticulated with theatrical exuberance, making his words jump forth as though even his vocal chords were choreographed with happiness.

Evelyn, right from the get-go, appeared to possess a whole slew of traits one would not expect in a choreographer. She moved with the stiff crankiness of a veteran drill sergeant (that someone forgot to address as "sir"), and her brow was crinkled with more stress than anyone in her mid-thirties should know. There were no fruit salad comparisons for this woman, except that Evelyn probably enjoyed putting slices of grapefruit into the mix; she was subtle in her evil ways. She wore a dark red coat that fell to mid-thigh, wrinkly black pants covered her thin legs, and a clipboard rested permanently in the crook of her elbow. If perchance the board was not there, she held her hands behind her back, fingers interlaced with seriousness. Tall, lean, and physically pretty with shoulder-length blond hair, an upturned nose, and a pleasant South African accent, she seemed like an absolutely lovely person to be friends with if she wanted it that way. She usually didn't.

"How on earth did she get into this show?" I overheard Evelyn exclaim, referring to a foreign skater who had difficulty understanding one of her often complex instructions. The confused Hungarian stood right in front of Evelyn and, despite the language barrier, was just as fluent in body language as the rest of us. Embarrassed and befuddled, the skater looked at the ice, whittling her blade into the cold warehouse floor.

Eventually Evelyn singled me out as her personal chew toy, although I never knew exactly why. Oh, all right, maybe I know a little bit. Accepting the rather unappealing roles she assigned me took a bit of getting used to, and I made the mistake of letting my disappointment show. I did my best to smile and remember that old saying "There are no small parts, only small actors," but it didn't help much. I wasn't an actor, I was an athlete. A few weeks passed before I caught on to certain trends in Evelyn's "favorites" department by watching those whom she sat next to in the break room, observing whom she smiled at most. Vanessa, Valentina, Viktoria, Irina, Fiona . . . all of them tall, thin, and beautiful, but not the best skaters of the group. Quietly I began to wonder what the middle ground was between ice shows and athleticism, because something strange was going on.

That first day, David and Evelyn proceeded to take attendance Ellis Island–style, stumbling over the international pronunciations and dubbing most of the Hungarians with new names. Unlike the contingency of Olgai that would saturate Hollywood on Ice, there was no name repetition among the men or women of Holiday's cast. Only in the world of professional skating would I find myself the sole Kathryn around, my name offering only a slight sliver of individuality in a place that favored conformity.

"Kathryn Ber*tyne*?"

"Yes, I'm here. But actually, it's Ber*teen*."

"All right. Whatever." There was a slight look of annoyance on Evelyn's part, as though to make it clear that it didn't matter what my last name was or how it was pronounced and that it had indeed been very rude of me to take up the entire nanosecond needed for *Teen*ing myself. Hell, I was just happy to be addressed as Kathryn for the first time in my life.

David and Evelyn then motioned for Viktoria, a Russian woman, and me to stand side by side. Their eyes traveled up and down our bodies as they whispered to each other and made inscriptions on their notepads.

"The rest of you can go on a five-minute break," David instructed, though no one else in the cast moved. The thirty-eight remaining skaters stood there watching Viktoria and me slip off our skate guards and step on the square sheet of warehouse ice. Although David and Evelyn did not explain what they wanted with the two of us, Viktoria and I understood what was about to take place. A duel of abilities, an impromptu audition to which only we were invited. The choreographers had studied our audition videos before we arrived in Bern, sizing up our talents and searching for whatever particulars they might need. For Viktoria and me, this was a skate-off, an unspoken competition to see which one of us performed better and would get a lead or, at the very least, an understudy role in the show.

Not having been on the ice for three days, my body felt unbalanced and cumbersome in my skates. After years of four-hour daily practices, three days without skating felt like years. The time difference, the process of getting settled, and the sleepless nights spent wondering what was to come had left my head cloudy and my body unsteady. Only when I looked to Viktoria did I find the inspiration that would carry me through this spontaneous performance; she looked worried and uncertain and began to speak in rapid Russian to another cast member. She sounded nervous. Perfect. Thank you, Vikki. Off came my sweatshirt and zip-leg sweats as the temperature of the rink melted away in the heat of competition. This was the moment every practice for eleven years had prepared me for, and there was no way someone else—a smoker at that—was going to take it away from me.

"Axel, please," David said. A short Russian male stepped up and announced that he would translate for Viktoria, although it was clear he was doing more coaching than translating. Garnering as much speed as possible within the sparse perimeters of the rink, I threw my body into a single axel and came down with a solid landing. Viktoria wobbled but pulled it off. In black tights and black velvet leotard, my body was dressed like that of a serious skater, whereas Viktoria's oversized sweatshirt and saggy leggings gave more of a uninterested appearance. The doubles came next, and I attacked them with artistic ferocity while Viktoria entered them with tentative reserve. On the spins, I had flow and speed while she was slow and cautious. When the choreographers asked to see what we had up our creative sleeves, I pulled out spread eagles, Ina Bauers, and edgy footwork patterns, smiling at the audience of skaters watching us, holding my posture steadfast and unwavering as I sailed toward each end of the ice. Viktoria unleashed fabulous spirals but repeatedly failed to vary her feet, direction, or choice of edge, a big no-no as far as amateur competitions and judging is concerned. She kept circling in one direction doing the same stunt over and over again (*Look kids, Big Ben! Parliament! Viktoria!*) until David motioned for us to stop.

"Thank you," he said, calling the rest of the skaters back onto the ice. The whole process had lasted less than ten minutes. A few of the English girls complimented me on my performance, saying I had clearly outskated Viktoria. For the rest of the day I daydreamed about the possibility of being a soloist. There was already a skater from Japan cast as the leading woman, but there was an understudy part and a small step-out solo waiting to be filled. After rehearsal I noticed that Viktoria was called over to the break room with her interpreter buddy and stood smiling and laughing with Evelyn and David. She had been given the part of lead understudy. I approached the choreographers to inquire about their selection, and in doing so must have sealed my fate. Viktoria's victory was not something I could let slide: this was my dream at stake here, and Fix-it Woman was out in full force, swinging her hammer o' justice without thinking about consequences.

Evelyn did not appreciate my polite interrogation, so David let me have the so-called truth — that I was too tall for what they had in mind. Too *tall?* Five-nine? Height, I had been told by former professional skaters, was usually an advantage in performance skating, as taller skaters could simply be seen more clearly by the audience.

That was my first clue that nothing in professional figure skating could really be called fair. How could ability be put second to physical form? Wasn't weight usually the main concern of show skaters? Weight was somewhat controllable, I thought to myself, but *height?* Something just did not seem right about it all, I thought as I watched Viktoria sign some release forms while Evelyn patted her shoulder. Viktoria seemed like a nice person. I congratulated her and asked her English-speaking friend if there was a Russian equivalent of "break a leg" while I silently wondered what Jeff Gillooly's going rate was these days.

David and Evelyn called all the skaters over to explain the ins and outs of the show before beginning rehearsal. We were officially welcomed to Holiday on Ice's 1997 holiday tour: *The Animals' Christmas Parade*. Some of us looked at one another tentatively at the word *animal*. Yet I had seen ice shows where the skaters wore tight, artistic costumes that depicted animals but looked human and elegant, and naively interpreted that Holiday on Ice would have a similar wardrobe. I didn't realize that I had signed on for an ice show that would stuff me into the most obscure costumes of inhuman proportion.

For as stifling as Bronxville might have been, it was nothing compared with the suffocating surroundings of a tiny rink teeming with skaters dressed as every four-legged entity known to man. By the end of the day, my dreams of professional skating were marred by the reality of the situation: dalmatians, ponies, squirrels, hens. . . . *The Animals' Christmas Parade* was not a place of skating; this was where the rejected mascots of minor league baseball teams were sent to die. In fact, the entire show might have made more sense if it was called *The Dejected Baseball Mascots on Ice*. But Evelyn wasn't really up for my suggestions, so I kept quiet and amused myself by feigning home runs and waddling around imaginary bases during the breaks.

Dejected mascots and all, there were forty skaters in the cast of Holiday on Ice. Evelyn and David had their hands full with the task of arranging us into costumes and positions, moving us about the ice so that we correlated with their notes on paper. With the multiple language barriers, we communicated through the international language of figure skating, positioning our bodies the way Evelyn held hers or following David's arm movements until all our postures fell in sync with one another.

There were never any disciplinary problems — we all snapped to attention when the music started and whispered quietly when we were not in immediate demand. We stood on the ice at all times; in turn, certain groups of skaters were called to center ice to work individually. The elephants huddled in one corner while the frogs took center stage, dogs were on call, and the clowns were on standby in five. Bits of personality slipped through the silence of our professionalism when the show's audiotape paused and began to rewind. Some people would burst into small spasms of dance or gymnastic displays, all for the love of warmth.

It was thirty-nine degrees in the rink, something I had difficulty adjusting to. Most of the skaters wore two layers of thin cotton tights and either a leotard or skating dress (tight shirts and sweatpants for the gentlemen) so the choreographers could better work with our bodies. I knew all about cold rinks and frigid weather, but those temperatures had always disappeared into the background of the day as my body warmed itself with the rigorous routines of freestyle practice. Here, in the warehouse of ice and brick, waiting our turn for instruction left us unoccupied for hours, and in skating, *unoccupied* is a synonym for *motionless,* which is a synonym for *freeze your ass to the point of gangrene.*

Every now and then the two balloonlike wind socks that ran the length of the ceiling inflated and grew noisy, and we were told heat came from their hole-poked bellies. Maybe so, but we were far beneath these inflatable rafters, and as far as I knew, European heat was no different than the American kind, prone to rising instead of drifting down. How nice and toasty the ceiling bricks must have been. When the music paused, skaters huddled among their countrymen and chatted quietly in foreign, frozen tongues.

Jalena, a young woman from the Czech Republic with a permanent grin and an unnerving habit of not blinking enough, was, like me, the only representative of her country. Her constant cheerfulness was probably a wonderful trait, but alas, my über-grouchy frozen brain reverted to an elementary-school level of snotty behavior and it was easier to pretend she had cooties than to sit next to her willingly. After witnessing the skate-off between Viktoria and me, Jalena must have fostered the idea that there were other solos available and decided to audition every few minutes. As soon as the show music paused and most of the skaters stopped moving, Jalena flung herself into wobbly double jumps with landings short of full rotation, aimed at Evelyn's peripheral vision. The incisions of her landings rang out with boisterous toe pick screeches, scraping the ice with such force that she made gutters of impact all over the rink.

This attempt at gaining recognition did not work in Jalena's favor, as the coaches rolled their eyes and turned their backs on the flying Czech. With every awkward leap, Jalena further solidified her chances of *not* getting into Holiday on Ice's permanent roster. When she finally took a breather from her gung-ho jumping bonanzas, she talked horses to anyone who would listen. I was her favorite target, as the chance to sharpen her English skills while reciting her love of ponies was something she seemed to look forward to with endless fervor. Keeping to myself the opinion that horse fanatics were right up there with Wicca practitioners and multiple-cat owners, I did my best to look occupied when Jalena skated my way, usually by attempting to even out the grout between the brick walls with my fingernails.

"Kaaaathryn . . ."

"Oh, Jalena, I'm sorry, I have to finish up this wall. Let's talk later?"

Rudeness was not my intention. Jalena was a sweet and caring person, but my professional skating predicament was making a despicable change in my otherwise neutral personality. I saw that Jalena was an irritation to David and Evelyn, and I figured that staying on their good side meant not associating with anyone the bosses deemed unworthy. As Evelyn turned her cold shoulder toward me more and more throughout the rehearsals, I caught on that some of the skaters avoided me just as I did Jalena, and deep down I knew I deserved it. In high school I had been the kid the principal called on to show new students the Bronxville ropes, and now I was the antithesis of friendliness to a Czech woman who had the same dream I did. Only in retrospect would I come to realize that, however irritating to anyone else, it took hard-core guts for Jalena to repeatedly fly into daredevil jumps and complicated spins, to unabashedly show her competitive nature and raw desire for skating.

I was getting a bad feeling about Petting Zoo on Ice. The only people whose company I could safely enjoy (from both choreographer-politics and secondhand-smoke standpoints) were the skaters who pacified me with false notions that everything was going to get better. Ivan from Mexico was a tall, thin man not much older than I who befriended me during our lunch breaks. He was hoping to tour permanently with Holiday's Green Division and said he had seen the show many times.

"You'll get called," he assured me. "You're better than their Green soloist. Don't worry, you'll get it." I returned the reassurance, even though I had never seen Ivan skate outside the small movements of Holiday's routines. Shows always needed male skaters and he had wonderful posture and graceful limbs. Ivan sometimes went running with me, and we held down each other's feet during sit-up sets. Now and then we sat together at breakfast, Ivan guarding me from Jalena as I saved him from Vincent from France, who had an enormous crush on the lanky Latino.

Daniel was a native Swiss who was always in a good mood and liked to talk about his many visits to America. We shared stories about our respective travels and skating dreams.

"I want to open my own show one of these days," Daniel confided. He was none too thrilled with the world of Holiday, either. "You can come skate for me, I'll give you a solo!" Small sentences with promises and maybes were exactly what we all needed to hear, especially while dressed up as deformed cartoon creatures.

I enjoyed most of the skaters when we hung out in small groups, but generally everyone traveled in national packs — the Hungarian buddies, the gaggle of English friends, the Finnish sisters — and I didn't mind the independence. Lord knows that after Bronxville school and family life, I had plenty of practice at alone time.

Until the second half of the production, I waited on the side of the rink, wishing for another role and growing colder by the minute, wondering how low my core body temperature could go before I died. In *Outside* magazine I read that just before people freeze to death, they grow delirious with hallucinations and get a warm, happy feeling all over. As clowns and marsupials skated by in conversation with horses dressed in overalls, death still seemed a far way off because the warm happy feeling never set in. When I sensed that there was enough time to take off one or both skates and revive my feet back into a semiconscious state of warmth, I untied my laces and rubbed at my stinky extremities.

My feet are like Quasimodo, lumpy and good-natured but a bit scary looking. On the back of each heel, bone spurs stick out like overprotective fenders while calluses run along the side: the human equivalent of the Toyota RAV4. The large bumps of heel growth came into being because I once spent too many months in a pair of ill-fitting figure skates. My feet grew three sizes in my first teenage year but because everything else on my body was equally confused, I didn't pay much attention to my toes' demands. So when my new skates seemed too small after only a month of wear, I figured that it was just the norm of figure skating and that I should get used to the feeling. When I finally couldn't take the pulsating discomfort any longer, I showed my suffering extremities to my coach, who asked if there was any trace of dinosaur in my genetic history because my feet looked like angry little *T. rex* claws.

Kind of like that seemingly unnecessary little morsel of toe that dogs have halfway up the rear of their paw, my bone spurs are useless but interesting. They jut my shoe size out one and a half times its normal length, so that my only option for footwear is to hit the racks at Payless for a devious mix-and-match from the shelves of different sizes. In addition to my protruding heel deformities, figure skating grew a mountainous shell of extra skin on my pinkie toes and other odd reconfigurations of my foot. The too small puberty-era skates so frightened one toe on my right foot — the ring finger equivalent, or the little piggy who didn't get roast beef — that it still continues to cower beneath its buddy to the right and won't come out from hiding no matter what I do to coax it into an independent lifestyle. This little piggy now resembles Gumby after a severe beating. There is also a grainy cluster of something bonelike yet smushy below the inside of my anklebone that has been there since I started skating and has lingered because it apparently has nowhere else to go and nothing better to do. A feeling I well related to inside Holiday's warehouse.

The English and Russian contingents had about ten skaters each, and they traveled in packs both within and outside the rink. I had met two of the British girls in the hotel bar the night before rehearsals started. Needing to escape my roommate for a few hours, I ventured into the bar and sat alone with my nerdy but comforting Coke until two women with the most beautiful hair I had ever seen entered the room and sat down next to me. One was blond and quiet, one was brunette and rowdy, and each had long, curly Rapunzel-like hair that hung glamorously down her back and tickled the butt of the barstool. I had just gotten my boob-length hair trimmed to my shoulders, and I longed for the abandoned inches upon seeing their tresses. Even without the little skate-charm necklaces, we knew we were all there for the skating tour. Skaters can usually sense one another's presence, since there are two kinds of auras skaters radiate: either the "I've spent my life in a cold bubble and therefore have no sense of the world outside but, golly, I'm cute!" or the more refreshing "I've spent my life in a cold bubble but am slightly conscious that there is life outside skating, but, yeah, I'm still kinda cute" vibe.

Clara was from England and adhered to the latter description, and Minnie was from Wales and leaned more toward the former. One worked in a skating show at a London-based theme park, the other had just finished a stint with Disney on Ice, where she spent years skating in the belly of a Mickey Mouse costume. We made conversation for a while, talking about the usual topics of how long we'd been skating, where we had trained, whether we had been in professional shows before Holiday on Ice.

As I left to turn in for the night, Minnie, who had tossed back a few gin and tonics by this time, said, "Damn this thing itches." With that, she took off her hair and put the long brown clip-on head of curls into her purse. Beneath her mass of curls was a cropped head of gelled-back hair, with an indentation where the barrette had once clung. Clara told me her true hair was as short as her friend's, but she kept the disguise attached to her head. Both of them mentioned that the longer, more feminine hair helped them get into ice shows.

It turned out that Clara had a wonderful presence on the ice — when she remained upright for more than five minutes. She had a strange habit of falling at the most unexpected times, like when she was standing still. Tall one minute and sprawled the next, Clara was a dyslexic jack-in-the-box of human movement. Here was the opposite of any skater I had ever encountered; she could deliver endless double lutzes with beautiful height and graceful landings, then collapse while doing a T-stop, a basic maneuver not much more difficult than it sounds. She'd nail flying camel combination spins, then wipe out on a single forward crossover.

In a concerned way I found Clara's spontaneous losses of balance rather amusing, like some sort of athletic narcolepsy. Instead of falling asleep, she only got as far as the verb. Clara seemed to notice nothing odd about her bouts with gravity and no one else brought up the topic, as if her falls were a genetic disorder it was impolite to stare at: a lazy eye, a giant goiter, Clara falling. People just looked away and waited till she righted herself. Even Evelyn, who I thought might wreak havoc on a wobbly skater, appeared not to care. This seemed peculiar, as falling usually went against the grain of most professional skating ideologies. Then again, falling has always been an area of interest to the figure skating audience, usually more so than for the skater. Something about witnessing the collapse of another human being is a continual source of intrigue for all sports enthusiasts, but only in skating does it seem like such a contradiction to the surrounding atmosphere of shimmery perfection. In football and hockey we expect physical plummeting; in basketball floor collisions look melodramatic but are still welcomed; and in baseball and soccer skidding wipeouts often precede or follow a successful play. In skating, it just looks altogether wrong.

The danger of falling in Holiday on Ice's Parade of Animals was relatively minimal for most of the skaters, as the steps were simple and most of the cast had been on ice skates before. With the exceptions of Jalena and Clara and Minnie, the rest of the women of Holiday on Ice were stable-footed with permanent heads of hair and a healthy indifference toward horses. There were three Hungarian women with a background in synchronized team skating, two bubbly Finnish sisters no taller than four-eleven, four very tan Brazilians, Mitsue the minute Japanese soloist, a South African redhead already hired on to Holiday's coveted Green Tour, and a pair of lively Italians who could barely skate but apparently loved trying and made up in personality what they lacked in skill. I wondered how they were ever hired for the show in the first place, as they were unable to do the most fundamental jumps and spins.

"Just look at them," Fiona, the long-limbed South African, said in answer to my question. "They're tall and thin." That was true; Vanessa and Valentina were just that, with spindly arms and legs that one would not hesitate to call skinny even beneath the winter sweaters they wore. Fiona was thin as well. So was everyone. I took a look around the warehouse as the show was put together, and noticed that the thinner skaters were often placed in the front line of numbers, while those less svelte were dressed in giant costumes that required little more than walking up and down the ice and waving at the audience of small children we were anticipating. Even the men were ultra-lean, especially the French and English contingents. The male Russian soloist, Roman, was short and squat, and Mitsue, his Japanese counterpart, was of the same dimensions. Viktoria, cast as Mitsue's understudy after our less-than-dramatic skate-off, was also petite. There was one woman my height, one of the quiet Hungarians, but everyone else was smaller and looked to be on the thinner side of healthy. All the years of running and skating had kept me lean but muscular, something surely favorable to professional skating, I had believed. About as favorable as my Mascots on Ice idea.

In the break room there was coffee and sometimes a plate of sweet pastries or cookies that one of the male skaters brought from the bakery down the street. The women did not eat these, and when we went for our lunch breaks they scattered about the neighborhood cafés in search of more coffee. At the time, I paid little attention to what people were and were not eating. I ate the measly breakfast at the Hotel Ambassador: a wheat roll the size of a kumquat and a pot of tea, and traded my miniature croissant for another wheat roll. I'd never liked those buttery little boomerangs and their empty, airy consistency. This Hungry-Man power breakfast was supposed to fuel me until dinner, through eight hours of skating and standing around an oversize freezer in the middle of a sub-zero winter.

On the other side of the hotel restaurant there was a buffet with fruit and cereal and eggs, but we were not allowed to eat in that half of the dining room. On the way out, though, I waited until the waitresses turned their heads and jetted over to pilfer some bananas or whatever I could get my hands on, to take with me. Turning a deaf ear to any server who approached me and defending myself with "No speak German, no speak German," I slipped away with my pockets full of fruit and napkin-wads of granola, feeling self-conscious of what felt both necessary and gluttonous.

On our half-hour lunch break, we all filed out of the warehouse and walked to the local shops and restaurants and produce markets. The Swiss November sky was usually the same color as the interior of the rink, gray and drab, hinting at the possibility of snow that never fell. Lunchtime found me with frozen toes, chilled bones, and an ache for warmth not unlike what I'd experienced on the mornings I had known so long ago at Murray's while tracing those loopy lobes of meticulous figures. At lunch I sat with Ivan or went off by myself to drink tea or coffee with lots of bottled water. I chose fruit over sandwiches despite the hunger I felt, not really understanding why an orange could suddenly make me feel better about myself than the turkey sandwich my stomach called out for. There was no time to analyze such thoughts; practice resumed quickly, refreezing our minds for the rest of the day.

When rehearsals ended at five, a group of us gathered at a place called Menora, a cafeteria-style buffet restaurant filled with amazing foods from all over the world. This restaurant came to be the site of my last supper, the last place I can remember eating normally, healthily, for a period that would extend long past my professional skating experience.

I missed the foreshadowing of my eating disorder that came in the form of my first costume: a furry, full-body circus-elephant suit complete with horizontally striped overalls and a pink bow tie. Prepared for glitzy spandex and the finest beading Holiday on Ice had to offer, I instead found myself in the belly of some sort of Euro-Dumbo, unsure whether to laugh or cry at this mammoth predicament. But by the end of the week, the elephant costume had become my favorite of the four creatures I was doomed to wear. The clumsy rooster, the angry duck, and the ditzy country bumpkin all paled in comparison to this enormous suspender-wearing pachyderm.

There were sixteen generic Babars in all, each with the same wide-eyed expression of excitable joy sewn onto its humongous face. The head weighed fifteen pounds and connected to the top of the fiberglass overalls with two interlocking plastic buckles similar to the ones found on the belts of backpacks. We looked out of mesh screens that constituted the elephants' mouths, our own heads bobbing where their tonsils might hang. One of our arms went through an armhole of the elephant, and the other went into its snout. Evelyn decreed that we figure out a way to move both our elephant arms and the trunk simultaneously, which posed a bit of a problem for any skater born with fewer than three arms. Sticking our left arm in the nose and our right arm in the elephant's right arm, then quickly switching positions into the opposite orifices, we did the best we could.

We began marching in unison, starting on the left foot, and while Evelyn stared at my furry legs with just enough intensity to make me question which foot was which, I concentrated more on my teeny-weeny baby steps than I had on my Senior Ladies long program. There was a herd of undifferentiated elephants circling around the rink in organized chaos, but Evelyn knew exactly where I was at all times, ready to yank me out to use as an example in her incessant speeches on the importance of knowing left from right. If only we'd had tusks.

"Happy elephants, I want happy elephants!" Evelyn dictated. What she got, with our wiggling trunks and erratic arm movements, was more analogous to an elephant allergy attack than a happy day at the zoo. Stepping and turning and bowing to one another was the technical portion of the elephant routine, all set to circus music complete with the sound effects of animal brays and whip-cracking ringmasters in the background. The whole scene took three minutes from the time we shuffled out onto the ice until we trundled back behind the curtain. Trying to balance the claustrophobic thirty-pound costume on the ice took more dexterity than I imagined, but it was not the skill I had trained for all those years of my amateur career.

The idea of human-powered, voiceless stuffed animals is just as eerie from the inside as it is from without. On my personal scale of creepiness, with *The Exorcist* rating a high of 5 stars and Mrs. Butterworth holding steady at 1, the animals of Holiday on Ice scored a good, solid 4½. I didn't like looking at the costumes or being stuck inside them, but every now and then someone would swivel her elephant head around 360 degrees while we waited backstage, breaking up the boredom with a small exorcism of much-needed humor. Still, deep questions echoed in my papier-mâché skull: All that hard work for this? What am I doing here? Am I ever going to get to *skate*? But if this was what it took to get started in pro skating, if playing safari dress-up was a step toward getting a solo, then all the dehumanization would eventually be worth it. *Suck it up,* I instructed all the doubting impulses zipping about my body. *Suck it up and be patient, Babar.* Quitting was just not an option.

Despite the animal-costume indignities, the only one to leave the show was Helen from England, who decided to return home after being cast as a rooster. She said she missed her boyfriend, but I assumed she probably missed herself as well. The rooster costume was ugly and demeaning, and its feces-colored feathery bodice hung like vertical roadkill among the rest of the wardrobe. Helen dropped out three days before the tour embarked for Paris, and Evelyn threw the rooster ensemble at me, smirking. Helen was a good ten inches shorter than I, but I believe Evelyn found great pleasure in shoving me, the only land-of-the-eagle American kid with Holiday on Ice, into the shell of a fabric chicken.

The rooster outfit itself was not really what made me feel so dejected; in fact, its ugliness was kind of amusing. But there was something else going on beneath the surface. I was the second-tallest female in the cast, so why didn't Evelyn cast one of the smaller skaters as the rooster? I began to suspect that the whole height excuse was just a cover-up for lies and favoritism. But if height wasn't really the main aspect of casting, then what was?

Having no other choice but to quit, which did not seem like a choice at all, I wiggled into this most horrific costume of white and brown feathers, complete with strap-on chicken feet that attached to my skating boots. There was even a creepy little nubbin of toe jutting out from the rear of the cloth heel, right in line with my bone spur. The rooster skull, which weighed more than the elephant head, was adorned with a bright red comb and two crossed eyes. Playing an androgynous elephant was one thing, but my ego was having a rough go accepting that it had to reside within the feathery skin of an optically challenged male chicken. I was the spitting image of the Looney Tunes' famously stuttering Foghorn Leghorn. All grace was lost inside the husk of this macho beast. The costume was so heavy and cumbersome that I was struggling for survival inside its hazy barnyard parameters.

The act was even worse than the elephant routine. In this Christmas farmhouse scene, a fox chased the rooster, a turkey, a peacock, and a cat around the rink. Nothing resembling skating took place, and the ticket holders in France never actually clapped while the farm antics were set in motion. I say, I say, I say, my roosterly self came out from behind the curtain, ran from the fox, and went back, back, backstage. I failed to see the entertainment of the act, but Holiday on Ice needed some way to buy time between the soloists' costume changes.

Time took on a new dimension during my stint with Holiday on Ice. I measured the days by rehearsal hours and broke down the minutes according to the duration of the show songs that ran through my head, even when I was away from the rink. Do I have time to go to the bathroom? *Sure, you've got at least three elephant parades before the movie starts.* When will the next train arrive? *Oh, in a few chicken solos.* When did you last speak to your boyfriend? *Yesterday, but he was at work, so we could only talk for a frog duet.* I had never been one to hurry time's passing. As an athlete rushing from practice to practice, time was something there was never enough of; it was never wasted or taken for granted. To suddenly count the minutes until skating was over left me perplexed and uneasy, yet I dismissed it as an adjustment period, something that would work itself out. *You can't quit now . . . this is everything you worked for! Remember all those hours of practice, all those shows and competitions? Remember the way it feels when an audience roars with applause and you are the reason for it? Remember the chill of the air at 5:30 in the morning while you stood alone on Murray's ice and your nostrils and eyelashes froze together? You didn't quit then and you're not quitting now. Be ready, be ready for anything.*

"You'll have more to do later, Kathryn," David assured me kindly, offering hope that a more human role might be in my future.

There were three divisions a Holiday on Ice skater could be assigned to permanently: the Blue Division that toured England, the Gold Division that traveled through the rest of Europe, and the illustrious Green Division that ventured all the way to South Africa. I had no color preference; anything was better than the freezing little ice cell in Bern or returning home to tell only of my days as a professional rooster. During the breaks, we whispered rumors about which skaters would make it where. Though my roommate was not as good at skating as she was at unleashing verbal diatribes on all things American, Ingrid was convinced that she would make it onto the Blue Tour, as her sister was a principal skater there. Sometimes nepotism was a bonus, if the preceding generation proved talented.

Realistically, there was no point in offering any sort of prediction as to who would end up where. The sucking-up had already begun, and the extra-smiley faces always greeted David and Evelyn whenever they walked into the warehouse. I partook in these events, doling out compliments to the choreographers, smiling with forced plasticity, keeping close check on my rights and lefts. I ventured into the office every day to chat with head honcho Christa and order something from the Holiday on Ice catalog, to show my pride and devotion to the company. Sweatshirts, warm-up suits, hats, all fantastically gaudy and completely unnecessary—I raked in the goods before any other suck-ups had a chance. In retrospect, buying the Holiday on Ice duffel bag was a bad idea and an even worse prophecy.

During the duck number Evelyn became irreversibly fed up with me, or so it felt at the time. For the Christmas pond scene, one of the most bizarre numbers in the show, I was cast as Angry Duck. I was one of six yellow furballs, each with his own emotion (angry, happy, sad, stupid, etc.), that marched out onto the ice searching for the hunter who had just shot—and killed—a baby duck! None of us saw the relevance to Christmas festivity, unless the poor duckling was supposed to represent the holiday dinner. But we were not paid to question the ingenuity of Holiday on Ice.

The act got stranger by the minute, as the six ducks waddled around the ice in search of the horrible hunter until the marching tempo broke loose into a blues beat. Then we momentarily became funky ducks, dancing and waving our muskets (in addition to our diverse facial expressions, we were all Revolutionary War–era army ducks), before going back to being serious birds.

During the swanky part, each duck was ordered to interact with the children in the audience. While we rehearsed in the spectatorless warehouse, we simply left out this part and stood facing the brick walls till the music changed. In France, where the tour took place, I ended up wrestling half the kids because they were more intent on trying to take off my enormous ducky skull than on shaking my friendly ducky hand. Had one looked closely during the audience-interaction part, it would have been quite clear that we ducks were not shaking the little French children's hands but rather playing tug-of-war with our webbed mittens. Making it back to center ice on cue did not always happen, as some of the older kids, hell-bent on finishing their duck lobotomy, grabbed onto our scalp-sewn, palm-size tuft of yellow fluff and opted not to let go. Most of the ducks were bald by the end of the tour, our neck muscles aching from struggling with the adolescent mad scientists.

In the middle of a day filled with continuous dress rehearsals, I changed out of the duck sack and hung it back up in its proper location until the next run-through of the number. Backstage looked like a rough draft of Greek mythology, with halves of costumes strewn everywhere and half human, half wannabeasts shuffling to and fro. Instead of the powerful centaur or the mighty griffin, Holiday's pseudo-Zeus gave to the world the weak-ass poodlesphinx and the harmless mallardonious.

When the second drill of the show began, my yellow duck feet were missing. I had my suspicions, as a few of my down-coated colleagues were not the most reliable or honest types. We all had to keep track of our own costumes, which proved to be beyond the mental capacity of some of the skaters. Whoever had lost his duck feet simply found it easier to take mine instead. I came out onto the ice anyway, not wanting to disrupt the rehearsal because of some misplaced boot covers that I could easily track down later. Suddenly the music stopped and Evelyn skated over and demanded to know why my skates were not webbed like everyone else's.

"Someone took my feet," I quacked, my best Donald Duck impersonation echoing out from the chamber of my furry head while I pointed my faux firearm over at Happy Duck. That didn't go over well. Forgetting that I was dressed as Angry Duck, I didn't realize that Evelyn might take my accusation far more seriously than I intended. Waving my prop around wasn't such a wise move, either. God forbid my papier-mâché gun might go off and kill the baby duckling already lying dead in the middle of the ice. From that point on, Evelyn branded me the unreliable goof-off and spoke to me condescendingly, if at all. I was the

American yahoo who was rude and rebellious and did not take her role in this fine production seriously enough. As I waddled back to the dressing room to hunt for my flippery booties, I took a long look at myself in the wall-size mirror next to the sewing machines. Angry Duck, indeed. The downward-slanted eyebrows, scowling mouth, the wrinkled little beak. It took me a second to notice that I had already taken off the giant birdie head and that my own reflection glared at me from the mirror. No wonder Evelyn didn't like me. I looked bitter and disgruntled and anything but happy to be where I was.

Holiday on Ice was not my dream, and on the days when things didn't go my way or rooster costumes came too plentifully, my internal defense mechanism to ward off disappointment—*the Ice Capades would have been so much better*—didn't help me give Holiday much of a chance. Evidently I'd brought a bit more baggage overseas than I thought. Maybe I did have a bad attitude. Maybe I was acting like a spoiled kid who expected immediate stardom. It certainly looked that way in the mirror. Maybe I could lighten up a little, learn to love the rooster. Be one with the elephant. Give Angry Duck a big hug. Finally it dawned on me that my cranky outlook and my perceived aloofness might be interpreted as completely disrespectful. After all, my dream to skate professionally was not something I wanted to pursue for all eternity, just for a few seasons. Yet for other skaters and for Evelyn and David, Holiday on Ice was their entire life. In the grand scheme of things, I was just a very eager visitor to their world. Perhaps my attitude had made it seem as though their world came second to my dreams. *Good job, Angry Duck. You've really started out on the right webbing.*

Neither Evelyn nor David was someone to rub the wrong way, for they both had direct ties to Christa, head of all casting and booking for the permanent tours. It was Christa who had hired me in the first place, who had seen my audition videotapes and sent a positive response in the middle of my Ice Capades meltdown. In the pit of my stomach, as I rummaged around for my ducky feet, I knew I was in the same boat as Jalena the jumping Czech: tolerated, but not for long.

Oddly enough, despite my sentencing into the rooster costume, the Angry Duck outfit, and the enormous elephant ensemble, David and

Evelyn had given me a short, thirty-second duet with Viktoria in the finale. Upon hearing the news that I would actually get to perform a couple of figure skating maneuvers apart from the majority of the cast, I was
overcome with a newfound enthusiasm for Holiday on Ice. But the excitement was short-lived, and I reprimanded myself for getting my hopes
up before getting the full scoop.

In keeping with the spirit of the entire production, the finale offered little normalcy and strayed quite far from the Christmas theme.
Viktoria and I were country girls from a big old country family who
stepped away from the rest of the cast members to briefly hurl ourselves
into axels and flying camels while the rest of the gang did a hoedown
with their honkin' barnyard friends. *Hurl* is a generous verb, for trying
to do any jump in the full-length skirt with multiple petticoats was a
challenge in itself, like asking a gymnast to perform a vault while wearing a straitjacket.

The dress was far from glamorous. The weight of the skirts combined with the velocity of the jump wrapped the polka-dotted fabric
around our bodies with more force than polyester is given credit for, and
the costume threatened the security of our landings. Our flying camels
were slow and lumpy-looking beneath the weight of the skirts, but we
smiled and stepped lively and put on our performance faces of false bliss.
If there was anything uplifting about the duet, it was that no masks were
worn and for the first time in the entire show I felt like a human being,
if only for a few moments. Too quick to gratify my professional skating
dream and too slow to fill me with the sensation of true figure skating,
the duet felt like a tease, a booby prize, a doggie bag from a feast I had
not been invited to.

As the cast whirled about one last time, Alexei, a Russian skater-
gymnast, barreled down the ice and whipped into the series of round-off
back-handspring back flips for which he was hired. Just as he finished,
the meddlesome duck hunter appeared once again and fired his shotgun
into the air, the whole cast collapsed onto the ice, and a blackout swallowed us up.

Evelyn insisted that we lie there on the ice until she went over our
corrections for the next run-through. Sprawled on our backs like forty
Claras, we stared up at the ceiling of the warehouse and waited to begin

all over again. When we took the show to Paris, the ending looked quite different. In the midst of the blackout, while we lay on our backs on Parisian ice, the children of the audience waved thousands of glowing green light-up toys in the pitch-black air. For a moment the entire rink looked like a foreign galaxy of neon stars, the zooming, twirling, and waving powered by unseen hands while voices echoed in a roar of appreciation. There was peace right then and there, as all rehearsals, costumes, personalities, and core body temperatures were temporarily forgotten beneath the stunning sky of plastic lights. Had the instant lasted a second or two longer, perhaps the entire show would have been worth it.

The hardest part of life within the warehouse was the standing and waiting for each dress rehearsal to get under way. In the days of training back at Murray's rink, coaches had no forbearance for the girls who hung on the boards chatting, talking, and wasting time. As skaters, we were there to skate, to shape ourselves into athletes, and those who lounged around were seen as lazy kids without motivation. Here, behind the curtain of Holiday on Ice, everyone moped with expressions beyond boredom and constantly whined for cigarette breaks. They talked about which bars to get plastered at after rehearsal, who they had picked up the night before, and how many calories were in a cup of coffee. I sat on the benches outside the heated break room, growing more and more numb from the damp chill in the brick-wall rink, not sure how I fit into my surroundings. Holiday sure wasn't Murray's, but I'd never expected it to be. I just didn't think the experience was going to be so like Bronxville. I was starting to feel terribly lonely.

Another skater sat on the benches, too, writing letters home. She was one of the girls hired from England, and we struck up a conversation. Felicia Hopkinson was one of the ten British girls in the cast. On the first day of practice she wore a blue jacket with yellow lettering that spelled out her alma mater, John Moores College, in Liverpool. My outermost layer was a roomy, maroon-and-gray Colgate sweatshirt that the university had given me as a gift for writing the graduation article six months before. I wore the sweatshirt nearly every day to rehearsal, the memories embedded in the lettering adding a little extra psychological warmth to the warehouse. With her shoulder-length blond hair, bright blue eyes, and the kind of cheeks that must have been relentlessly pinched by aging relatives throughout her childhood, Felicia was cute and unassuming.

Felicia and I discovered that we were the only two college grads among Holiday's skaters and felt fortunate that we had our education to fall back on after the skating experience. Felicia was a good, solid skater, strong in the technical areas of jumping and spinning. Yet she could turn on the charm and whip out the skater smile when necessary, so it was easy to see why Holiday chose to hire her. She was also about five-four, which Holiday favored more than the five-five-plus population. Neither of us wanted to be a professional skater her whole life, and we spent our break times talking about our non-skating-related interests. Felicia aspired to be a pilot but had always dreamed passionately of skating professionally first. Holiday on Ice was England's version of the Ice Capades, touring through her hometown every year since she could remember. Flying could wait, this was the time for skating, Felicia believed, just as I had put off plans of graduate school and dreams of journalism. We spoke of looking forward to France, wondering what it would be like to finally perform this mutually detested show before an audience. For the remainder of our time with Holiday on Ice, Felicia and I became inseparable and spent our sparse free time walking the streets of Bern, talking about flying and writing, and hiding from Jalena and all her pretty horses.

The first thing I did when we arrived in Paris was step in a pile of poodle shit, which, no matter how much I tried to laugh it off as dumb klutziness, proved a pretty accurate omen of what the next year would bring. When our tour bus pulled in to Paris in early December, I had been eager to disembark and survey the streets for running routes. While I scraped the tread of my fouled Asics along the curb, the rest of the skaters filed past me with looks of disgust, as if I had deliberately flung myself into the poop. By this time I was somewhat of an outsider to the cast, a fact Ingrid often reminded me of.

"No one here thinks you'll make it as a show skater," she offered matter-of-factly one day, between her theories that America was destined for utter failure and that Belgian chocolate was far superior to "that Hershey shit."

"Yeah? Why won't I?"

"You're too healthy," she replied. "All that running crap, and you never party. You won't last on a regular tour." My individuality, it seemed, was mistaken for aloofness by some of the skaters, and I recognized the familiar tone of Ingrid's declaration. Up to that point I had dismissed all of Ingrid's philosophies with equal disregard, as they affected me about as profoundly as the cellulite cream did her buttocks, but this comment stuck and felt like an immediate throwback to my high school days. Running, sightseeing, not partying . . . I wasn't trying to be snobby or act superior to anyone, I was just trying to be myself. Usually I leapt at the chance to prove people wrong when challenged, but Ingrid had a point. I was healthy, healthy to the point of freakishness in the eyes of some. My mother smoked enough for the two of us, drugs just didn't entice, and alcohol never entered the picture.

Peer pressure backfired way back in the sixth grade and made a lasting impression when a classmate of mine teased me for not wanting to take a sip of beer at her older sibling's party. "You're gonna have to try it sooner or later," she said. I did not like being told what I had to try, and I was so horrified that someone could judge me by whether or not I drank that the very idea of alcohol turned irrevocably sour. More so with every taunt through adolescence. To this day, I have never tasted it.

My idea of partying, when I really went crazy, usually involved slugging back three or more caffeinated sodas in one evening. I wasn't *trying* to be a straight arrow, I just was. I had some control issues, in the sense that I liked being in control of my own body at all times. That was something I could trace back to an obsession my mother had about what or how much I ate as a teenager. About that time I began to guard my body fiercely, deciding that I would be the only one who ruled what went into it. Not to mention that my personality was of an addictive nature: skating, running, rowing—these were things that my endorphin-junkie body craved so voraciously that if I could not have them on call all the time, I felt restless, deprived, and out of control. When I loved something, whether it was a sport, activity, or fellow human, I wanted more of it and as often as possible. Drugs and alcohol, if by chance I found their effects pleasing, would probably take me down faster than my attempt at a triple axel, so I just avoided chemical temptation altogether.

Holiday on Ice was not going to break my long-ingrained patterns of alcohol abstinence or my happy addiction to endorphins. Despite Ingrid's prophecy of my future in show skating, I felt that I got along well with a fair number of the skaters. Ingrid was the only one with whom I occasionally clashed. I helped some of the Russians with their English in the dressing rooms, and in return they showed me how to put on eye shadow and cheek blush so it no longer appeared that a packet of Skittles had exploded on my face. Trivial yet confidence-building, Irina and Livia's makeup pointers made me feel like the most attractive rooster no one had ever seen.

Although I knew I could survive on any tour just fine, the question I was refusing to entertain was whether I wanted to be on a tour like this one. So far, the world of professional figure skating was anything but what my imagination had conjured up over the course of a decade. I could forgive the nutty themes and weird costumes, but where the hell was the skating? Surely things would get better, more Ice Capades–like. There was always the permanent tour, and even though Evelyn was not a warm, fuzzy person, she could not deny that I had more talent than most of the women in this peculiar animal parade.

We awaited our room assignments outside the Paris hotel, and my soles were nearly free of feces when I heard my name combined with Ingrid and Mitsue, the Japanese soloist. Mitsue was the only Asian woman in the cast, and a good skater, with powerful jumps and playful antics of choreography. Maybe five feet tall on a good day, she was adventuresome and individualistic. She didn't spend much time with the other skaters, choosing to explore the city instead of sleep in or party late, but because she was the soloist, no one spoke ill of her lack of group-bonding efforts. Ingrid took the pullout couch, and Mitsue and I grabbed the twin beds in a separate room. I wasn't sure which was more difficult to listen to — Ingrid's terminal America-bashing diatribes or Mitsue's constant replay of and backup singing to the Rent soundtrack, so I spent most of my time with Felicia or out running through the streets of Paris. At night I came back to the suite to find Ingrid frying fish heads in the kitchen or Mitsue lying on the couch and moaning about her stomachache with an empty bulk-size packet of Gummi Bears by her side. Both my roommates refused my offers of fresh bread from the shop on the corner unless it had been toasted crispier than a crouton.

"Fresh bread has more calories than toast," Ingrid alleged.

"No, it doesn't," I balked. "It's exactly the same. Geez. Do you want some or not?"

"Clinton looks like he eats too much bread."

"Okay, thanks, I'll let him know."

"And too much fast food. They show that on TV."

"Ingrid, the president eats a lot of things he shouldn't."

Our hotel was ten blocks from the Palais Omnisports in Bercy, an incredible anti-Murrayan structure that was as artistic outside as it was spacious inside. Pyramids of mirrored glass punctured the bubble-dome stereotype of what a skating rink should look like, and a slate walkway encircled the outer perimeter of the rink—perfect for running laps. Usually I hated running in circles, but the streets of Paris were heavy with foot traffic and filled with people who stared in disbelief that a person would voluntarily run without being chased by something. Circumnavigating the Omnisport was quiet, safe, and solitary. I ran in the mornings, circling the Omnisport from the outside or finding my way inside to run up the stadium steps over and over until my legs ached but would still be able to carry out three ice shows that day.

Some days I made my way to the banks of the Seine and ran its length along the city. I never traveled anywhere without a pair of shorts, a trustworthy sports bra, and a couple of size ten Gel-Lyte Asics packed in the bottom of my bag. Ever since seventh grade intramural cross-country, running had been my passion second to skating. Through the city streets of a foreign town, my feet knew the way in the manner that only a runner understands—as if there can be no wrong turns or wasted steps, because running isn't about maps and direction but rather chance and duration, and all I could do was heed the compass inside me.

The thoughts that passed through my head as I ran through Paris were different from those I had when running in New York. Something had changed, and I found myself running because it proved more a necessary comfort than a physical enjoyment. Comfort, however, grew closer to obsession, and if I was not running, I was walking everywhere to keep my mind and body occupied with things other than the tour and all its disappointment. At the end of a day with Holiday on Ice, I was exhausted from standing around and climbing in and out of stuffed animals. I thought about the days filled with the figure skating I used to know, when my body would ache with the satiating fatigue of physical exertion. The serene calm of a postathletic state was a reward in itself, and I would fall asleep every night with the peace of knowing that my body had squeezed all it could have out of life that day. There, in the streets of Paris, I walked and ran to escape the very questions I was trying to figure out.

The holiday show would end in three weeks, and then what? What if Holiday did not re-sign me? Where would I go, what would I do? Was that to be the end of all I had worked for in skating? Sometimes I ran to answer these questions, other days I put on my sneakers in hopes of outrunning their constant need of contemplation. Besides, running would burn away the calories I had taken to counting, a concept that had never crossed my mind when I had run in high school or college. Things were changing. Evelyn had brought a scale into the rink the day before and called a few of the women to stand on its plastic platform. She wrote the numbers into a book and dismissed the person on the scale with a curt thank-you.

Between shows or on the occasional afternoon off, I did what all good Bronxville citizens were supposed to do while abroad and visited the finest, most regal institutions of tourism. I wandered through the Louvre, the lovely overstocked museum so dense with stuff that even the hallways leading to the rest rooms were clogged with priceless artifacts. I looked for the *Mona Lisa,* who hid herself behind bulletproof plastic and a thousand other tourists. She was much smaller than I had imagined, and twice as sarcastic-looking as the textbooks depicted. I dawdled through Notre Dame, more fixated on sighting Quasimodo's ghost than the flying buttresses I was supposed to take note of. The Eiffel Tower, where I opted to take the stairs instead of the elevator, was a lot of fun but I skipped the historical plaques on the way up because timing my ascent was more of a thrill. I was failing miserably at tourism and did not to give a twaddle about anything antique or historic. I used these sights as distractions from my thoughts rather than as educational experiences, though the latter was something I usually enjoyed. Paris was miserable because I was.

Erik, the booking manager for Holiday on Ice, had been ignoring me throughout the latter half of the Paris tour. He was the go-between for Christa in the office and Evelyn and David out on the ice. It was the second-to-last day of the Christmas show and still some skaters were waiting for their next tour assignments, which would begin in two days' time. Ingrid had already been cast in the same tour as her sister, traveling through Europe. Mitsue was on her way to the Green Division in South Africa, and Viktoria was assigned there as well. Everything about these assignments was reassuring and my confidence was high; my skating level was more advanced than Ingrid's and Viktoria's, and if they were cast, all I had to do was wait for Erik to bring the good news. South Africa, England, Europe, it didn't matter, but I needed to know soon so I could send word to my parents whether I needed the suitcase with the T-shirts or the one with the sweaters sent from home.

"I'm sorry, Kathryn," Erik finally broke when I cornered him in the Omnisport parking lot after he tried to slip out a back door. "You haven't been assigned."

"Okay, so then you'll know tomorrow?"

Erik shook his head. I stared at him.

"Why?" My anger came out louder than the disappointment it covered.

"Well, uh, American visas are really expensive; we just don't have the means to hire you," he fed me.

"Then pay me less." Salary had never been the drive. If it had been, I'd have been in trouble trying to rely on my weekly three-hundred-dollar paycheck. I had a better shot at becoming a millionaire poet than making a decent living as a pro figure skater. I was going to get a so-called *real* job and go to grad school after the tour, anyway. But this was the time for skating, and with everything slipping away, I was ready to do it for pennies. *A* penny. Whatever technically constituted professional status. I could live off stolen napkin wads of granola—not a problem. Just *please* don't take away my skating dreams.

Erik, running out of excuses, fumbled for his keys. "Casting doesn't work that way, I'm sorry. I hope you enjoyed your time with Holiday on Ice." As he got into the car, I leaned down to his window for one last question, prefacing it with a request for his honesty.

"Is it my weight?" Evelyn had put me on the scale the day before, staring intently at the number that arose. The moment of silence that passed between my question and Erik's answer was the answer in itself, but he came up with some words he believed might soften the blow.

"Show skating isn't for everyone."

"What happens to a dream deferred?" Langston Hughes asks in his famous poem. "Does it dry up / like a raisin in the sun? / Or fester like a sore— / And then run?"

With Holiday on Ice cutting me loose, my dream was rapidly heading toward the raisin stage. All I had worked for was suddenly shrunken down to the perfect yet unfortunate analogy of a dehydrated grape. Dried-up raisins, open wounds, and the blistering chafe of an ill-fitting dream. When it came to fat dreams and malnourished realities, Hughes was on to something. Maybe it was better to put a suffering dream out of its misery, to blow it up from the outside before it exploded from within. I wasn't ready to pull the trigger on my skating, though.

In the conference room of the Omnisport, we dressed for the last time in our elephant suits and other mammalian garb. The mood was mixed: those who had signed with the permanent tour were all smiles and stepped into their beastly costumes with more liveliness than the rest of us could stand. Those of us rejected by Holiday on Ice sulked in our furry trousers, frustrated by false promises and sketchy choices. Most of the Russians were promoted to the permanent tours, as were the slinky-bodied Italians. Some of the seasoned show skaters explained that the Russian visas were much cheaper, almost half of what it cost for some European and American work permits. The majority of the English girls were released, the Hungarians and Brazilians were also dismissed, and Jalena was headed back to her horses in the Czech Republic. Some of the most talented skaters were let go, while some of the weakest and thinnest were rewarded spots on the tour.

From the hallway, the sounds of the gargantuan arena drifted into the conference room adjacent to the ice. The spectators had begun to take their seats, and the faint shouts of children discovering the echo effect of the spacious rink reverberated into our dressing room, reaching our ears but creating less excitement than it had on opening night.

I took my ever smiling elephant skull to the table and lay it facedown, propping myself up on a folding table to tie my skates for the last time under the jurisdiction of Holiday on Ice. At the next table, a conversation within my eavesdropping boundaries was taking place.

"The show," Alexei said, in his thick Russian accent, "is like *seerkoos.*"

Having no idea what a *seerkoos* was but honing in on the words that followed, I lumbered over to him as quickly as I could, smoothing out the fur of my elephantine stomach as I listened to him tell another skater about the show he was returning to after Holiday on Ice's Christmas tour ended. His parents were veteran performers, former circus entertainers who had toured with the Moscow Circus back in the sixties and seventies. Alexei had been brought up in ice rinks and circus tents, adapting the skills learned from one into the arena of the other. Holiday on Ice had hired him to perform his special gymnastic routine, a series of round-off back handsprings that traveled down the ice and ended in a layout back flip. What looked like an unfeasible stunt to perform on the slick surface of the ice was made possible by special gloves with tack-size nails jutting out from the palms, like track spikes for the hands that gripped into the ice upon the correct equation of impact and velocity. The crowd loved Alexei, and so did Holiday on Ice. The Russian women gasped at his flexibility and eyed his limber body and mullet hairstyle with seductive admiration. My roommate Ingrid was Alexei's first conquest on the tour.

I listened as he explained a little about the acts of Hollywood on Ice, how some parts of the show were freestyle skating routines and other numbers of the *seerkoos* incorporated hoops and rings and balancing acts upon the ice with props one might find in a Ringling Brothers act. Although there was plenty of glitz and glamour in the first half of the ice show, the post-intermission routine revolved around the theme of Flintstones on Ice and catered to children's entertainment. Sounded like a great combination, something very similar to the Ice Capades, which had beautiful skating performances infused with Smurfy antics for all ages to enjoy.

I recall Alexei saying something about a tent, that Hollywood's rink looked like a tent, but I heard only what I wanted to, dismissing this odd tent fact and focusing on his verification that yes, there were freestyle routines involved — real skating, with jumps and spins and choreography and applause. Do they do double jumps? Yes. Triples? Sometimes. Who is the lead skater? Are they looking for more athletes? Would they hire me? Alexei nodded to all my questions.

"They are always looking for skaters," he assured me, again. Failing to fully dissect this statement and peer into the intricacies that lay just below the surface, I set my mind on getting into Hollywood on Ice as a last attempt to recapture my festering dream of professional skating that had not yet panned out as planned.

Alexei gave me the contact information of Hollywood on Ice, a Canadian woman who had toured with Hollywood on Ice off and on for the past ten years. Pam was the line captain of the skaters when she was on tour, and when she was home in Canada, she helped recruit for the show.

"Did Alexei tell you that Hollywood on Ice is like a circus?" Pam said over the phone. One of Holiday on Ice's elephants lumbered by me in the hallway, where I was calling Ontario from a pay phone.

"Yes, yes, I understand." For God's sake, Hollywood on Ice couldn't be any more of a circus than the Parade of Animals I was in the midst of. Pam explained that the show was performed beneath a giant tent and a stage of ice that was 60 by 45 feet, kind of like the Bern Warehouse. As long as it was real ice, not the synthetic sheath of unmeltable plastic crap that Vegas-type productions and Caribbean cruise ships used, I really did not mind. If it wasn't ice, it wasn't skating. As long as there was frozen water and real figure skating that didn't resemble an incarnation of Old MacDonald's Farm, I would be a happy camper. Pam mentioned that the pay was three hundred dollars a week, which, without the burden of hefty animal costumes, somehow felt like a huge raise from Holiday's identical salary.

"Are you willing to commit for a year?"

"Can I stay longer?" I asked, my goal unfolding before my eyes. The Ice Capades and Holiday on Ice had proved disastrous, but now, in the eleventh hour, something permanent and tangible had arrived to erase the ache of a dream deferred. A year was perfect, but if the experience of Hollywood on Ice was as promising as it sounded, I could always delay grad school again. Some dreams could be safely deferred without the threat of explosion.

"When do I start?"

After the phone call with Pam, a plane ticket to Argentina arrived and I was expected in the beach town of Necochea two days after New Year's 1998. The trailer, in all its glory, was only days away from engulfing me into its boxy world of spandex, sequins, scales, solitude, and all that was to come with the package deal of professional figure skating that I had yet to truly understand.

※

Chapter Five

What Might Have Once Been Dino

The airport in Mar del Plata, Argentina, was small and hot, not much bigger than a bus station, and my failed attempts at keeping my sundress free of sweat marks engulfed me in nervousness about first impressions. There was still a two-hour car trip to the site of Hollywood on Ice, and I was determined to start off the tour on the right foot. Sweaty armpit runoff was not something most professional skaters seek to bring to first-time management meetings, so I walked around the unair-conditioned building with my arms outstretched and flapping slightly, impersonating the planes landing outside.

In the sweltering lobby, I waited for the arrival of Felicia's flight from London, keeping a lookout for the cheeky little Brit with a blond ponytail and penchant for Adidas sweatshirts and Naf Naf (the Gap of France) clothing. Felicia was the only other member of Europe's Holiday on Ice Christmas show who decided to try her luck with Hollywood on Ice. Of course, there weren't too many alternatives left, unless skating naked in casinos and cruise ships peaked our curiosity. It didn't. Ice and nudity just did not seem like a wise combination, at least from the employee standpoint. Yet there was still the opportunity of Hollywood on Ice, which we were promised covered all genitalia and actually involved figure skating.

Getting into Hollywood on Ice was a much simpler process than my initial audition for the Ice Capades, or the audition video I sent with

FedEx haste to Holiday on Ice in Europe. There had been no face-to-face meetings with Hollywood's management, no Ice Capades–style auditions, only a confirmation from one skater in Holiday on Ice to another in Hollywood on Ice that my skating talents would please the manager of the South America–based show.

Felicia arrived with the same look of excitement I wore, and we jabbered eagerly about our immediate future as we awaited our ride to Hollywood on Ice. I held no lofty expectations, other than Hollywood simply had to be better than Holiday. Anything would be superior to sweating away in the belly of an elephant. As we kept a lookout for a yellow Mustang that we were told would whisk us away to Hollywood, my backpack holding two pairs of skates grew heavy. I took it off, fiddling nervously with the buckle, clicking it together and releasing it over and over again. I had lost the original buckle while in Europe and needed a replacement. Remembering that our elephant heads attached to our elephant overalls by a large plastic snap, I snuck into the costume shop of Holiday on Ice on the final night of the show and sawed one off with my pocketknife.

We reminisced about our short stint with Holiday on Ice, and how god-awful the whole ordeal had been, as we kept a lookout for the promised yellow Mustang and a driver named Fernando. Our nerves were ready to snap three hours later, when no Mustang of any color or breed had appeared, the sun was beginning to set, and our nervous tension started swinging toward the other direction of excitement. Maybe the karma gods were at it again, withholding the coveted Mustang for all the bad horse juju that I had bestowed upon Jalena. Between the two of us, Felicia and I had a cell phone number that no one answered, two suitcases with some figure skates inside, and absolutely no idea of what to do if our fluorescent chariot failed to show up at the tiny Argentinean airport.

Thoughts of the Ice Capades entered my head and just as I wondered whether Hollywood had permanently shut down during my flight, a canary-colored convertible rolled into the airport parking lot. A short man of dark Hispanic complexion dressed in a suit and tie got out and loaded us into his car. Thinking that Hollywood's headquarters were somewhere in the general vicinity, Felicia and I grew a bit weary after the first hour passed. Fernando was not the talkative type.

"How much longer?" we asked.

"More," he answered. "More longer."

Two hours later we pulled into the town of Necochea, a beach resort 120 miles south of Mar del Plata. It was dark out, but at the single stoplight we had encountered during the entire journey, a poster advertising Hollywood on Ice clung to a wall beneath a streetlight. Two women, legs elongated in split-jump formation, crisscrossed paths in midair over the ice of a full-house arena. The poster was not a photograph but a painting that appeared photographic from a distance. The women, clad in sparking blue outfits that revealed strong bodies, were physically awe-inspiring. These women were part athlete, part superhero — they had quads like runners, backs rippled with the lats of rowers, calves like Lance Armstrong's, and arms chiseled with the strength and grace of a butterfly swimmer. I took immediate reassurance from this premonition of Hollywood on Ice. Strength, it appeared, was welcomed here. There would be no more scrutinized dinners, no more celery-stick snacks, no more feelings of internal hunger and physical comparison that had begun to infiltrate my thoughts in Holiday on Ice. This poster was proof that the skaters were not only strong but happy. I paid no attention to the upper right hand corner of the advertisement that had begun to unfurl and droop weakly above the word *Ice*.

Fernando pulled up alongside a humongous circus tent with streamers of lights cascading down, music emanating from within, and a bright red-and-yellow sign that screamed HOLLYWOOD ON ICE for all to see. He told us to wait there for a few moments, or if we wanted, we could go across the street, he said, pointing to a small convenience shop. Not much else was open, as it was Sunday, a day that would soon begin to harbor a not-so-pleasant correlation with poor nourishment. Nervous but famished, Felicia and I entered the shop and picked out some orange juice and a large flat loaf of bread, too tired to notice the quizzical looks of the woman behind the counter when we asked for two plates and two paper cups. We did not want to experiment with any ethnic food on our first night in South America and figured that bread and OJ were a safe bet. I picked out our dinner and told Felicia not to worry, my high school Spanish education was still with me.

As we sat on the curb chewing my botched attempt at a meal, raw pizza dough, and sipping from a bottle of undiluted orange drink concentrate, staring at a circus tent pitched in a dusty field in a foreign land of which we knew only of hot airports, yellow Mustangs, and cloudy darkness, Felicia began to cry.

"I think I'd like to go home now, Kathryn," she confessed in muffled sniffs.

"Wait, Liss, it will get better . . . wait until we get inside. It'll be okay, I promise," I said, offering her some more concentrate.

The manager's office of Hollywood on Ice was a small, cramped trailer with fake wood paneling and a dingy yellow carpet; a square little desk with an enormously rotund Mexican woman behind it; and two stiff chairs set before her. I took one and Felicia, now dry-eyed, took the other. We smiled and nodded and waited, not realizing that this was pretty much the same thing we'd be doing on the ice for the rest of the year, only with more makeup and less clothing. The woman snuggled behind the desk was Lora, who oversaw the entire show. She was not a woman of many words, most of which were Spanish, but there in her office Lora spoke to Felicia and me in broken English. Fernando, the publicist, sat alongside her and translated.

"Passports," Lora said to Fernando.

"Passports," Fernando said to us, and held out his hand as Felicia and I turned over our documents to him. "For safekeeping, no?" he stated. At the time, I did not know that it is illegal for someone to keep another person's passport under lock and key. Lora pushed some papers toward Felicia and me.

"Contracts," she said.

"Contracts," Fernando clarified. We read them quickly and signed the bottom. It all *seemed* normal enough . . . no missing shows, no being late, no smoking while in costume. We pushed the papers back to Lora. There was no moment of welcome, no well wishes, no "how was your trip," no "happy to have you here" bits of sentiment thrown our way. We had traveled halfway around the world, but just a quick once-over and a brief exchange of formalities was the extent of our greeting. Soon a young woman appeared in the doorway. She wore shorts over fishnet stockings, and a T-shirt covering what looked to be something very tight and sparkly. Her dark shoulder-length hair was pulled into a loose pony-tail and an expression of blankness tugged at the otherwise attractive features of her face. She was wearing her skates, blue plastic guards protecting the blades.

"Krystal," Lora said, pointing to the woman.

"Krystal," Fernando agreed.

Krystal was summoned to take Felicia and me back to the dressing rooms and give us the informal tour of Hollywood on Ice. Whatever personal notions of professional figure skating glamour had endured through Holiday on Ice now deflated rapidly as we walked from the office to the backstage area. We did not go through the lobby, which was streaming with vendors and merchandise and an aura of validity. We skirted the collapsible building, making our way around the circus-tent-like structure while stepping over ropes and bolts and other construction hazards that threatened our verticality. Krystal was quite deft at the process, swinging her legs over each rope with timed perfection. When we reached the rear of the building, Krystal found an obscure angle of the tent, parted a flap, and held open a corner of darkness for Felicia and me to enter. Before we ducked into the bowels of Hollywood on Ice, Krystal offered a note of caution.

"Look out for all the trash around here," she said. I looked down, but the ground was relatively clean despite the maze of rope and pegs. Krystal was not looking down. She waved her hand toward the Mexican workers walking about the grounds.

Beneath the curtain there was a narrow wooden ramp that led up to the platform of the backstage area. There were two large trailers on either side of the ramp, and as our eyes adjusted to the dim lighting, I saw something dart under the trailer on the left but could not identify what it was. At the top of the ramp, a black curtain loomed in front of us. Just beyond its flimsy dangle was the ice we had not yet seen. Krystal pointed to the trailers and the seamstress tables on either side, and as her voice grew complicated with the inflections of instructions and warnings and advice, out from the dressing rooms they came: a few at first, then in large numbers, until Felicia and I were at the hub of what seemed to be a besequined alien colony. When people talk of extraterrestrial encounters, I think of my first glimpse of the cast of Hollywood on Ice.

Women with feather headdresses and exuberant eyelashes smiled falsely through reddened lips. Men emerged half naked, wearing white tuxedo pants and top hats to match, cigarettes dangling from the corner of their mouth. A small dark-skinned man wearing the bottom half of what looked like Barney Rubble walked by, carrying the head of what might have once been Dino. Somewhere in the distance a chicken squawked and the yap of a small dog echoed through the shadowy backstage, providing the slightest comfort that we just might still be on Earth, although the chicken noise brought back bad rooster memories.

With foreign accents and broken English, hellos came forth with quiet resonance while the stares came down much louder. Names went in one ear and out the other, but we knew they would all come around again, so we smiled, shook some hands, and helloed back. We were ushered into a trailer by Krystal, and then right back out again as music began to pulse through the speakers. The show was about to begin and Krystal pointed the way to the exit ramp and the bleachers, where Felicia and I watched both performances from the audience that night.

As we walked out between the gigantic trailers, I looked to where I had seen something move in the darkness earlier. My eyes had grown accustomed to the poor lighting, and there in the darkness under the trailer was a man. Beneath each dressing room camper was a row of bunks not more than five feet long and three feet wide and only about two and a half feet tall. Coffin-size. They hung down from the trailer like a row of side-by-side drawers, and in each compartment was a pillow and some blankets, a dull lightbulb, and maybe a radio. In the first bunk the man was sleeping, his body taking up almost the entire cubicle. The others were empty. These were the homes of the ice show workers, the ones responsible for packing up and putting together Hollywood on Ice every time the tour switched locations. According to Krystal, this was where the trash lived.

There had been no trailers in Holiday on Ice; the rinks it toured were already in place and there was no need for the company to construct its own. Hollywood's setup was a bit unusual, but I welcomed the peculiarity of it all. Stepping beyond Bronxville's dainty margins was part of the initial draw, part of the literal goal of exploring all the places skating could take me. Getting away from familiarity is the most necessary component in chasing far-off dreams, and Hollywood on Ice seemed perfect, lying just beyond the borders of all things customary and secure.

※

Chapter Six

The Museum

The house I grew up in was a large stone-and-brick structure built on the hillcrest of Hemlock Road in Bronxville, and I spent the first twenty years of my life there. I became attached to 14 Hemlock in a strange way, as the house enveloped my creativity at an early age, though its aesthetic boundaries later pushed me away from feeling truly comfortable within its walls. Having no other siblings to play with while Peter was away at boarding school, I spent my days exploring the house with unfaltering zest, convinced there were time-travel portals lodged somewhere between the antiques my mother hoarded. While looking for buried treasure under the attic floorboards or playing Ghostbuster in the basement with my backpack, an old garden hose, and all the lights on, I spent days creating games and stories about these vast places within our home. I held skating competitions in my socks on the slippery foyer floor and ran about our outdoor property as Wonder Woman (complete with tinfoil wristbands), freeing strategically placed stuffed animals from cotton-thirsty invisible enemies. Horsing around was something I was not allowed to do inside, and perhaps these grounds were where I first discovered the joy of running, years before competition had anything to do with the activity. In fact, my home may have indirectly encouraged my desire to be athletic, to be outside, to be away from all things inert and breakable.

In the decades we lived there, our house on Hemlock never changed. My mother, the interior decorator, spent her days reworking the homes of clients into her own visions of aesthetic perfection. She was good at her profession and boasted an impressive list of satisfied customers all over the country. Office buildings in New York City, fancy hotels out West, mansions owned by famous baseball players or politicians along the East Coast and other wealthy highbrows were among her numerous credits. My brother's college dorm rooms and my freshman-year cubicle of living space were also on the list. She would have had a field day with the trailer, after regaining consciousness from fainting. Pete and I referred to our house as "the museum," wondering if it were possible to love and hate our home with simultaneous passion.

Once the furniture was arranged in our house sometime during the mid-1970s, the decor was never altered again. Why bother to improve on perfection? The style of our home was not reminiscent of the fashion-challenged decade when my parents acquired the house. My mother had her standards, and the seventies weren't up to par. The overall theme of her fun park was Victorian, with other eras named after foreign queens worked into the decor, too. My father remained patiently indifferent to the surroundings of the museum, always managing to muster a loving thank-you no matter how many embroidered trout pillows and refurbished crystal doorknobs he received on his birthdays and Christmases. When Peter or I forgot our father's age, all we had to do was wander the museum, count fish pillows, and add them to the year my parents got married. For our mother, the same equation worked for gardening/home interior books—until she started buying them for herself at random. One year we realized that she couldn't be 528 years old, so we had to use a new formula that involved finding the square root of the number of her Lord & Taylor jewelry boxes.

Living in the museum required a nonrefundable lifetime membership and a strict set of commandments Pete and I had to abide by. The rules were unwritten, but they were as good as carved in stone. There was no running in the museum. Eating was to be done in the kitchen, and non-clear beverages were not permissible outside of it. The dog was not to be riled, the cats were not to be fed overdoses of catnip. Arts and crafts were to be done in the basement or outside. Glitter was the antichrist; Satan lurked within the vials of washable finger paint.

Newspaper was to be put down prior to any creative undertaking, even over the pavement of the driveway. On the rare occasion when permission was granted for an outdoor water balloon battle, all the bits of rubber shrapnel were to be accounted for, collected, and given a proper burial. Pachysandra was not to be stepped on or run through, and the fragile rhododendrons were to be avoided at all costs. (There is nothing fragile about a rhododendron, which survives the winter by curling its leaves in tight little tubes of warmth. These tough plants are like perennial warriors. Rhododendrons would have made good figure skaters.)

Inside, skirted tables stood like elegant chintz tepees and were not to be hid beneath, while the master bedroom was off-limits to any derivative of the word *play*. Forts constructed of old sheets or boxes were issued temporary building permits but were to be bulldozed by nightfall. Posters and artwork were prohibited from my bedroom since Scotch tape, stickum, thumbtacks, and other such destructive weapons threatened the life of wallpaper. My bedroom was to be cleaned every Thursday evening in anticipation of our curator's most crucial visitor, Bernadetta. One might say Bernadetta was my mother's best friend, so the house had to be spotless prior to her arrival. Bernadetta was our cleaning lady.

My room did not physically change for twenty-one years, save one detail. The crib was moved out and an antique maple bed frame was moved in. True antique beds are interesting structures, as people were smaller and shorter in the eighteenth and nineteenth centuries. When my body stretched itself out to five-nine, my bed did not accommodate the change very well. Neither did my mother. It's an *antique,* she explained. I slept diagonally until college.

In the museum, we could look but not touch. There was little tolerance for spills, dribbles, collisions, and other childhood earthquakes. Precautions were prevalent throughout the house, almost part of the decor itself, down to the last possible detail. Paper napkins were folded into neat squares and placed over the cork blocks that separated the tabletop from the villainous coffee mug . . . even our coasters had coasters.

There were sixteen rooms in our house, and my mother was the curator of her entire collection. She could be everywhere at once, always aware of dirty hands coming too close to her white walls, framed paintings, tippy sculptures, or expensive artifacts. The museum was visually splendid, but not an appropriate place for children.

In second grade I had a friend who lived in an apartment building, and I told my mother I wished we could live in one, too. She drew back in horror and warned me not to say such things. What she considered cramped, privacy-lacking, and low-class about apartments was exactly what I loved. Apartments had other families and kids to play with, all right next door. What could be better than that? I marveled at the concept of playrooms, bunk beds, and the plastic furniture my playmates possessed. I remember playing at a friend's home one day when she suggested, "Let's bake a cake!"

"Indoors?!" I asked in a low whisper.

The museum had its high points. Despite the permanent displays and collections of culture and frivolity, it was a beautiful house. It made my mother proud. New guests were given lengthy tours, and the response was usually positive. The tours were mandatory for my guests as well. As my mother led them from room to room and pointed out what not to touch, I trailed along in hushed embarrassment. Despite the strictness of the museum, my little buddies loved to come play at our house. They were mesmerized by some of the eccentric decorations, such as the collection of papier-mâché fruit and vegetables that sat like petrified produce in wicker baskets upon the butcher-block countertop in the kitchen. Wide-eyed, my friends would run their hands over the basket of fake peas as if they were stale emeralds.

Not until I was a teenager did I notice that my mother, the warden of visual perfection, was slowly transforming me from a museum spectator into an exhibit. Her professional focus had begun to seep into her everyday life, especially as she watched the body of her young tomboy contort into the shape of a woman. Just as the furniture was polished, the accessories dusted, and the wall hangings adjusted to the angles of visual perfection, I too was observed and altered accordingly. I was the one piece of modern artwork misplaced and mismatched within the Victorian age, clashing in personality and appearance with the museum.

On the awkward evenings of high school dances when a friend-boy would come to escort me to an overly decorated gymnasium or cafeteria, I slipped out of my T-shirts and jeans and skidded into a dress. The next step was smudging makeup over my face, which I would come to perfect only in the later years through the ritual of preparing for skating performances. The final preparation was the descent down the spiral staircase after the doorbell had rung and the nonsuitor had been ushered into the foyer. By the bottom step, my mother said how pretty I looked, a flattery similar to being told I looked smashing in my Halloween costume. My mother complimented my appearance only when I was dressed up as somebody other than myself, whether it was a formal party dress or a tinselly skating outfit.

What I longed for in those years when childhood was physically fading away was not to look pretty but to *be* pretty. I wanted to be like the house, a structure of unchanging comfort. Sweatpants and baseball caps were far from beautiful and, therefore, I grew to believe, so was the girl who liked to wear them. I ached to hear the phrase "you are pretty" cry out from the one who seemed an expert on beauty's definition, but museums are quiet places.

I was an exhibit from the cultural establishment of our home, and it was vital to the curator's image that I be displayed properly. I was framed and adorned in name-brand clothing by a woman who would do anything to exorcise the tomboy from her daughter's body. I could have any pretty outfit I wanted, on the condition that I first try it on under my mother's surveillance. If my muscles rippled through the fabric of the garment and added any curvature (other than my breasts) to my ladylike frame, the outfit was rejected. Muscles were not proper for a woman; the "bigger and better" concept of female strength was not commonly accepted in my mother's generation, having only just begun to surface in mine. Yet strangely enough, both my mother and grandmother had been athletes in their youth.

In the countless dressing rooms of stores that bore the names of Calvin, Donna, Anne, and Ralph, I turned in a slow circle, like a pig on a barbecue spit, and waited for my mother's final jurisdiction. Occasionally I passed with flying colors. More often I settled for the next size up after she observed that my behind was too muscular for whatever I tried to cover it with. There was an awkward silence of disappointment on her end if the tag on the larger garment was stitched with a number larger than six.

Back home, I hung these clothes in the closet and slipped into my baggy pants and droopy Ts, the limp fabric engulfing my athletic features into three general categories — arms, legs, torso. The furniture I sat on was better dressed than I was. Our sofas and couches looked well kept and polished, but when I sat down, some would creak and sag beneath the reality of my human dimensions, as if to tell me my growing body was too much for them to bear, just as the squeaky moan of the trailer chairs in Hollywood's dressing room brought back this feeling of ungainliness. Just as the concept of *home* lives within the structure of a house, I lived somewhere deep within the decor of my exterior. Inside the walls of myself creativity festered and confidence grew in small buds that I hoped would bloom eventually, unshakable as the rhododendrons that grew outside our home. I longed to be in the free, open space outside the museum. Skating rinks were perfect, a sheet of ice spared of obstacles and limits where I was the artwork, the visitor, and the curator all at once.

Necochea was a stopover village for Hollywood on Ice on its way to the bigger cities in Argentina. Home for the skaters was a run-down motel on a dusty, deserted backstreet, made up of two stories and one raspy set of stairs that sagged upon impact but still seemed safer than the phone-booth-size elevator to its left. This was the kind of hotel most Bronxvillians might have referred to as a slum tenement. I thought it was perfect. Almost.

"Kathryn, how do you say *ant* in Spanish?" Felicia asked, sitting on her bed in our small *habitación,* writing what looked like a letter. It was our first week with Hollywood on Ice, and we were settling in to the newness of this foreign culture and acclimating to the concept that hotel and home were now one and the same. Some rooms had flimsy doors that wouldn't lock, decorative windows that did not open, and showers that constituted a ceiling-centered spigot that rained down over everything, cleansing both body and bathroom all at the same time.

"*Tía,*" I responded, thinking she meant *aunt.* "Is that who you're writing to?"

"No, that is what is crawling all over our floor. There are bloomin' *tías* roaming everywhere." Looking down, I noticed a mass of little *hormigas* cruising about the cracked tile, making their way over to the table where we kept our boxed food. Thinking that I was walking on sand that we trekked in from the beach, I had failed to notice that the crunchy noises beneath my feet were, or had been, alive. In the lobby a small woman with a broad smile appeared when I dinged the bell.

"*Señora, tengo hormigas en mi habitación.*" I've got ants in my room, lady.

"*Sí, hormigas.*" Yep, ants.

Following this productive conversation, Felicia and I had no other choice but to adapt to our tribe of new roommates until Hollywood on Ice picked up shop and headed to the next town three weeks later. Ants indoors were new for me but didn't seem all that bad despite the fact that they never asked first about sharing my granola. At least they didn't crap all over the place, like the pigeons of my past. Hollywood on Ice would never quite be able to surpass those birds. Yet there was something more to the ants and the shabbiness of the hotels where we bunked. The cramped quarters, the noise of neighbors, the grunginess of the decor . . . of all the Hollywoodisms that began to nibble at my sense of comfort, our hotels were not among them. After all the years in the museum, it was nice to finally feel at ease in an ant farm.

✤

Chapter Seven

Pandora's G-String

There was a clause written into my Hollywood contract that I wear a G-string when performing. The high-cut costumes of Hollywood on Ice were designed to show as much leg as possible and there was no room for extra mounds of cottony bulge. I refused to wear a G-string at first, embarrassed by its sexiness, and instead pulled all of my full-coverage underwear into the crevice not designed for it. When my "granny panties," as Ingrid used to call them, chafed and slipped, I finally converted to the first amendment of my showgirl's constitution and donned the stringy floss that turned out to be spectacularly more comfortable than initially imagined. The sheer spandex outfits left little to the imagination. As the stretchy cloth rose over hilly buttocks and plunged into valleys of cleavage, the fabric itself was a fearless explorer of uncharted territory. I tugged at the boundaries of these costumes, hoping only to help the wayward material achieve manifest destiny across my body.

Fishnet stockings encased each leg with thousands of tiny threaded windows. These tights somehow managed to nip and tuck any body into "perfect" contours, gripping the expansive upper thigh under control while flattening the buttocks into as much of a plateau as possible. The fishnets ran from waist to toe, covering the outside of the skate and attaching between the blade and boot with an unseen safety pin or eyelet hook. Wearing the tights over the outside of the skate gave the appearance of longer-legged showgirls, keeping with the odd social ideal that a body stretched to its farthest dimensions is more attractive than when it appears within its original borders.

The men in the audience liked these stockings. In Argentina it was not uncommon to hear a masculine voice call out, "Feeeshnits, feeeshnits!" The appeal of Hollywood on Ice throughout South America seemed quite high. The continent is known for both its warm weather and its appreciation of the scantily clad. The whistles from the audience confirmed this, as did the occasional grope from a lingering spectator (often a teenage boy on a dare from his buddies) as the cast exited the grounds for the evening.

In Argentina I quickly caught on to the fact that children are revered in a different way than they are in *los Estados Unidos* of America. Young kids in the southern continent are regarded as tiny saints and are treated so even when they act like little demons, which too often reminded me of the Bronxville social system. Parents in Argentinean cities tended to giggle instead of discipline, often instigating instead of reprimanding, or just turning their head when their kid pelted innocent bystanders with goop-filled plastic bombs.

Hollywood on Ice spent the month of February in the oceanside resort of Mar del Plata, a popular vacation site for the wealthy Buenos Aires community. February, which is summertime in the Southern Hemisphere, also brought Children's Week. Not *day,* as they celebrate in Japan and some European countries, but a full seven days honoring nonadults. Children of Argentina commemorate their existence throughout the week by playing pranks, most of which consist of water, mud, or shaving-cream-filled-balloon-throwing festivities.

Most skaters walked to Hollywood's performance venue, a mile from our residence at El Hotel Gatex, and every day someone in the cast came into the rink covered with the contents of one of these kiddie grenades. Once confronted by three small boys who encircled me with squishy ammunition gripped in their palms, I noticed that their mothers were only a few feet away and patiently waited for them to intervene on my behalf. Only laughter came from the ladies as the boys drew back their launching arms and began a unified countdown. I escaped the situation by offering free tickets to that night's performance. The children lowered their balloons and accepted while the parents asked for extra tickets. After giving them directions to the ticket booth where they would be able to pick up the passes that I would, oops, forget to leave, I was on my way to the trailer. Felicia was not as lucky and often entered the trailer drenched in the runoff of Children's Week, changing out of her wet clothes, swearing British curses, and muttering insults/casting spells on the world of professional figure skating while wiggling into her fishnets.

During our performances most children in the audience were completely spellbound — for the first ten minutes. The show was two hours long. If a routine outlasted their attention span, the squirming began and eventually the kids slipped from the thronelike laps of their parents and wandered to the edge of the stage, where there was a feeble five-foot steel fence providing a barrier between the ice stage and the audience. Its dull, vertical slats were merely intended to provide a passive warning, not aggressively halt those who yearned to climb or slip through the spaces. But rather than being a deterrent, the small railing invited the children to ascend its flimsy construction and they did, the parents retrieving their offspring only if they began to wriggle out onto the ice itself.

Most of the kids stood at the fence, harmlessly drooling at the glitz and glamour before them while others made faces that ranged from utter scorn to imitations of severe mental retardation. They wanted us — the forever-smiling cookie-cutter showgirls — to break character. Sometimes we did, making faces right back, but only if we were facing the side seats and management could not see us head-on. We did not smile at the devilish children who threw things onto the ice and gambled with our fate. Popcorn was the trip kernel of choice, easily obtained from the vendors in the audience. Soft missiles of wilted helium balloons were also popular, but unlike the popcorn, these colored spheres were easier to see and kick away. Yet even the pale kernels rarely upset a skater. The real danger was calculating the rise and fall of the peso.

Pesos, centavos, bolívaros, reales: coins were the most feared object, for the metal stuck to the ice and buried itself like a small land mine in its surface. One fleeting brush between blade and peso would send a showgirl flying. This possibility was the height of entertainment to a youngster but perhaps the end of a career for a skater. One creative delinquent in Mendoza, Argentina, threw an enormous beetle onto the ice, where its black body thrashed against the white surface until it froze, limbs forever skyward. We warned one another, ventriloquist-style through our clenched smiles, about such hazards. *Beetle, seven o'clock!* The beetle incident occurred right after the movie *Titanic* debuted and I warned Felicia in my best English accent, "Icebug, straight ahead!" Felicia nearly met the same fate as the doomed ocean liner when she unsuccessfully tried to free the frozen insect carcass with her toe pick.

For a moment in my mind I was back at Murray's, remembering pigeon poopie and pine needles and whatever else the feathered gods in the rafters threw our way. Small comforts were hard to find in Hollywood on Ice, and if they came by way of dead bugs, so be it. For a moment I was home again, and the audience transformed into something more familiar and appreciative of what I had once considered show skating, to a time when there were no hazards of cryogenic beetles and the crowds that came to watch the skaters were sometimes skaters themselves, circling around the very rinks I pretended were my own.

Throughout my childhood and well into my teens, I visited Rockefeller Center in far-off New York City, twenty minutes south of Bronxville, at least once every winter. The small rectangle of ice submerged in a metropolitan well of skyscrapers often had a line a quarter of a mile long and an hour's wait to set foot on the rink. The vibrant colors of the national flags surrounding it, the colossal fir tree dotted with delicate lights, the Christmas carols emanating from the restaurant and lobby below, the statue of golden gods entwined in permanent fluidity — everything about the place denounced the drabness of an urban winter.

No matter how cold the New York City winds blew, I wore my favorite tights and skating skirt of the season and pounced into center ice, unabashed by the crowds circling me in full clothing. I was a figure skater; this was my territory. Weaving through the people, I spun and jumped with both caution and recklessness until my eyes watered and my nose went numb and plasma flowed liberally from my crispy nostrils. Spectators above the rink looked down and clapped for the little girl who looked so cold and happy. Usually the rink was too crowded to do much jumping, and I moved to center ice and practiced my spins. Again and again I arched my body backward, dropping into the crook of a layback spin, keeping my eyes open to watch the city swirl above me; skyscrapers whirled freely, lightly, as if made of anything but steadfast metal and immovable concrete. When I brought my body upright, everything else spun for a second or two longer, eventually settling back into the permanence from which it came.

"Aren't you dizzy?" someone always asked.

"Nope." In truth, skaters do get dizzy, but we grow used to the feeling and understand its temporary grasp. Just as downhill skiers adapt to the speed, platform divers conquer the height, and gymnasts overcome the fear, skaters master the effects of centrifugal force with practice and discipline. Though rinks change and weather conditions come into play, ice is ice and there is little that can truly hinder a skater's sense of place. Unless, of course, the skater happens to be dressed as a psychedelic flounder the size of a Volkswagen with partially obstructed vision. Such cases may cause an uncomfortable level of dizziness and require direct hands-on involvement from the audience.

"Really," Felicia complained, sliding the enormous fish costume over her head, "they have got to do something about these eyeholes. I can't see a bloomin' thing." There was no time to offer agreement — this was the fastest quick change in Hollywood on Ice, jumping from the Michael Jackson number to the Little Mermaid scene in thirty seconds. Every costume in the show was skintight and partially revealing except for the seven minutes we spent as sequined fish in *Debajo del mar,* or as Hollywood on Ice borrowed from Disney, "Under the Sea." The sparkly, bulky fish skin was all-encompassing, from head to ankle. *Debajo* our fish attire, all we had on was a long T-shirt and our trusty fishnets. The Little Mermaid scene came right before intermission, during which we lounged in partial nudity to free our skin from the evil clutches of tootight spandex. There was no need to wear much under the fish outfit, it covered us like a mitten from head to skate and the audience never saw anything other than an occasional calf muscle.

The routine was simple, reminiscent of Holiday on Ice's Angry Duck choreography. Six showgirls took to the ice as fish (sans musket), three on each side of the stage, while the *Serenita* and her less-than-handsome prince skated about in the center. Olga #1, the one with a high-pitched screech and unquenchable desire for other people's boyfriends, did a good job in this part of the show and never lived up to our hopes for a catastrophic wipeout that would necessitate sending her back to Russia in a body cast. As for the fish, we swayed to the funky reggae beat with all the ichthyological excitement we could muster. During the chorus of the song, we traded places with the fish across the way, spun around a few times, and exited the ice stage. Pretty basic.

Felicia was right: the eyeholes in the costume were in terrible condition. Trying to see through the giant yellowed-plastic bubbles was like trying to see through a latex glove or other protective prophylactic. Holiday on Ice had used mesh screens that made it relatively easy to see out of the rooster and duck costumes, but Hollywood enjoyed giving the skaters small challenges, like blindness. Only light and shapes could be vaguely detected from behind the synthetic fish eyes. Luckily, running lights illuminated the final six feet of the ice stage before we hit dry land behind the curtain. These minilightbulbs were crucial to the fish, as the Little Mermaid scene ended in an otherwise dramatic blackout. Without the footlights, we would have no idea where or if we were coming or going.

"Where's Felicia, eh?" Jody asked as we sat in the trailer, awaiting the second half of the show. Felicia and I had performed only three shows with Hollywood on Ice, and Jody from Red Deer, Alberta, was our lifeline to tour survival. She had been with the show for seven months by that point and clued us in to all we needed to know about the routines and the people who surrounded us. Felicia never wandered too far from either Jody or me.

"Dunno," I said, peeking out of the trailer. In she walked at that very moment, hair disheveled, makeup smeared, T-shirt and tights ripped and dirty. Something rather sharkish appeared to have attacked our cheeky little British fish.

"I'll be fired for sure," she wailed, explaining the circumstances of her appearance as tears plowed narrow troughs through what was left of her makeup. Felicia was the last fish in line off stage left, the farthest one from the running lights at the other end of the stage. A malfunction had occurred on that side, and the lights blew a fuse. In the throes of dizziness and poor vision, with the rest of the rink blacked out, Felicia walked the wrong way. Thinking she was heading backstage, she stepped off the ice and smack into the audience just as Olga came out for her Mermaid solo. In all accuracy, Felicia did not quite make it to the audience. The safety fence that dissuaded small children from charging the ice broke her fall. Apparently it worked well as a dam from the other direction. Falling, Felicia managed to get one fin and one skate stuck in the railing and was unable to do anything but flail about helplessly as the proverbial fish out of water that she was. Eventually a man from the audience approached the fence and freed her from the metal net, thankfully adhering to the catch-and-release method. He lifted the fish costume off Felicia so she could untangle her foot from the fence, and as her T-shirt rose up in the process of defishification, a half-naked human was revealed in slow motion. Breaking character and unveiling the inner workings of a costumed outfit was the greatest taboo of professional performance, something we had been warned about continuously ever since one of the other skaters, Bella, lost her lobster head during a fall earlier in the week and was issued a fine and a last-chance admonition.

Felicia's story explained the odd burst of applause and catcalls that echoed back to the trailer during a typically quiet time of the show. In the buff from the waist down, with a fish costume in one hand and a figure skate in the other, she could return to the trailer only by hopping up onto the ice and walking across to backstage. Felicia did her best to dodge Olga and Grígor, trying not to be "part of their world" as the song played out their duet. Making her way across the small frozen sea, which must have seemed no less harrowing than crossing the Atlantic Ocean, Felicia swam back to the trailer.

With great gobs of airless laughter and tears streaming down our faces, Jody and I rolled off our chairs and onto the trailer floor, doing what we could not to pee in our fishnets while we tried to restrain our spasms of hysteria and comfort our fallen friend. Falling on the ice was one thing, falling off it was another. Never before had clothes come off upon impact from a spill, and rare was the fall that practically necessitated the Jaws of Life. Jody assured Felicia that she would not be fired, that in retrospect, her unplanned nudity had most likely boosted the ticket sales for weeks to come.

At that moment, Olga stormed through the trailer in her seashell bra and finlike tights, glaring bullets at the misguided fish who had stolen the attention Olga constantly craved. While Olga unleashed a torrent of Russian angst, Felicia tried to smuggle in an apology but Olga would hear none of it. The *Serenita* had been upstaged by a naked flounder and there were no words to describe what a painful ordeal this was. Between Jody's laughter, Felicia's unnecessary apologies, and Olga's princess airs, the trailer was alive with emotion specific only to this world of ice and fish. Felicia's fall released a loaded tension that night. All week we had been learning the steps, perfecting the footwork, finding the rhythm, and paying attention to all the details thrown our way. Hollywood on Ice appeared so put-together, so precise, so flawless at first that Felicia's fall brought a new reality to the picture.

Perhaps it was a forewarning, a quick glance at the bone beneath the skin of the show. Flying fish, cranky mermaids, and human audience participation — it all swirled together. And yet in the trailer, most everyone took this zany nuttiness in stride. Had I realized from the beginning that nothing about Hollywood on Ice made sense, perhaps I wouldn't have tried so hard to fit in to its expectations. I should have been the one to fall off the stage, as it likely would have knocked some sense into me.

But in the newness of it all, prancing in front of a packed audience while dressed as a human was actually intoxicating compared with the previous bodily oppressive experience of Mutant Pet Shop Escapees on Ice. The crazy trailer was my own personal Pandora's box, and I tore off the lid to play with all the sparkly things inside before realizing that it was really just a pile of brightly colored broken glass.

Despite the male ogling, the juvenile pranks, and the nondisciplinarian mothers, the audience was the livelihood of our show. Personally, I did not care about how much money the crowd brought in or whether a show sold out or had a few vacant seats. Every town was different. We performed for huge crowds that hardly clapped and small gatherings that cheered us to no end. I enjoyed performing in the small villages better, for the people were excited to have such an important-looking show come to their humble home. The adults watched with true interest and bought their children glow-in-the-dark toys, which they cherished and waved during the blackouts between numbers, so the whole arena glimmered with neon happiness. The children in small towns did not throw anything onto the ice except their full attention. They waited for us after the show, holding out pens and paper and smiles. They asked, "*¿Donde están Beety y Veelma?*" wanting to know if the two famous Flintstone women would be coming out of the dressing room soon. Those who did not bring autograph material simply tilted a cheek in the hopes of being kissed, the South American equivalent of a handshake. In La Calera, Chile, the children followed us from the *supermercado* to our hotel down the street, smiling and pointing at the blond *gringas,* sometimes shouting, "*Olleywoodonice, Olleywoodonice.*" Others just ran up to a skater, touched her with a timid hand, and ran away again, laughing gleefully at their brush with "fame."

A boy of fourteen came to every performance we had in his city of Necochea. He sat in the same seat every night and looked longingly at all the skaters. He would talk to us on our way out each evening, asking us questions about the traveling life we led, wondering if he could come along. *¿Puedo trabajar con Hollywood on Ice?* We smiled and said we'd ask, although I don't think anyone ever did. After we moved on from his town, one of the men in the cast said the little boy had come to him and begged to go with us. The boy had confided to a few of the skaters that he was gay and did not want to stay in his hometown and bring shame to his family. It was better to run away and never come home, the boy had said. I wished we had been able to stow him away in the trailer somehow, for a little while anyway.

The audience loved certain numbers in the show more than others and expressed their excitement with hoots of appreciation, boisterous chanting, and rhythmic clapping for the routines that stirred their blood. The Michael Jackson dance number was first on their list, and they agreeably overlooked the fact that "Michael" was a blond Caucasian with a pudgy waistline. Lenny had skated as the King of Pop for so many years that such specific details as physical similarity no longer mattered. As long as the audience didn't mind, neither did management. Not only that, but "Michael" ventured onto the ice in a manner that distracted people from the lack of resemblance. Lenny rode a compact purple ATV across the rink for no apparent reason but that Hollywood thought motorized vehicles on ice somehow added to the profundity of the skating show. He circled the perimeter on the little lavender lawnmower-gone-bad while the skater dancers came out and wagged some tail. Len was notorious for scouting the audience for attractive ladies while he skated, selecting one to pursue after the show. Never ceasing to amaze me at how successful he was, he often escorted one or more women back to his hotel room.

The crowd also went wild for Ruslan and Olga #3, who performed an acrobatic duet complete with hooks that attached to their clothing and elevated them high above the ice in contorted positions. In Belarus, Ruslan had been a gymnast, not a skater. He could barely stand up on skates, but that was all he really needed to do to get from backstage to where the hook spiraled down to center ice. Then he was airborne, leaving the intricacies of skating far below. Teenage girls screamed for Ruslan, who wore no shirt, just sequined, tight turquoise pants. The men hollered for Olga, whose costume barely covered her G-string. She could skate much better than her partner but was also a former gymnast converted to show skating by Hollywood on Ice.

Barbie was a popular routine for the children, as was the Little Mermaid, whose beautiful princesses and fire-breathing sea dragons captured their attention almost as completely as goo-filled balloons. The parents enjoyed the showgirls' dance routines and laughed along with their children at the Flintstones' antics. At the end of the show two lucky audience members were selected to ride in the Flintmobile (a well-constructed rendition of the prehistoric golf cart) and have a Polaroid snapped with Dino. Watching the expressions of these children, ecstatic and wide-eyed, reminded me of my own trips to the Ice Capades when I was younger. Well into my teenage years I had still longed to be selected for the kiddie train.

The consciousness of an audience indirectly formed my love for the stage, for performing. And because skating was pure athleticism disguised as theatrical exhibitionism, all aspects of professional skating seemed more than appealing. But for the first few weeks of the show, I did not take pleasure in the spectators at all. I was too busy counting crossovers, memorizing entrances and exits, and trying to keep up with all the convoluted choreography (left arm up while right foot flexes, hold, hold, repeat on three in the opposite direction, now backward, two, three, four). When my mind finally adapted my body to the routines and the performance became less of a chore and more of an exciting experience, I was able to look into the audience. Slowly the blackness gave way to shapes and took on human form and faces. While my feet did what they had committed to memory, I peered into the crowd, searching for eye contact. Fantasizing that people I knew were actually in the bleachers made it easier to adjust to the fact that I didn't know a single person on the continent. I sent letters to friends and family and said, *Come see me!* Knowing they couldn't just hop on a flight to South America did not stop me from hoping that perhaps some night, somewhere, the stage manager would come backstage and tell me I had a visitor in the lobby. Sometimes it really happened to other skaters in the cast, even the Russians. Hollywood on Ice's audience was always big enough to pretend that just one member of the crowd might be there for me.

Sunday morning, December 11, 1986, was way too cold for someone to be wearing a single layer of spandex and a pair of nylon tights, but for all I knew it could have been a humid afternoon in July. I felt nothing of the temperature, nothing of the New York winter percolating though the open seams of Murray's rink. Nervousness dulls all weather conditions and regulates core body temperature of its own accord. This was the day of my first figure skating competition, and I took the ice in my long-sleeved purple dress with the pink vertical stripes and zigzagged about the empty oval for one minute and four seconds, doing two-foot spins and waltz jumps that looked like accidents in the process of happening. When it was all over, I heard something interesting. Clapping. It came from my family and a few skating friends in a far corner of the rink, but in my small, cold ears it echoed like thunder in a frozen canyon. I curtsied just to get some more of that sound and took my time getting off the ice. In that moment I became aware of another side of figure skating: being watched. Apparently I wasn't just out there jumping around by myself; real people, not just judges, could actually *see* me. It was a rather foreign concept to a little girl with busy parents, a little sister used to being ignored, a little kid who spent enough time by herself that she believed her stuffed animals could talk. Applause was a revelation, a verification of noted existence, and the audience was its source.

From then on, I gave a show to whoever took the time to watch, as the notion of presentation began to infuse its way into my skating. With radar perception, I knew when people came into a rink. Whether I recognized friends, strangers, or the hockey players waiting in the boxes to take the ice next, I pretended they were all there for me, me, me, and every practice session turned into a personal exhibition when spectators wandered by. Was I looking for success, to be defined as "good" by others' opinions? No, not in the early years. I only wanted to show, not show off, just show what a spin looked like, what a jump felt like, what a body could do on a pair of blades and a sheet of ice. Strangers provided one sort of audience, and family threw a whole other log on the fire. My brother, mother, and father — an utterly diverse cornucopia of personalities — always managed to influence my level of showmanship, whether or not they were physically present at a show or competition.

My brother came to see me perform three times in my life as a figure skater: twice when I was eleven, then again when I was twenty-one. The first time was at my first competition, and the second time was a practice session, a morning when Peter brought the video camera he was using for a school assignment. I had just turned eleven; Pete was eighteen, with his shaggy teenager hair and mid-eighties denim jacket. Although we share the same dark brown hair with a reddish tint, no one ever thinks we're related. Our genes divvied up the facial features of our parents quite evenly, without repetition. He got Dad's short forehead and ears, Mom's blue eyes and lengthy nose, and I got the exact opposite: Dad's brown eyes and little smile, and Mom's long forehead. But I liked it when people squinted and lied politely, *Oh yeah . . . I can see the, uh, resemblance,* as it always made me feel connected to Pete, as if it was some kind of proof to hold on to during the times when he was mentally disconnected from the family.

I spun and leapt with novice movements before the camcorder's electronic eye as my brother watched. I commanded, *Lookit this! And this! Didya see that?* Within moments I had twirled myself through all the half leaps and toe turns and uncentered spins I had learned, and wished I knew more so he would stay longer and not lose interest.

"Do that," Peter said, pointing to an older girl who sailed over the ice in perfect spiral formation, free-leg extension graceful, skating leg solid, both arms outstretched, and posture fluidly erect. I couldn't do a spiral like that. Instead of my body resembling the lower case letter *t,* it looked more like an upper case *K.* In Sanskrit. I was all slants and angles, without the translation to grace. I did the spiral anyway, with scare-crowed knees and Pinocchio elbows jutting every which way. Peter soon put down the camera and went into the lobby. He emerged later, after calling the local radio station with a request. Not many people call in at six in the morning, and immediately Jethro Tull's flutey classic "Skating Away on the Thin Ice of a New Day" came tumbling out of Murray's scratchy speakers. I did just what the title asked, listening to the words and making up little spazzy movements to the intricate tempo. I had never heard the song before and felt even more entranced by my older brother's seemingly bottomless depth of knowledge, as if he himself had written the music and lyrics during his brief visit to the lobby. Maybe *I* had inspired *him!* The song became my favorite, although that morning it was Peter who would skate away and, as I thought, lose interest in anything having to do with me.

Peter's absence, however, helped shape my skating and my dedication to the sport over the years. He was my invisible standard, a silent shadow in an empty rink whom I wanted to impress, someone I longed to hear praise from in the way only a younger sibling craves. As things began to change in his behavior, when he was about fifteen, no one in the family knew that bipolar disorder was charting its course through my brother's mind. To me, Peter was Peter — wild, crazy, happy, angry, fierce, and sometimes mild Peter. I had no comparison for sibling normalcy; it was just the two of us. Peter was my only foreshadowing of what it was like to be *older.* I was fascinated with him and wanted to be more involved in his life — a life that was spinning its eccentric web far above my understanding. But this was a quiet yearning, one that I did not know how to express. So I settled for being ignored, quietly harboring the dull hope of one day being rediscovered.

When Peter went off to boarding school, I wandered through his bedroom despite his instructions to "stay the hell outta there." Of course, the warning to stay out of Peter's room held little threat during the weeks he was away. I entered his lair in silence and respect, just wanting to look. Textbooks, board games, and clothes—there was nothing unique about his stuff except for the fact that it was *his*. I would climb on a chair and look at the books on the top row of Pete's shelf: Bradbury, Rand, Hawking, Mowat. I loved to jump up and reach for things just outside my grasp—doorframes, light switches, top shelves of closets. And in the emotional sense, I reached for Peter.

Yet my brother was absent in another way, too; he experienced occasional lapses in judgment caused by the chemical imbalance of his manic depression, which was kept secret from me until I was in my twenties. Peter struggled with the disease from his early teens but went undiagnosed until he was nearly twenty. Before he found the right medications and therapy to regulate his alternating moods, he lived in the extremes of elation and despair. Peter gave me memories of water-balloon fights, hide-and-seek tournaments, and watching goofy teen movies together. But there were also black eyes, stomach punches, kicks to my shins, thrown furniture, and being chased with a knife during his darkest moments of mania . . . things that went unspoken about, the archives of our museum.

My parents did not know what to make of his behavior, and it was not uncommon to come home and find the house in disarray after one of his tornado-like rampages. My mother left upturned tables, downed bookcases, shattered mirrors, and ripped-out plants to show my father the extent of the damage that *his* son had created. My father dealt with Peter after I went to sleep, though the volume of the arguments and the sound of broken glass sometimes warranted my mother's peeking into my room and whispering, "Katie, why don't you lock your door tonight?" Wanting to have a friend come over to play after school meant calling first to see if Peter was there. If he was, I invited my friends another day or asked if I could go to their house instead, to spare them and myself the eruptions of expletives and airborne antiques.

When he was happy, Peter was the best older brother a tomboy could ask for, teaching me how to skateboard down our driveway and build go-carts in our garage. But his condition could alter so quickly and the delicate balance between sanity and what lay beyond could flip like a switch. I thought that I was the one he got so mad at, that I sent him into these reeling moods of unpredictable violence and sadness. Peter was the recalcitrant son, and by contrast I was left to fill the void of the good child, the normal kid, the daughter who had it all together, the one who was always in control.

As part of the bipolar condition, my brother reached highs where nothing seemed unattainable. My father had the credit card receipts to prove it. Peter would go on spending sprees, buying everything from electronic equipment to purebred puppies, all on a manic whim. Since Peter was careless with money, I became awfully frugal for a Bronxville child, saving my baby-sitting money and allowance cash in crumpled wads in tin cans just in case my father ran out of his own and needed my help.

Skating was expensive: ten dollars a morning, lessons three times a week, new freestyle and patch skates at least once a year, new dresses, new music, summer training in Lake Placid. There was no room for me to compete with Peter's crazy spending, and I feared my skating privileges might disappear altogether because of their cost. At the end of every morning practice I stepped off the ice exactly two hours from when I got on, so I wouldn't waste a minute of the expensive ice time. Looking back, I wonder how many new jumps did I land then, how many new spins were at last understood in those final minutes of practice that might never have come to fruition if I didn't have that strange sense of pressure? With a mind given to such erratic volatility, Peter was able to give me the one thing he did not have himself—the gift of consistency, as he unknowingly shaped my life as an athlete.

Pete was a good athlete in his own right, although team sports befuddled his condition. His peers knew nothing of his mental illness, and small instances of competitive angst or ambitious rivalry could set him off into fits of rage or sudden gloom. His talents lay in individual endeavors, and his interests and hobbies often bounced from one activity to another with such fervor that my parents, in attempting to bolster his healthy desires, gave in to his spontaneous urges, no matter the financial burden. Musical instruments, art projects, rebuilding cars, new windsurfers—

Peter was good at everything but rarely stuck with what he started. As if covering for Peter's unfinished projects, I felt a need for continuity and a pressure not to quit. For the most part, sticking to my activities was a good thing and made my youth multidimensional. I did not skate or play softball or run or act in plays, I did them all at once or not at all. Why choose? Still, I often wondered about quality versus quantity. What if I'd spent that extra track practice time skating instead? Would I have landed all those elusive triples? Won more medals? Maybe I would have gotten tendonitis instead, or broken some critical bone. The comfort I now find in the very questions that once left me perplexed is that I am able to ask such questions at all. Had I lived solely for skating and not glimpsed the world outside, there might not have been any what-ifs at all . . . which is the only thing worse than the what-ifs themselves.

I won my first skating competition that day in December 1986, but I did not exactly blow the field away. Actually, there was no field. Murray's organized its small competition by level and age group, and since the other Freestyle One competitors were fresh out of kinder-garten, I got my own, separate, embarrassment-free age category of Freestyle One: "eleven and up." Complete with the strenuous require-ments of two-foot spins, waltz jumps, and forward swizzles, my program went smoothly. So to speak. Peter was there to witness my winning mo-ment. My parents bought me flowers and I left with a plastic medal around my neck and a wobbly home video that my brother narrated for the entire minute I was on the ice. *She's rounding the corner, gaining speed, looks like something big is coming up. . . . Ladies and gentlemen, would you look at that! Now she's skating backward! Tremendous!* As soon as I stepped off the rink Peter was off and running as well, having dutifully put in his time as a required spectator. He would not see me skate again for another decade, as his invitations to do so were either for-gotten or dismissed by plans of greater importance.

But Pete was in the front row of every audience I created when training—he was watching, cheering, applauding with pride and wild fervor for his little sister, throwing flowers on the good days, offering comfort on the tough ones. The hope that I might someday impress my older brother with my skating was in the back of my mind at every practice, every competition, just in case he happened to walk in the door right then. In my first few days with Hollywood on Ice, the ones still brimming with the hope of skating a solo, I was sure my brother was seated just out of my range of sight, a little left of center, somewhere in the tiers of the ice show's darkened tent filled with shadowed strangers.

On one end of my familial spectrum was Pete's absence. On the other, my mother's perfect attendance at shows and competitions over-compensated for the void my brother left. My father was right on the middle mark. Until I left for college, for better or for worse, there was always some family member in the audience when I competed. My mother got nervous during my competitions, spending more time outside the rink smoking than inside watching. When my group of competitors took to the ice she came indoors and wrung the schedule of events program until it tunneled itself diploma-style in her palm. Making her way to the top of the bleachers, she played judge far above the real ones who sat with their scoring sheets in hockey boxes or elevated rink-side platforms. According to her decorating instincts, she classified the girls not by name or performance or musical selection but by their outfits and body types.

Scoring procedures in low-level or nonqualifying competitions are nothing like the televised events. Judges do not use instantaneous flash cards or electronic tabulations that rank skaters directly after their music stops. There is no kiss-and-cry well where skaters await their scores and wave at the cameras. In fact, there are no cameras. No thrown bouquets or teddy bears, no Evian bottles crinkling with the grip-induced pressure of it all. Just a lingering coach on hand to hug the disappointed, congratulate the happy, and quiet the prima donna perfectionist who blames her falls on off-center hairbows, as hell hath no fury like a preteen scorned. At these competitions, no skater knows exactly how he or she fared until all the competitors have finished their programs. The judges take their sweet time tallying the marks, which are then sent to the computer room, retallied, and finally taped up on a wall amid a crowd of nervous parents, sneaker-wearing skaters, and bored siblings who cannot wait to go home from this place of ice and weirdness.

* * *

My mother always had immediate results. In her program guide there were notes next to the names of the girls in my group listing how many times they fell, whether they smiled or frowned, and of course what color dresses they wore. Costumes were never red, orange, yellow, green, blue, purple, or pink but were listed in the decorators' spectrum: crimson, ginger, saffron, chartreuse, azure, mauve, or magenta. There were numbers alongside our names that stood for the unofficial places my mother ranked us with check marks, pointy stars, and rutted circling denoting personal preferences. Waiting for the official results to come up, I scanned her computations with nervous intrigue. She'd wager on the bright cobalt girl to come in first, I'd probably come in second, but the pastel peach lace-and-ribbons blonde might have snuck in there, too, even though she had giant teeth and bad skin. The chubby periwinkle princess was definitely out of the running, and the teal-and-silver-striped kid with the feathery hair ribbons had nice skating but big legs and fell on just about everything and no amount of artistry could fix that much damage so don't worry honey you're safe for a medal thank God I just hope they are not as tacky as last year's flimsy cheapos I'm going out for two quick puffs holler when they're posted will you, dear?

More often than not, my mother was accurate within a few place standings. The difference between my mother's judging and the marks of the certified officials was that my mother could not tell an axel from a cartwheel.

Every jump in skating has the same landing but a completely different entry; the swooping double edge of a salchow, the razor-sharp line of a lutz, and the loop that seems to explode from nowhere all have distinct beginnings. Some jumps are harder than others, and thus scored differently, but my mother lumped them all together, and a fall was a fall was a fall. To her credit, my mother knew her spins — the names like layback and sit spin were a bit easier to match up to a skater's body position. But she was forever lost in the world of jumps and knew only that triples were indeed quite difficult. Despite her limited knowledge of figure skating's scoring system, my mother was a participant in my competitions, a part of my audience.

*   *   *

My father enjoyed his role of watching my eleven-year progress through amateur skating. In competition, no matter if I skated a clean program or how many times my little spandex heinie Zambonied the ice over two and a half minutes, my father always thought I'd won and told me so.

"You definitely beat all those kids. Hands down. You looked great out there." Often I was the one who had to sit him down and explain the reality of the situation.

"Dad, I fell six times."

"Yeah, but you got right back up and . . . "

"Dad, I sucked today. It's okay."

"Well, aaaall right. Next time, then." And there were plenty of next times when my father's opinions truly had some validity and I did come out on top. Or topish. He told me that I recovered so quickly from falls that if anyone in the audience blinked, they would have missed my slipups. I think my dad blinked a lot. Regardless, he was always there. While we waited for the results to be Scotch taped to the concrete rink walls, my dad and I worked on his high-five technique, which took over a decade to perfect. Instead of softly arching his palm up to meet mine, he rammed his hand straight out, as if stopping some imaginary car no one else could see.

"Oww, Dad! Follow through, *follow through!* Bend the wrist. Loosen the fingers."

"Sorry. Show me again."

"Why is this confusing to you? Should we warm up with pat-a-cake?"

"Aaaaall right, let's try again, Miss Smarty Pants."

"Hey, the results are up!"

My parents shared a meager amount of technical knowledge of skating, but my father understood something more about the sport: the athleticism, the grit beneath the artistry. But in all its multifaceted dimensions, skating provided something for each of my parents to appreciate—athleticism and artistry—and allowed me to unite them. Or at least try to.

◆

Chapter Eight

The Birth of Captain Graceful

On the third shelf in my right-hand closet back in Bronxville sits a blue plastic visor with ICE CAPADES painted in white on the brim below a row of tiny colored lights that actually flicker on and off with a D battery, sold separately. It has been there for over nineteen years. My parents bought this hat for me during one of our annual pilgrimages to the show. I used to wave at the skaters in the Ice Capades, hoping only that they might wave back, not knowing that the future would bring an audition with the company. I was seventeen, a senior in high school, when I got the chance to act on the promise I'd made myself years ago on a merciless, graceless Murray's winter morning: *I'm going to be in the Ice Capades.* One of the coaches at Murray's, Stacey, left our little rink to take a year off and skate with the Ice Capades during the 1992 season. It was Stacey who gave me the numbers to call and the names to drop, and within two weeks I had an audition booked. She also offered a bit of advice that lodged in my memory but that I didn't pay much attention to at the time.

"If you decide to go with the Ice Capades," Stacey said, "just stay strong. Be true to yourself." Then she looked me over for a minute, her eyes circumnavigating my body, even though she had seen me at Murray's every day for seven years and knew exactly what I looked like. "You'll be fine," she decided.

My audition for the tour was at the Nassau Coliseum on Long

Island, a massive arena with rows of seats stretching farther out and higher up than my nearsightedness could process. I was one of three girls auditioning that night in January 1993. A handful of executive board members all dressed in black seriousness watched my performance, studying my form and appearance while scribbling notes onto clipboards. I followed step sequences led by their choreographer and was timed for how quickly I could pick up new patterns and skills. The girl on my left had sloppy arm positions and kept her head down the whole time. She wore a white T-shirt over a blue leotard and a pair of dingy taupe tights. T-shirts and dirty leggings weren't going to cut it with the Ice Capades. The woman to my right had a long skating skirt that fell to her knees and a neat white sweater with long sleeves. She messed up the footwork patterns but knew how to play the game. She held her head high and smiled, and never let her posture sag even during the break. I understood the unspoken rules, too — skill meant nothing when presented without style and charisma. I was never very good at learning new steps immediately and footwork always took a good deal of repetition, but once memorized, the movements and patterns were permanently ingrained in my mind. A former Ice Capades skater prepared me for the quick memorization segment of the audition by offering stellar advice: mirror the first five or six steps perfectly and then just cross your fingers and improvise until the panel says, "Thank you, Kathryn." As long as it looked as though I knew what I was doing, I'd be okay; but if it appeared that I was thinking too much and skating with trepidation, they'd cut me immediately.

I wore a snug black leotard and new Danskin tights, sunset tan size B. Skates freshly polished, hair sprayed back, and makeup slight and proper. Small gold hoop earrings, no dangling bracelets or floppy necklaces that might take an onlooker's focus away from the body they decorated. In technical and artistic measure, my skating level was higher than the other two girls'. Sheer luck, of course, was also on my side that night.

After the footwork patterns and the basic forward and backward skating came the jumps and spins, each progressing in difficulty and style. I forwent the attempt at my triple toe loop; the Ice Capades wanted more overall consistency than I could have offered on that one, so I stuck to the doubles, combos, and artsy-fartsy stuff. Oozing with overdramatic facial expressions of boundless joy as my insides seethed with competitive fire, my alter ego, Captain Graceful, stepped up to the plate and performed with confidence.

As I rifled through all I knew how to do in figure skating, time flew out the window, making it impossible to tell if the audition had lasted all night or if I had just stepped on the ice. The Coliseum spun around me in its expanse of empty seating and endless possibility, a funnel of greatness, and I wanted to savor every moment. *Remember the colorful seats, the bleaching lights, the smell of leftover hockey and heat-lamp hot dogs, the custodians working the nosebleed section, and the* scrrch, scrrch *of their twiny brooms falling down, down, down to me. Remember.*

As the other women were called to perform their athletic feats, I feigned an attentive gaze their way but let my peripheral vision wander into the grandstand and bask in the light of daydreams that were about to come true. When we were finally told to relax and "take five," I assumed that the results of our performances would be mailed or telephoned within a few weeks. Therefore, I was amazed when the casting director called me over with a smile, a wave, and a six-word statement, one word for each year it had taken me to get there: "Congratulations, Kathryn, you made the show." Silent yeehaws and yipeekaiyays tore through my body and I desperately wanted to hear how they would echo in the Coliseum, but I exhaled calmly and shook the casting director's hand. He first said that I skated very well, then asked if I wanted to go to college. I did, that had always been part of the plan.

School was terribly important to me. Math classes were spent calculating the ratio of time to effort it would take to land my first triple, sketching blueprints of creative new spins on graph paper, and using my compass to draw out figure eights, which were deeply rutted into my notebook by the end of the period. I failed two semesters of algebra but kept wonderfully productive by writing short science fiction stories about a mean-spirited math teacher who got sucked up into the alien posing as an overhead projector. In physics, I reported on the gravitational component of binary star rotation and how it correlated to the manner in which a figure skater spins (instantaneously forgetting most of the theory after handing in my paper, but still feeling pretty snazzy about being able to use a phrase like "the gravitational component of binary star rotation").

My English papers argued that Penelope had issues of low self-esteem and that had she been an athlete, she might not have sat around unweaving her life away, waiting for Odysseus. Juliet had passion and leadership and would have made a good team captain even though her take-one-for-the-team attitude didn't end up doing her much good in the love-life arena. Ophelia was too wishy-washy and sure could have used some swimming lessons. King Lear would have been literature's most destructive soccer dad. For free-topic history papers, my peers chose subjects such as the Great Depression and the Cold War while I explored the development of female athletics and their political, social, and economic roles in any society I could dig up, from central Kansas to western Liberia.

I had twelve applications out at universities around the country (six my choices, six my mother's), but it was months before the thick and thin envelopes started rolling in. The director of the Ice Capades was very encouraging about college plans and pointed out that he preferred his skaters to get their education first, because Ice Capades had too many skaters quitting the show midseason to start or finish school. Either way, I made it into the show, he said, and it was my decision to sign on immediately or wait a few years. I chose to wait. The interim would not only bring college at its regularly scheduled interval but would also give me four extra years of skating improvement, exhibitions, and amateur competitions before turning professional, something that would benefit both me and Ice Capades. Could it get any better? I had my cake and could eat it anytime I wanted. (Baaaad analogy that turned out to be. Unless rice cakes count.)

The director went over my audition performance with me, critiquing my skating technique and assessing which maneuvers were stable and which elements needed work. Left-foot spirals and left tango stops could use a little fine-tuning. He then said he would see me in 1997, adding, "You've made a smart decision; education comes first. We'll be here when you graduate."

The audition itself had been a graduation of sorts, a rise above amateur standing, a passage into the elite, a justification of commitment. Or perhaps it was all a mirage, where for forty-five minutes a casting director mistook an awkward duckling for a graceful swan. When I was twelve, almost six years before my audition for the Ice Capades, *graceful* was the last adjective anyone would consider while watching me skate. I was in the middle of a six-inches-and-thirty-pounds twelve-month growth spurt, and I had no idea what my body looked like in motion. Linda, my coach, did. She was blunt and honest.

"You are the most ungraceful person I have ever coached," she told me one morning at six o'clock while we put together an intermediate-level program as my limbs flailed in unruly spasms of what puberty and I thought were artistic movements.

Linda shook her head. "Like this." She demonstrated, her arm rainbowing above her head in a soft, flowing arc. "Like you're a pretty skater in the Ice Capades."

"Oh. Like this?" I zoomed out my arm and clocked an oncoming skater in the face. Linda put a hand over her own face. "You just don't have *it*," she reiterated. She retracted these impression-making words years later, but they were a turning point for me on that frigid winter morning. At that very moment I decided I was going to get *it*, whatever *it* was. Some sort of superhero alter ego burst to life when Linda labeled me helplessly uncoordinated, and Captain Graceful was born from the shadows of doubt and ignorance.

"*I'm* going to be in the Ice Capades!" Captain Graceful bellowed. Linda rubbed her temples, and I kept trying to maneuver my appendages without giving nosebleeds to my little friends.

Captain Graceful, no doubt a distant relative of SuperStarbutt, was the kind of hero who enjoyed proving others wrong, and we took up the challenge Linda did not realize she had offered. According to her, one was born either with or without grace. Either you had it or you didn't, and if you didn't, good luck ever finding it. I understood but disagreed. According to me, one was born either with or without determination, and there was plenty of that swimming around in my gene pool. My grandmother had been a seven-time New Jersey state diving champion in the 1- and 3-meter springboard. My mother was a state champion and junior national champion freestyle swimmer, and my father had begun rowing competitively in his early fifties. If he could find his angle of grace and power at that stage of the game, then surely I could grow into mine.

According to Captain Graceful, skating skirts weren't all that different from little red capes, and there was really nothing stopping me from gracefully leaping over Linda's expectations in a single bound. Well, a few thousand single bounds.

From that moment on, grace became my obsession. I wouldn't jump without a unique footwork sequence preceding the entrance and I wouldn't spin without an arm position that no other skater had ever thought of using. Even the tedious, annoying basics — forward stroking, backward crossovers, left-foot spirals — became part of the challenge to better myself, to find grace and make it my own. I went back and did these drills again and again, paying attention to the details that had bored me only days before. Mimicking the choreography of the Olympic skaters on TV — the theatrical command of Katarina Witt, the bold athleticism of Surya Bonaly, the gentle refinement of Caryn Kadavy, and Scott Hamilton's unsurpassable love of sport, I studied their posture, their grace, and brought their essence to my practices. *Those* skaters had *it*. I watched these champions perform not just on television but also in ice shows and holiday specials year in and year out. The Ice Capades never hired the ungraceful — I knew that much even at twelve. Ice Capades, then, would be my validation, my proof that I could set a goal and reach it, no matter how long it took to get there.

Most skaters supplement their training with ballet, but Captain Graceful had a better, Cliffs Notes idea that would save time and allow for more on-ice practice. Instead of choosing junior high school electives such as woodworking and home ec, I took seventh-period drama class and learned to *act* like a ballerina! It was a perfectly safe and happy way to find grace while staying as far away from pink tutus as possible; I simply traced the perimeters of ballet, hoping that I might get away with a carbon-copy version of the original study.

Captain Graceful and I were not quite as high-profile as Superman and Clark Kent, or Spiderman and Peter Parker. Those guys defended world peace and the good of all mankind. Captain Graceful worked on smaller fronts, mostly for inner peace and the good of surviving adolescence. We were more like Michael and Kitt, from *Knight Rider*. I didn't talk into my watch and have her pull around when things got tricky, but we definitely depended on each other in a human/nonhuman way. When

I needed the Captain's confident edge, I forwent the phone booth and sticky webbing and just asked if she'd take over my mind to battle the dark forces of Negativity. She would show up, jump in my brain and body, do her confidence-boosting thing, and take off when she finished what she needed to do. Sometimes she showed up without my calling for her, but for the most part she gave me my space. All she asked of me was that I stay strong and healthy, because there isn't much of a market for weak superheroes.

Captain Graceful told everyone about our dreams of skating greatness, about how someday I'd be a professional skater. Declaring this out loud to anyone who would listen was scary and exciting and made me step up to the challenge of my confession; it was like grasping a piece of my future before it arrived. It was the Captain who took charge when answering every dreamless, programmed adult who asked, "And what do you want to do when you grow up, Katie?" *I'm gonna be in the Ice Capades.* "Ohhh, how precious! Now what do you really want to do?" *Are you deaf, Carol Brady? I'mgonnabeintheIceCapades!*

As I continued my quest for polished style, something interesting happened to my skating. My arms, once rigid with fledgling stiffness, began to relax. They curved with softness during slow music and snapped into poses of strength when the tempo picked up. My feet, which grew too big and too clunky too fast, began to find their balance with toes pointing into well-rehearsed lines of balletic composure. Even my neck complied, holding my head higher than the average teenager deems necessary. Grace became my sweet desire of personal perfection, the slow thrill of working toward something so far away that getting there and failing to do so carried the same weight of inspiration.

Grace was not a passing fixation. After years of practicing style and poise, allowing my body to explore its limits of space and boundaries, elegance became second nature. Pre-preliminary, preliminary, pre-juvenile, juvenile, intermediate, novice, junior, senior . . . I climbed through the levels of figure skating, never missing an opportunity to compete or exhibit whenever or wherever I had the chance. I knew I was getting closer to *it* when at a competition in New Jersey, an elderly judge with cavernously thick glasses approached me after the free skate, touched me on the arm, and said, "You skated beautifully, Jenny, your artistry has improved tremendously."

Neither the Captain nor I had any idea who Jenny was, but grace by association seemed like a step in the right direction, so I thanked her and quickly walked away before the real Jenny materialized. From time to time Linda acknowledged improvement but always stopped just short of using the one word she knew I was after: *graceful.* Even the sound was beautiful, with its gritty growl of a beginning and the hiss of hidden competition at its end . . . *grrrr race.* This was a word with power in its roots, something that could be captured and tamed, but only through respect and patience. And a whole lotta prayerlike begging—*Don'tfalldon'tfalldon'tfall*—during spirals, spread eagles, and, most formidable of all, axels.

The axel jump, one and a half rotations from a forward-edge takeoff, is a big deal for the beginning skater. It's right up there with menstruation, a sign that significant changes are on the way. The axel is the gateway to the doubles, just as the double axel brings passage into the world of triple jumps, as the time it takes to master the jump creates a sort of purgatory between the levels of advancement. After the body finally gets used to the feeling of spinning itself 360 degrees in the air, along comes the axel with its exclusive forward takeoff, throwing another 180 into the equation. The jump was named for the man who first performed it way back in 1882, a Mr. Axel Paulsen of Norway. Personally, I think the jump might have been something of a penicillin-like discovery, an accident of sorts. I'd wager that Mr. Axel Paulsen slipped off his edge while getting ready to do some other jump and just happened to pull off a last-minute landing. I support this theory with the fact that they named the jump the "axel" instead of the more respectful "paulsen," as if some bystander observed the first flubbed leap and doled out a little sarcasm, "Nice one, Axel!" then turned away, muttering, "Moron." Yet the jump has survived gravity, time, and bad nomenclature and is today respected as the most difficult maneuver of the single, double, triple, and soon to be quadruple rotations.

The single axel is often the make-or-break point in a young skater's career, the jump that defines who will work through discouraging falls and who will unlace her skates and find a new activity beyond the rink.

In the farthest right-hand corner of Murray's rink, I landed my axel on a Friday evening freestyle session in the late fall of 1987. I quickly grabbed a witness, a little boy a year or two younger than me named Ian who had already landed his axel some time ago. "Watchwatchwatch," I demanded. The jump was anything but straight and pretty: I hunched my body in the middle of the air as though I had been shot in the stomach at the apex of flight, and my arms bent into little wings that did not fly, an unlucky duck plunging toward the hounds. Looking as if my knees were physically conjoined, my legs remained tightly pressed side by side instead of crossing over each other at the ankle. My butt, beneath my green-and-purple (excuse me, *leaf*-and-*lilac*) paisley dress, stuck out as if an invisible bully had pulled an imaginary chair out from under me. Odd as it was, all this distortion took place in less than one second. Had the ice rink been a swimming pool, my axel was a cannonball to everyone else's swan dive. I was a gravitational disaster, an exception to the laws of physics. The only aspect of grace was perhaps the gentle flow of my braid in the breeze of the landing, after it recovered from smacking into the back of my head. Regardless, I was upright, on one foot, 540 degrees (one and a half revolutions) from where I had started, and quite pleased with myself.

"Looks kinda funny," Ian said of my newborn axel, "but it's clean." And alas it was. Cleanliness was the gift of a fully rotated jump, whereas cheated jumps suffered insufficient rotation but were still landable by shifting blade and body weight at the exact moment of impact and swooshing out the extra bit of rotation on the ice instead of in the air. I raced over to display my new jump to Linda, and she watched me perform my very special axel and offered her congratulations with more excitement than I'd ever heard before.

"Good job," she mumbled, and turned her attention back to the student she was working with. I was giddy from all her praise. Wow, *two* words! An adjective *and* a noun! That was just the response I needed.

Brevity did something for me, as long as there was honesty inside. Some coaches squeal with excitement for their skaters' achievements; some never crack a smile or offer even the faintest accolade. Linda acknowledged when things were good, when they needed work, and when they were just plain bad, but her tone was never harsh or condescending. There was always possibility in her voice, always something to take from what she said. She also offered monetary incentives, such as *I'll give you twenty bucks if you land a double axel right now.* The less she offered, the closer we were to a successful landing. Linda's prize-money offers for my triples were usually in the low thousands. Sometimes she said nothing at all, using other forms of communication to get her point across. One of her toe picks pressed into the back of my knee meant "More knee bend, please." A tug on my arm meant "This hand stays back, please." A shove to the lower back or shoulder meant "Get your ass in gear and move a little faster, please." My muscle memory recorded her nonverbal speeches in detail.

Linda was trustworthy and reliable, and I cared deeply for her over the seven years we worked together. In that time she went from being single to married and then to being the mother of two young boys, all while teaching figure skating at the crack of dawn and second grade for the rest of the day. Linda filled a void in my life and family structure somewhere between big sister, mother, and teacher, and although we were never "friends," I believe she gave me the knowledge of what to look for in one. We spent hundreds of mornings together, tracing circles in the ice, choreographing programs, understanding all movements of the human body and those of an unseen alter ego, watching the sun rise over Murray's and the darkness set in later each day.

When Murray's closed for the summer in early May, in the years before I could drive and before I trained in Lake Placid, Linda shuttled me and a few other skaters up to the Terry Connor Rink in Stamford, Connecticut, or over to the skating club in Darien, both about a forty-minute drive from Yonkers. On the way over in the mornings, we ate breakfast in silence and listened to Z100 on the radio. We never really spoke about skating when we weren't on the ice. On the way back I fell asleep somewhere between Cos Cob, Connecticut, and White Plains, New York, exhausted from four or five hours of daily practice. I slept until we rolled into Murray's parking lot, when the wind that whipped into the open windows of her sapphire Camaro slowly died down and the engine's stillness woke me from the deep peace of athletic exhaustion.

By my early teens I was a competition junkie. I entered every figure skating meet in the tristate area, searching out the ones that offered multiple events. New Jersey, Connecticut, Delaware, and every New York town from the Canadian border to the Long Island beaches. Nothing seemed too far away, and each summer I traveled farther. I competed in Dallas, Chicago, Detroit, and San Francisco, just to see what other skaters looked like. For regionals and qualifiers, performing my technical and free-skate programs was a given, as were figures, but most every amateur nonqualifying competition has a few other categories aside from the "serious" ones, and it was not uncommon for me to enter five or six per weekend. Artistic, Showcase, Dance, Footwork, Compulsory Moves—these were the fun routines, the less-strenuous side of competition that made skating seem a little bigger. They gave competitors the "second-chance feeling," taking the pressure off any skater who feared that her entire existence came down to just one, all or nothing, three-minute program.

Artistic and Showcase allowed lyrical programs that were more like exhibition routines; we were judged primarily on style over technical difficulty or content of jumps. We brought our favorite sloppy love songs to artistic competitions—"Lady in Red," "Unchained Melody," "One Moment in Time." Our bodies writhed with choreographed emotion that was well beyond our preteen ability to comprehend. What did we know of heartache and yearning, secret promises, and whispered desires? Not much, but in terms of the passion we felt toward our sport, we understood every love-oozing stanza as if it applied to our personal romance with skating. During artistic programs, we held on to the moves that held us captive, holding spirals and spread eagles twice as far as we did in free-skate programs, free from the demand of hurrying along from jump to jump. We spun a revolution or two longer, stretched our limbs a little farther, reaching out toward everything that skating made us feel within. And when we wiped out in the middle of an overly emotional leg extension, we did our best to make it look like something artistically planned, getting up with an extra-pretty roll of the wrist or dramatic elongation of the neck, laughing somewhere inside, just beneath our sheer embarrassment.

Footwork programs allowed no jumps or spins, only quick maneuvers of the feet for a minute or so. Compulsory moves, the opposite of artistic programs, meant competing with specific jumps or spins that were prechosen by the judges, which we performed individually and without music, not unlike a hockey or basketball skills competition in which every thing from slapshots to free throws are judged singly and separately. Pairs and Shadow Dance were categories that allowed two skaters to perform a freestyle or dance routine side by side, without all the lifting and touching. This was helpful for beginner ice dancers, as there was always a shortage of male partners. Shadow Dance allowed two girls to "dance" together but not face-to-face. At age thirteen I competed in Shadow Dance and came in second place at a large Lake Placid competition. Amy and I were ecstatic to win the silver, but not so thrilled when we found out we were the only ones competing in the event. We watched the videotape later and came to agree with the judging. Our thirteen-year-old limbs flew hither and yon and our timing was completely off. Milli Vanilli had better syncopation than we did, and we were lucky the judges gave us any medal instead of outright disqualifying us on the grounds of complete incompetence in figure skating.

Yet the best event of all, hands down, was Interpretive. This was not a category for the self-conscious skater, as it called for instantaneous creativity and the ability to throw caution to the wind. The rules were simple and exciting. A group of competing skaters was herded onto the ice, where a mystery tape was played twice over the loudspeaker. We all got a chance to practice to the music for a few minutes, then we were ushered into a locker room (from which we could not watch the other skaters) until it was our turn to go out and make up an impromptu program to the music we had heard just moments before. The music for Interpretive ranged from classical to pop, jazz to blockbuster movie theme songs. We were judged on creativity, how well we adapted to the music, technical elements, and whether we were able to stop when the tape did. Interpretive was a hybrid of spontaneity, raw emotion, and musical chairs, and I loved the event with all my heart. Something about putting it all on the line, right then and there, selling myself to the audience and judges, and gathering up the courage to possibly be laughed at gave me a confidence that seemed unsurpassable.

Murray's kids were all very good at Interpretive, as well we should have been, after all those mornings when tapes froze in the cassette player and we skated along to other people's programs just to keep warm. We practiced artistic programs while swerving around bird doo and executed compulsory moves while vaulting over sun-melted puddles, and every session called for shadow dance as the rink was crowded with so many skaters that it was not uncommon to be side by side with someone for the entire practice.

My first time in Interpretive, at age thirteen, Billy Joel's "Uptown Girl" was the chosen music. *This one's in the bag,* I thought to myself. Between spins and jumps I pranced around as if I were Bronxville's gift to figure skating, nose in the air, chest following suit, flippantly tossing my ponytail, waving my hand dismissively, pulling blasé facial expressions, and rolling my eyes at Billy Joel's tribute to highbrow-female desire. Now, just end with the music . . . spiiiiin, hoooold, okay Captain Uptown, aaaaand stop!

I came in first out of twelve that day, on a Sunday, at a competition in Morristown, New Jersey. It was as if my entire young life had been preparing me for Interpretive all along . . . making up a game to play by myself, creating all the rules as I went along, not caring what others thought, standing in the spotlight . . . nothing compared to the readiness that Interpretive called for. Be ready, Captain Graceful, be ready for anything.

The eagerness with which I threw myself into each competition was not something I carried over to my job with Hollywood on Ice. My body was doing more waving and smiling than skating, and my mind was not sure how to handle the transition from the athletic, amateur version of figure skating. Walking into the trailer, my enthusiasm was about equal to that of a tollbooth collector working the graveyard shift of an E-ZPass lane. Once I had memorized my steps, I realized that the show ran on autopilot and that all the skater showgirls had to do was show up and get into place. The cast started filtering in half an hour before the curtain went up. Actually, in Hollywood's case, it was parted manually side to side by two Mexican workers who stood in the middle and ran with the split curtain in opposite directions. One worker was quick and lively, but the other was not quite as spry in his movements, so there was always one skater who had to push either the HOLLYWOO or OD ON ICE curtain out of her way in an effort to make it to the ice on time. It must have looked funny from the audience to see about thirty mannequin-still showgirls and one lone woman wrestling to free her headdress from the attacking backdrop.

The show worked like this: skate a number, quick change, skate another number, quick change, skate another number, quick change . . . until two hours passed and we quick-changed back into our civilian clothes. Not every skater was in every number, so at some point we had a break that was a few minutes longer than usual. My rest time came three numbers into the show, when I sat out the Michael Jackson routine and tried to figure out the lyrics to "Smooth Criminal" in the acoustically challenged rink. The burbled chorus of Michael asking some chick named Annie if she's okay, if she's okay, if she's okay, *Annie—ow!* sounded to me like, *And here I go a walkin' a walkin' a walkin', just me! OW!* Apparently my interpretation was shaped by what my subconscious wanted me to do.

Between the Michael Jackson and Barbie skits and the Little Mermaid scene, there was a comedy routine (think clowns and confetti buckets), Pam's solo to "Memories" from *Cats* (which ironically was the slow part for my Senior Ladies long program), and a most incredible act by the Sirota family. Alexei and his parents, all former circus employees, took to the ice for their daredevil hoop act. A human-size steel hamster wheel with raised inner rungs used as handles was rolled onto the ice. The family of three then stood inside the sturdy circle, one behind another, wearing skates of course, so that together they looked like the famous drawing of Leonardo da Vinci's medical anatomy man. Their feet were all shoulder-width apart, Alexei's arms were straight out to the side, his father's slightly above, his mother's arms above that. In this position, the wheel, nubbed with little metal spikes, traveled up and down the ice, propelled by the momentum of body-positioning physics within. The family rolled all over the place, as Alexei occasionally stepped out of the contraption to do a back flip on the ice, then stepped back in. The background music was an electronically speeded-up, techno-enhanced *Flintstones* theme song with a dub-over voice singing "Familia Sirota" interspersed throughout. Whoever did the dubbing was obviously misinformed as to the happy and lighthearted theme of the act, for the deep, throaty voice sounded like an angered demon from a horror movie. The routine was visually entertaining but pretty much unrelated to skating except for the floor being made of ice.

Next was the *Flashdance* sequence, bringing my role as a punk rock bimbo—to which I was so able to relate. The best part about it was something that Felicia got to experience firsthand: riding a bicycle over the ice. As the rest of the cast was in a quick change, two skaters, Felicia and tiny little Yulia, the backup pairs soloist, kicked off the routine by mimicking the mid-eighties movie, where the lead actress rides her ten-speed to work at the welding plant. To a harmony of bicycle bells, Felicia and Yulia circled the ice on a couple of old Schwinns with little nails jutting out from the tires to create traction. Being careful not to get their sparkly leg warmers caught on the chain ring, their toe picks stuck in the spokes, or blindly crash into each other because of the dark Wayfarer sunglasses they wore, the two skaters pedaled shakily about the rink with obvious nervousness and effort.

"You're so lucky you get to ride the bike," I told Felicia, half joking. At least she got to look athletic.

"Yeah? You have a go on the bloody thing!" she responded, cursing on about the wedgie it gave her. I never did get to ride the old bike but somehow got over the loss.

I trotted back on the ice for the Little Mermaid antics; yet before donning the sea-horse costume, eight of us put on black, hooded cloaks and whooshed over the ice carrying a hand-sewn cloth jellyfish that dangled from a stick. The billowy anemone was made of white rayon, and the rink went to blacklight, to get that "under the sea" feel. The glowing jellyfish circled the rink only a few times, and then we hopped off to get ready for the big oceanic shindig. Shuffling backstage in our cloaks, we entered the trailer in quiet succession, looking like a herd of Grim Reapers returning from a long day of doom. After la *Serenita* and her prince skated a pairs solo and saved the sea kingdom from the wrath of Ursula the sea witch (played by Lenny), there was a fifteen-minute intermission before the Flintstone frolics began. A few more solos, more skimpy costumes, more waving, then curtain.

Of course, we were lucky if we made it out onto the ice for any number at all. Toe picks got caught on everything from the trailer's sorry excuse for a carpet to the electrical wires that lay like camouflaged snakes around the backstage mats. Even the matting was mislaid and jagged, wood and nails jutting up from cockeyed angles of exposed floorboards. No one used skate guards, as too many quick changes hurried us from one backstage area to another. We wore rubber guards only en route to the bathroom, a separate minitrailer at the opposite end of the grounds. Serrated blades and scarred boots replaced the skates once cared for with tenderness and respect. Everything behind the curtain was a lawsuit waiting to happen, a pitfall of impairment where our toe picks felled us regularly into the darkness of props and trailers.

There was no time clock in the trailer — we were free to leave after the last show of the night. There were no see-ya-laters to any of our fellow employees, as that was just a given. The job atmosphere of skating was quite a contrast to the amateur one, where skaters lingered at Murray's for as long as we could. No one wanted to hang around the trailer or any other part of the Hollywood tent, everyone just wanted out — and as quickly as possible. Most of the skaters loosened their skates, yanked them off, and chucked them in their drawers without wiping the blades or putting them away gently. Respectfully. Every careless thud of blade on drawer made me wince. As I watched the skaters hurry away from it all, I wondered if they felt the same ache for the old days of skating that I did, or if all those memories had been forgotten. Or worse, worn away by apathy, never again to be resharpened.

Though he was fifty years my senior, sparks flew every time I walked into Mr. Kohler's shop. They were the literal kind, as fiery beads of metallic friction shot into the air from his skate-sharpening machine and landed on the concrete countertop of his garage-turned-workshop in Nyack, New York. Six or seven times a year Mr. Kohler ran my patch and freestyle skates through this machine, which looked like some sort of misplaced train engine, complete with pistons and wheels that clamored and buzzed with noisy importance. Setting the contraption and positioning each blade according to how much of its hollow needed grinding, Mr. Kohler sharpened every edge to perfection. The science of sharpening was a mystery to me, with its intricate measurements and levels; all I knew for sure was that this was the man who gave me balance.

The ritual did not take very long, only a few minutes per boot, unless there was a traffic jam of skaters waiting. Mr. Kohler was a very important man in the figure skating communities of the tristate area, one who necessitated appointments, but scheduling ran over from time to time as proud skating moms took too much liberty with the sharpener's question "And how is your daughter's skating coming along?" The loud whirring of the machine dissuaded conversation while Mr. Kohler performed his duties, but afterward he patiently listened to all the stories of who won what competition and who landed which jump for the first time, "uh-huhing" in his thick German accent, re-revving up the machine as a subtle clue for those who talked too long. He was interested in his skater clients, but professionally distant, passing along good news and happy tidbits but never spreading gossip from visitor to visitor. He was solid and confident in his work, never asking how our blades felt, because he knew he never failed his skaters. My mother and I either waited in the workshop or ventured to the local McDonald's, bringing a cup of coffee back to the man who held my fate in his hands. If we stayed put in the workshop, she read the travel magazines Mr. Kohler laid out while I dug into the box of plastic skate guards or picked out a new pair of woolly tights. (It was impossible to have too many pairs of woolly tights.)

There were bottles of skate polish and sole-waterproofing kits for sale, as well as spare laces and boot covers, stacked boxes containing new skating boots from the SP-Teri company, and blades from MK in England. Endless pairs of used skates that Mr. Kohler resold for his clients marched side by side under the shelf and told their stories. Well-worn boots with creases, buckling leather, and faded laces stood next to stiffer-looking boots with no repolishing marks and unfrayed cords, showing which owners were serious competitors and which had quickly decided the sport of figure skating was not for them. I never resold my skates to Mr. Kohler, not only because each pair was broken down to sockish consistency but because there was not much of a market for size ten women's figure skates. Instead, my old skates formed a bladeless kickline along the wall in our garage, artifacts of a former life that were too old to be used again, too loved to be thrown away.

Mr. Kohler's hands were weathered but ageless, like the rest of him. He was a grandfatherly man who did not seem to grow one day older in the decade I knew him, and there was something wonderfully comforting about his unwavering character. He never wore protective goggles when he operated the sparking machine, because the lenses of his glasses were thick enough, and the blue apron he donned over his plaid shirts seemed practically sewn on. What we knew of Mr. Kohler was that his daughter was a skater, he liked his coffee black, and he went skiing for two weeks every year but was sure to put up his vacation schedule months in advance so that panicky mothers and princessy skaters could plan ahead for the travesty of his absence.

The drive from Bronxville up to Mr. Kohler's tiny town of Garnerville just outside of Nyack took about half an hour. Before I could pilot the car on my own, my mother navigated the trip. I had my first and only one-sided discussion about sex on the way to Mr. Kohler's. The song "Feel Like Makin' Love" came onto the radio midway through the journey and my mother took this opportunity to voice her opinions about the topic. Ironically, the song is sung by a band called Bad Company, but my mother didn't know that and I didn't know what irony was, so the conversation was fatefully unavoidable.

"You know, there is an appropriate time and place for making love and people should not do it until they are ready, no matter how much they might feel like it," my mother ennunciated slowly. I was fourteen, many months away from my first kiss and light-years away from what had so inspired Bad Company. I responded with a nod and squirmed noticeably in the seat of the station wagon, and that was the last we ever spoke of sex. Instead of the Birds and the Bees, I got the slightly off-kilter version of the Buick Skylark and Dee. I don't think either of us was ever happier to see Mr. Kohler. Both my blades and the general atmosphere of teenage embarrassment were back in balance after a few minutes of sparky distraction and my mother's wise decision to go pick up two cups of black coffee.

There were other sharpeners I used if I had to, while training far from home during the summers, but I always returned to Mr. Kohler before important competitions or figure and free-skating tests. He was the last person to touch my skates before I left for the tour. Extra-sharp, please, I requested.

᭟

Chapter Nine

The Challenge of an Altered Dream

The Ice Capades was the first time I saw group figure skating, as the show was not a series of random figure skaters performing on the ice one at a time but a mix of soloists, chorus lines, and group routines. Theater and athleticism: every aspect was something I wanted to experience, from the precise synchronicity of the skaters in the background to the intense focus of the star shining alone at center ice. I aspired to be a soloist, but the backup dance corps of skaters seemed pretty interesting, too. Just getting into the Ice Capades was the primary focus, and working my way up from there. The only thing I ruled out for sure, because of my height, was skating as part of a pair team unless they found some five-two guy I could throw effortlessly into triple salchows and hold over my head in flamboyant lift combinations.

The only team element in Hollywood on Ice was the unspoken bond of bored complacency that the skaters shared with one another. Other than that, it was every skater for himself, whether vying for a solo position or merely keeping lightbulbs from being hijacked in the trailer. Still entranced by the newness of it all, Felicia's and my excitement was tolerated but met with the gentle shakes of the head from other skaters that seemed to say, *Have fun while it lasts, girls.* During my first week with Hollywood on Ice, time did what it does best in a new setting, turning everything surreal as it passed by in clumps of undifferentiated hours. Felicia and I spent the first few days under Krystal's tutelage, learning the steps to all the numbers in the show. For hours on end we pranced around the square of disposable ice under Hollywood on Ice's traveling tent. Vacant bleachers watched our every move, and for the first time I found no reason to fill them with imaginary people. All I did was step and sway, smile and wave. There were no feats of athleticism at which to marvel, not even an axel, so I turned away the images of loved ones that usually showed up in my mind to watch me skate. Perhaps I could invite them back when the steps were learned and the show was complete, but not now. On breaks, I removed my skates from my feet, which swelled up so much in the Argentinean summer heat that the only way to shrink them down again was to walk around barefoot on the ice until the ten-minute break was over.

A few technicians dawdled about the grounds, popping their heads between the tent curtains now and then to get a glance at the two new *gringas*. Felicia was an instant hit as her blond hair invited catcalls and whispers of "*Tssst . . . Hola, linda, linda.*"

"*Me llamo Felicia.* Fel-*iss*-cee-uh," she cried in frustration, screaming at the worker who had *linda*-ed her one too many times.

"Felicia, *linda* means 'pretty' in Spanish," Jody explained.

"Oh. Righty, then. Linda it is!"

I was cast as one of the six "showgirls," all of whom were taller than five-eight. With this title came such honors as standing on flights of stumpy stairs and waving up a storm while the shorter yet more numerous "skater dancers" kicklined and booty-shook up and down the ice. *Soon,* I thought, *soon there will be a skating part.* It couldn't be like this all show long, just cross-steps and pivots. During our choreography breaks Krystal went backstage for a smoke and Felicia and I worked on combination jumps and death drops, trying to figure out the dimensions of the small, bumpy ice rink and how to set up for such elements when we were eventually called to do them. Yet each scene came and went without step-outs or solos, and our skills went unrequired. I flailed fishlike through the Little Mermaid scene, bebopped through the Flintstones number, and flopped my way through Barbie, but when the turquoise-sequined finale costume plunged into the valley of my posterior, the show had come to an end without any real skating. Not for me, anyway.

There were two soloist numbers: one belonged to the line captain (either Pam or her sub, Sunny), the other to Olga #1 and her pairs partner, Grígor. The most strenuous jump that either of the female soloists performed was a single axel, and when I witnessed this, my competitive instinct kicked in. Survival of the fittest is a well-understood concept among athletes; those who improve move on, and the rest watch the others pass by. At Murray's the better skaters always got the best ice-show solos, just as the fastest runners and the strongest rowers were always given the opportunity to race their counterparts. Watching the show from the audience, I knew that Pam and Sunny were good skaters but that my level of showmanship and jumping abilities were a tad higher. I skated over to Krystal and asked when I could schedule an audition for a solo spot.

"But that's Pam's number," Krystal said with a confused look.

"Well, I'd like a shot at it. Or at least an understudy position." *Let me just show you what I've got,* I tried to explain. I was an athlete, and this was my confidence. If management did not think I was talented, then fine, but not to have an opportunity to display what I could do was a strange concept. My request was met with blankness and never granted.

Something will change, that was the mantra I chanted in my head. *Something will change and I will get to skate in this show as a soloist. In the meantime, I'll do whatever they say . . . wave, prance, smile, whatever. Be patient, Captain Graceful, be patient. You just got here. Put your cape away and calm down. You've got the talent, now just wait for the right time.* I was being impatient and I knew it. But patience felt like passivity, like inactivity, and inactivity left skaters physically cold and mentally forgotten. This was *my* dream since I was twelve, and there had always been a solo in the plan, and that was that. Patience, schmatience. Though I had barely arrived at the big-top circus of Hollywood on Ice, the disappointment of the Ice Capades, and the solo-less Holiday made it feel that my experiences in professional skating were anything but new.

At the end of my first week with Hollywood was the Sunday weigh-in. Sunday evenings in the trailer meant stepping on a scale while one of the workers wrote down our weight. Felicia and I rolled our eyes, snorted a laugh. *Gee, fun.* We had been at the trailer all afternoon, try-

ing on all our sparkly new costumes and taking pictures to send back
home, little snapshots that proved our status as professionals. We stood
in the hokey showgirl poses that Krystal taught us—-right leg out in
front with the knee slightly bent and the toe just touching the ground,
rear leg anchoring our weight, hands on hips with the fingers in back,
suck in the gut, stick out the chest . . . click. While I slithered out of the
turquoise-and-black finale bodysuit, Sunny, the acting line captain in
Pam's absence, asked how things were going.

"Oh fine, getting used to it all, ya know?"

"Good. Great. Okay," she sang in a happy singsong tone that instantly negated her lyrics. "Listen, just so you know . . ." Sunny brought
word that Lora had made an executive decision that I was to lose weight.
"Don't worry," Sunny chirped. "She says everyone has to lose weight."

"How much?"

"We'll let you know when you can stop."

"But it's *muscle*."

"You're a showgirl now, not an athlete. You just need to be a little
more feminine, softer."

I'd like to think that a grand cacophony of warning bells went off
in my head upon hearing this response and inadvertently deafened me,
and this is why I did not immediately run from the dressing room. *Not
an athlete? I'm a figure skater, for Christ's sake. Showgirl, my ass! You can
dress me up in a giant sequin, but that doesn't mean I am a sequin. I'm an
athlete. More feminine? There is nothing wrong with my body, you big
mean dummy.*

But my attempts at justification fell on deaf ears, and everything I
carried inside in regard to weight turned immediately to anger as if a
switch had been flipped. Holiday on Ice's issues with weight and height,
the Ice Capades' nonissues, an audition fiasco during college for Disney
on Ice, my mother's obsession with my appearance, skating, rowing, running, muscles, softness, femininity, scales blind to strength and proportion—everything whirled together and made little sense. These were the
very muscles that had allowed me to get into professional tours, championship meets, national competitions. Why were they now inappropriate,
something to get rid of? The request that I lose weight came as a smack
in the face. But athletes take pain in stride. Back down? No way.

If Hollywood on Ice wanted me to lose weight, then fine. I could fix that. I would be the best damn weight-loser this tour had ever seen. Grab your cape, Captain Graceful, and hang on. Nothing gets in the way of my dream. A decision had to be made. Accept the challenge of an altered dream, or give up? Accept. Giving up was for quitters. Only I had it all backward. Blind to the fact that professional skating was failing my body, I believed only that I was failing at my goal. Had I not worked so hard, so long, to be where I was? I could not let food or weight be my breaking point. An athlete never believes she can fail. She takes no shortcuts through dedication. If less of myself was what it took to get noticed, then that's what I'd give them. *No one takes my goals away from me,* I thought angrily, fumbling through the wooden drawer at the end of the trailer and pulling out the scale to note my starting point.

The line captain of Hollywood on Ice, Pam, hollered, "Weigh-ins!" at six o'clock sharp every Sunday and we all left the dressing room and headed for the toilet. There, we rid ourselves of any excess weight one last time before we stepped on the scale. Most of us just urinated, hoping our bowels might move, too, even though on Sundays there was nothing in our system to move. Other skaters put either a laxative or their index finger down their throats. Instead of concerned voices inquiring about the well-being of the woman next to us, "Hurry-up!" and *"¡Vamos!"* echoed through the stalls when any skater lingered too long. Only flushes and sighs of mental relief sounded through the bathroom as the skaters made their way back to the trailer with the scale.

We were tense and irritable and silent. No one talked about weight or the hideous methods of reducing it. Talking about weight led to talking about food, a subject no one liked to bring up, for it made us hungry just to think about what we no longer let ourselves consume. Sometimes food conversations began as whispers in the dressing room, inevitably growing louder and attracting more participants as our voices carried through the trailer, the stale air suddenly circulating with the memories of groceries we used to know. Instead of recollecting past birthday cakes or looking forward to an elaborate dinner of the finest Chilean seafood, we spoke of mundane, familiar fare that had somehow become forbidden luxuries: pretzel sticks, peanuts, ham and cheese sandwiches, vanilla ice-cream cones.

There were not many conversations like this, though. It was easier to lie, to tell one another that we weren't hungry. The unspoken rule that no one ever broke was asking another skater about the number at which she tipped the scales. The answer would have been a lie, anyway. Weight was a sensitive subject, and the reasons varied from skater to skater. For some it was the threat of fines, a reduction in one's paycheck for being over one's target number. For others, it was personal. As an athlete, I felt as though every muscle in my body had its own individual heart. Now, Lora demanded that I break each one, as if the lifelong relationship between my body and my sport meant nothing at all.

꙳

Chapter Ten

Sundays Past, Sundays Present

Before the warehouse in Bern, before the pallid square of ice beneath Hollywood's big top, are the memories of rinks scattered about the country where I laced my skates on benches in lobbies that seemed to be both foreign and familiar at the same time. All rinks differ but slightly in their internal architecture, and those familiar with skating know exactly where to go and what to do the moment they step inside.

In the summers of my teenage years, Lake Placid was my training venue, where I worked with Tommy Litz, Mary Emes, Gustave Lussi, and other greats of skating tutelage. I willingly crammed three daily freestyle sessions, two hours of patch, one nightly ice dance practice, and optional weight training and ballet classes into every day I spent at the U.S. Olympic Center. The magnificent building housed four rinks beneath its colossal roof: one dedicated to figures, and the rest divided among the freestyle skaters and hockey players. In the sporadic moments not spent on the ice, the figure skaters traveled in adolescent flocks to watch the Can Am hockey camp kids and counselors zoom around the historic 1980 Rink. We flirtatiously walked the long way to our freestyle sessions on the USA rink, past the penalty boxes and locker rooms of the teenage hockey players. Any money our parents sent us we spent in the pro shop, buying overpriced skating garb and little souvenirs inscribed with LAKE PLACID, HOME OF THE 1932 AND 1980 WINTER OLYMPIC GAMES.

Waiting by the 1932 Rink or the Lussi Rink until our session started, we looked at the display cases that contained hundreds of black-and-white photos of figure skating's past. Sonja Henie and Dorothy Hamill were easy to spot, as were Peggy Fleming, Dick Button, and the infamous shot of the 1961 U.S. national team, beaming teenagers and proud judges standing in front of the ill-fated airplane that took their lives shortly after the camera took their picture. There were photos of the Ice Follies, the grandfather of the Ice Capades, and we marveled at the flimsy old skates that laced halfway up the calf and the abundant skirts that hung down to the same point. So much about the sport had changed, but there in that display case greatness skated forever. Each summer Captain Graceful stood before those glass windows and daydreamed about being on the other side.

At lunchtime I found Nina and Rachel, two skaters from Murray's. We ate our sandwiches outside in the summer sun, giggling at the tourists who gathered to pose at the IT'S NO MIRACLE, IT'S REAL SNOW! sign above the little pit where the Zamboni dumped its collection every few hours, and listened to weary mothers futilely implore, "Joey, no! Stop eating that!" In the distance the Adirondacks turned deep green and purple as the afternoon clouds rolled by, obscuring our view of the Olympic ski jumps that hovered like a couple of regal brontosauruses keeping watch over their historic land.

My days began at seven, and by the time I skated my last freestyle session, the upstate summer sky had long turned dark and breezy. My parents did not accompany me up north, which was fine. At fourteen, I was a veteran teenager and my parents were still suffering through their awkward stage, so it was probably best that I gave them some space. I boarded at a house especially for figure skaters, where thirty pubescent girls spent the summers camp-style under the watchful eye of the owners of Lysek's Hillcrest Inn. Mrs. Lysek checked on us and turned out our lights at night, and Mr. Lysek made pancakes each morning and knew no one by name, only who was a blueberry, chocolate chip, or plain girl. Letters and care packages cluttered the dining room table. Some moms sent cookies and brownies. Mine sent J. Crew catalogs with circled outfits that might look good on me, always worn by tall models with long brown hair. Now and then Mrs. Lysek asked how our day had gone, but other than that, we were on our own, which seemed like a great privilege.

Summers in Lake Placid were routine and consistent. I almost moved up there to finish high school at the National Sports Academy and train at the Olympic arenas, but despite the fabulous skating facilities and the lack of Bronxville's social problems, Lake Placid did not have the one thing that I really needed: Murray's. At its core, figure skating is about consistency, and Murray's was so embedded in me that no place else could possibly satisfy my long-term training.

Hollywood on Ice had no archive of its skating "greats," no photos of its past, only a brochure-like program from the early eighties that was annually reproduced for the souvenir stands, displaying showgirls who were no longer there. Lenny's was the only recognizable face in the booklet.

Like two ailing hippopotamuses and a litter of their box-shaped babies, the trailers and trucks of Hollywood on Ice lumbered into dusty lots in remote corners of South America and wallowed on the outskirts of towns until it was time to roll on again. Villages did not ask Hollywood on Ice to come — we just did — and management crossed their fingers that the townspeople were in the mood to see an ice show with seminaked women and figure skating acrobats. On tour, when one skater asked another how life was going, it usually connoted weight loss. *How are you doing? Oh, a few pounds off target, and you?* I hardly expected Lora to tuck us in at night or make us flapjacks for breakfast, but our clashing definitions of figure skating and professional ice show management made it clear that we were not the most compatible employer-employee combination.

At the core of my intolerance for the world of professional skating was the inconsistency of Hollywood on Ice. My disdain for weigh-ins and the generally unathletic nature of the show might be easy to understand, yet what ran deeper was my frustration that there was nothing concrete or permanent about the tour. The only constant was the start times of each show, seven and ten-thirty, and on weekends a third show at one. Otherwise, there was not a single predictable or plannable moment, and those characteristics had been the two most nurturing of my amateur career.

No one knew when and where the next Hollywood venue would be, how long we would stay there, or if the tour might suddenly be canceled altogether because its geriatric owner in Mexico conked out and left no funding for continuation. No one knew if they could stop starving themselves. No one knew if there would be enough revenue for paychecks that week, or whether we'd be given handwritten IOU slips again. No one even knew if their dressing table lightbulb would still be there at the end of the night, let alone if their life goals and dreams were playing a nasty practical joke on them. Ingrained in my previous lifestyle, consistency had become the backbone of all things good and respectable. Going to a rink every day and trying to be the best I could, that was consistency. Going into the trailer and trying to decide if it would be a laxative or diet pill day, that was the kind of consistency I could do without.

The hotels Hollywood put us up in were mostly old and nondescript and, like most of the architecture in South America, one- or two-story structures that looked more like a family duplex than a commercial building. The rooms usually had two beds, a bathroom, a window if we were lucky, and sometimes a closet. In Bahía Blanca and Santiago, Felicia and I had a television and we gorged ourselves on CNN, MTV, and the subtitled late-night reruns of Emmy escapees like *ALF* and *My Two Dads*. There was never a kitchen or a fridge in the room, and though this bothered some of the skaters, I found the kitchenless situation ideal.

Fridges, cabinets, stoves, and microwaves made the thought of food overwhelming and tempting, and it was much easier to set my bowls of fruit and boxes of instant powdery stuff on a hidden closet shelf than in some right-there-in-your-face kitchen. Most of the Chilean and Argentinean hotels had a small dining area somewhere in the lobby or a communal oven, but I did what I could to avoid such places. Losing weight was the goal, and all kitchens became scary spaces. At the time I was too caught up in the weight-loss process to ponder the history of my kitchen discomfort, which in fact stemmed from my pretour days on the other side of the equator.

The kitchen in our house in Bronxville was old and beautiful. The stove was set in a large butcher-block piece in the middle of the room with a barstool countertop on the opposite side. We had a pantry at one end and a round wooden dinner table at the other, an alcove that gave way to my mother's office in one direction and a TV room in the other corner. Across from the butcher block, there were finely refinished hardwood cabinets that snapped open and shut with a *ka-pung* sound. The cabinet that stored all of Taffy's Alpo, Saddy and Bushy's Meow Mix, and Zigmund's hamster pellets had an additional squeak, which the dog's and cats' bionic hearing could apparently detect from across the neighborhood. The manner in which the animals came flying toward dinner when I opened the kibble door was the same way my mother showed up when I opened the other cabinets to feed myself. *Ka-pung*—

"What are you eating?"

"Cereal."

"You just ate dinner."

"I'm still hungry."

"Really? How come?"

"Dunno."

The feel hungry/eat food logic that had seemed so natural to me as a child began to dissipate over the teenage years, as my self-consciousness rose to a level I did not understand. My mother kept a subtle vigil over my food intake, not responding to my requests for second helpings.

"Are there more peas?"

"In the freezer."

"Could you make more next time? I really like peas."

"I made plenty."

Her portion sizes were infinitesimal, and I often went in search of seconds or thirds, growing frustrated if there were none to be found.

"Here," my father usually offered, dishing part of his food onto my plate. Sometimes I accepted, but I usually declined because I felt guilty taking his dinner away from him. My mother was a pretty good cook, but I did not want more food because it tasted good. I was truly hungry— *Viking* hungry—from the numerous physical activities of my day, and my stomach was far from full after the five bites it took to clear my plate. Stouffer's side dishes for one were distributed three ways, and I firmly believe that my allocated pork chop came from a guinea pig or some other appetizer-size mammal. Artichokes made a rather consistent appearance at the table, a deceptive vegetable with its plentiful exterior and 5 percent edibility ratio that never quite satisfied me. *Boy, that was a tough work-out . . . pass me an artichoke, will you?* My dad showed me how to cut the heart of the vegetable out from underneath the indigestible prickly layer. *There's more meat in there,* he'd whisper, as if he, too, was scavenging for more sustenance.

Dinner, as a family activity, changed over the years. The meal started out with four participants, then dwindled down to three when Pete went to boarding school. When skating took center stage and practices went till 7:15 on Monday, Tuesday, and Friday nights, dinner was a solo operation. When we ate together at the round wooden antique table a few nights a week, conversation spanned the usual how-was-your-day gamut. My parents mumbled about which clients they had seen that day. On the rare occasions that he was home, Pete, a computer whiz, talked about the most recent technology advancements. I revealed my latest test grade, unless it was in math, in which I simply said, "Almost," and everyone left it at that. The air between my parents was not tense, just kind of vacant. They made little eye contact or personal conversation, and it had been that way for a while, since Dad moved into the guest room and Mom explained that it was because I got up so early to skate.

Although we ate together only a couple of nights a week, the scrutiny of my meals did not lessen. My simple solution to hunger was to make more food for myself, so when my requests for bigger portions went unheeded, I just picked up where my mother left off. We always had cereal, or something frozen hiding in the freezer. The food was there, but physically getting it became a problem as I felt hawk eyes on me every time I went for some replenishment.

I began to sneak about the kitchen, formulating excuses as to why I needed to eat so they were on hand when my mother came to investigate the *ka-pung*ing cabinets. Hunger, as a reason, did not seem valid anymore. When I had used up all the old excuses—*I ran six miles today at track, skating practice tonight was really hard, I'm tired and I need some energy, I just wanna have some popcorn with the movie*—a new method emerged. Shame. Instead of just going to the cabinet and grabbing a granola bar or handful of Cracklin' Oat Bran, I pulled on the handles and pushed on the wood frame just above the latch so that the door opened with a much more muted *ka-pung.* I was the Indian warrior of our kitchen, Silent

Eating One, creeping about on tiptoe through a lush expanse of cabinets tripped with audible booby traps. Hunting down my food was easier than covering my tracks.

There was no way to shut the cabinet door without making a loud click, so I left the cabinets open, just a crack, the wooden doors merely brushing up against the latch, as if to let my guilt of consumption slip quietly out of each one that I left ajar. It worked. My mother, Crouches With Radar, could not detect the sound of my silent refueling. Sooner or later she would come into the kitchen anyway and nitpick about my newest habit of not shutting the cabinets all the way—but that was all right by me. I had long since finished my snack and there was no one around to judge my caloric intake. Silent Eating One left no shred of evidence, no trail of trail mix, no proof of crumbs along the sofas while a satisfied Crouches With Radar went back to her smoky tepee to drink cup after cup of diluted tea and puff away on her appetite-suppressing peace pipes.

In our otherwise ordinary kitchen my relationship with food began to change, though at first only slightly. Food began to make me feel ashamed, and I grew terribly self-conscious about eating in front of other people. Would strangers judge me and ask me why or what I ate, or look at me the way my mother did when I went for more? "Why?" is not a valid question when it comes to the act of eating, as without eating, no one usually lives too long. That's *why*. Yet somehow hunger and satiety and the need for fuel all seemed to fail as reasonable riposte to the act of eating. What was once a given had become a point of rumination; what was once so natural and pleasurable began to feel foreign and unnerving. Within the *ka-pung*ing cabinets, somewhere between the oatmeal cookies and the pasta packages, stacked behind the soup cans and towers of tuna fish, hid the concept that food had something negative to do with the shape of my body. In time, this thought worked its way to the front of the shelves and crowded out all other choices of sustenance.

A cranky old man and his much nicer wife ran El Hotel Gatex, the humble two-story establishment facing the southern shores of the Atlantic Ocean where Hollywood on Ice stayed in Mar del Plata. Felicia and I were in habitación #3, directly below the small dining room that

The Bertine family, 1997: Grandma, Mom, Dad, Sarah, Me, Pete

Murray's in all its early-morning splendor

Captain Graceful, age twelve

*Almost passing for greatness, age sixteen,
North Atlantic Regional Competition.
This is the layback photo Scott Hamilton
and Paul Wylie commented on.*

Skating at a Colgate hockey game, 1996

The epitome of strength: the 1997 Colgate women's varsity crew, in the heat of competition. I'm fifth from left. Muscles were not frowned upon here.

*Generic Foghorn
Leghorn on my head,
elephant-ass trousers
on my right.
Holiday on Ice.*

*Home sweet home . . .
the trailer of
Hollywood on Ice*

Posing with Felicia in front of the Flintstones set

Felicia getting ready for Hollywood's Flashdance *number*

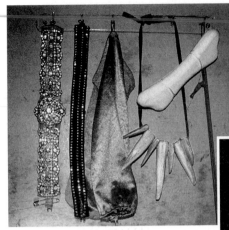

The family jewels of
Hollywood on Ice

Showgirl finale costume,
three weeks into my stint
with Hollywood on Ice.
Clearly, my obesity is
quite offensive.

Moscow's finest pairs skater

On the bike, Tucson Triathlon, 2000

*On my way to an age-group win,
New York City Triathlon, 2001*

*Now coaching, I am able to warp
the minds of the young.
Pictured here, Briana Langley,
Tucson Figure Skating Club,
age seven.*

gave a pleasant view of the brilliant coastline running the length of the city. All the other hotel guests were served free coffee and pastries each morning in the dining room, but the skaters were more like the orphans from *Oliver Twist* who hoped for a smidgen of gruel if lucky. We were allowed one cup of tea and a single slice of toast about half the size of a normal piece of bread. Mmmm. Brown water and a communion wafer! I've known pigeons that survive on bigger rations. *Please, sir, may I have some more?* Nope. The old man went so far as to lock the pastry cabinet when he saw us climb the stairs to the dining room. I never found out whether Lora had made a cheaper, breakfastless deal with the hotel owners or whether she paid them more to make sure we didn't eat.

Other than the weekly sweat runs on the eve of a weigh-in, when the Olgai and others went out for a jog in full sweatsuits on a summer evening, no one on the tour worked out. Only Ruslan and Olga #3 did stretching exercises and push-ups to keep their muscles toned for their gymnastic routine. Some of the cities we visited had gyms, and Felicia and I took aerobics classes every now and then, but I could no longer bring myself to use the strength-building equipment that I had once so proudly maneuvered. Trapped in an environment that equated muscle weight with fatness, I knew that lifting would only worsen my dilemma with the scale, so I stayed away from the weights and quietly cherished the memories of a time when strength was something to be proud of, something reflecting personal greatness.

As an athlete, I first discovered "weight" during the Lake Placid summer between eighth and ninth grades. In the basement of the enormous Olympic Center was a sizable weight room with a bunch of oblong metal muscle-promoting contraptions. The solid structures were intimidating and overwhelming; not having a clue as to which limb went where or pulled what, I found the entire weight-lifting concept a bit scary. I simply did not want to be there in that room of sharp edges and loud clangs. But I knew that lifting weights made one stronger and that stronger skaters were better skaters, so it was worth a try.

Dana was a handsome, easygoing, muscle-bound athlete in his mid-twenties, hired by Lake Placid's skating program to be the strength coach for any skater who wanted to supplement her overall training. Weight lifting was optional but recommended by the skating coaches, and I signed up for three weight sessions a week with Dana.

"Hold this," Dana said, handing me a metal pole nearly twice my height. I took the pole, which I later learned was a straight free-weight bar, and held it up vertically with one end leaning on the floor. Okay! Weight lifting wasn't so bad!

"No," Dana said, laughing, "like this." He reclaimed the bar and held it in front of him horizontally in an underhand grip down across his thighs. "Now watch," he instructed, bending only his elbows and repeatedly curling the bar from his thighs to his chest. He did this with such ease and effort that in his grasp the bar seemed no heavier than a ballpoint pen. "Okay, your turn."

Dana gently lowered the free-weight bar into my copycat stance, and like a cartoon figure I held on to the bar as it sagged my entire body to the floor. Dana, now a bit wiser to the strength of a young stringbean skater, smiled and gave me an identical bar that was about ten pounds lighter — still a little on the heavy side but much more manageable. I tried lifting it again as Dana stood in front of me, ready to catch either the bar or me, whichever fell first. I was able to lift the bar to my chin only one time before my arms wavered in protest.

"Kate," Dana said, pointing to the bar that had originally dragged me to the floor, "by the end of the summer you will be able to do three sets of eight reps with that free-weight bar without my help." I did the math as quickly as my nonmathematical brain could calculate.

"That's twenty-four repetitions!" I exclaimed after a few minutes. I had no reason to doubt Dana, but it seemed a bit of a stretch. Yet he knew about weights and I didn't, and I sure liked the sound of the challenge.

And so as the summer passed, every other day I became better versed in the lingo of weight lifting. The abdominal machine replaced my ignorant nomenclature of "that thing," the hamstring curl was no longer "the bench and leg doohickey," the tricep push, lat pulls, and deltoid cables replaced "all those hangin' wires and stuff."

Dana weighed me in the beginning of the summer on the old scale in the corner of the gym. I hopped on in my little spandex skating dress, Dana wrote down a number, and I hopped off, simple as that, without a care in the world about the number or what anyone else thought of the digits, without the slightest foreshadowing of what was to come ten years down the road. I was not a number back then, I was a healthy, happy, soon-to-be-strong little thirteen-year-old.

At the end of the summer, on my final day in the weight room, I went through all the exercises I had worked on for the past two and a half months. Leg press, hamstring curl, hip flexor, back extensions, abdominal crunches, push-ups, lat pulls, triceps curls, bench press, and finally the free-weight biceps curl with the bar of promise. After gradually adding more repetitions to my sets all summer, now was the big test of achievement.

"Ready?" Dana asked.

"Yup."

The first set went smoothly, the second set was a bit harder, and on the third, I felt the ease slip away with my concentration, wondering how I'd be able to get up to eight reps. My arms began to shake with tremors of exertion, but the bar went up twenty-four times, just as Dana said it would. Celebrating, I bounced around the room and raised my arms in biceps-protruding stances, showing my little hills of muscle to anyone who would look, anyone who didn't need glasses. *Now,* I thought, *I'm strrrrrrrong.* Dana reweighed me and we discovered that I had gained nine pounds of muscle. This seemed very impressive to me, and I told all my skater friends about how strrrrrrrrong I had become, and that each one of those nine pounds was proof of my hard work.

When I returned home, I put on a new skating leotard I had bought in Lake Placid and told my parents I had a wonderful surprise. From upstairs I called to them to sit in the living room. I bounded downstairs in my new black outfit and began leaping about, showing off my body, hurling myself into skateless jumps over the brown carpet and striking poses of grace and power. With every whirl, I announced, "Look at me, I've gained nine pounds of muscle! *Muh*-scle! I am superstrong! Wahooo!" I flexed my arms and legs, patted my flat tummy, which was little-girl smooth, but now showing some signs of indented ridges.

My father applauded and laughed at my silly prancing, showering me with compliments of "You look great, honey" and "Ooh, how strong" and "Look out, Hulk Hogan!"

For a while my mother was quiet and I assumed she was enjoying my goofy parade of pride. She was studying my body, no doubt admiring my healthy, somewhat-less-stick-straight frame. *She must be searching for just the right compliment,* I thought. Then she said,

"*Nine* pounds?"

I stopped dancing. Her tone and facial expression was my hard-core introduction to the reality that some people do not think muscle is a good thing on women. By thirteen, I already knew that my mother liked skinny people more than heavier ones, but my new body weight wasn't *fat,* it was *muscle.* Something one had to earn through hard work and consistency. I had earned this. All summer long I had wanted nothing but muscles and strength, yet in that one resonating moment, I wished for nothing more desperately than a robe.

I know the exact moment I became an athlete, the scene so vivid in my mind that I am sure it happened only moments ago. In September of 1982 Miss Gibson shuffled her third-grade class outside to the kickball field for recess. I didn't think I was very talented at kickball and proved myself right during my first two times at the plate, watching mournfully as the bright red rubber ball rolled right past my outstretched leg. With the honest bluntness only eight-year-olds can get away with, a call came from center field as I approached the plate for the third and final time.

"Move in, mooove in! She can't kick" came the cry from Luis, a skinny little kid who had somehow garnered popularity through snottiness, and I watched curiously as my classmates took three zombielike steps closer to where I stood. With those words, something peculiar came over me, and this time the ball did not roll by. Not only did that ball sail directly over Luis's head, his outstretched arms, his wiggling fingers, and his pathetic little jump to block it, but it seemed to grow wings and fly, fly, fly through the heavens. Luis had to retrieve my home-run ball, as I discovered the remarkable power of athleticism in the time it took him to return — out of breath — from the farthest end of the playground.

In time, I learned that that surge of emotion and physical intuition I had experienced was nothing more than plain old adrenaline set in motion. Only it didn't seem so plain to me, and the addiction was quick and irreversible. I needed adrenaline, and because of kickball, I had a lead as to where to find more. Sports. There seemed so many to try, so many to choose from, and I wanted to play them all and be great, great, great. I was an athlete and there was no turning back, and there was a little bit of kickball in everything that came after that day. The kick of the leg was the same kick that soon launched my body up into double axels, the run of the bases was the burst of speed I would pull out in cross-country meets, and opponents that only I could see gave me the adrenaline that I needed.

As I skated fast around a rink, crossovers gaining speed and carrying my body swiftly from one maneuver to the next, adrenaline let me surpass the graceful talents of Dorothy Hamill, edge out Michelle Kwan for the world title, and nail triple-triple-triple combinations, all in the arena of my mind. The best part about the endorphin rush was letting it dribble over into everything else. After winning the presidency, granting world peace, curing cancer, stopping violence, housing the homeless, feeding the hungry, finding the antidote to eating disorders, chatting it up with Larry King, Bob Costas, and Oprah, and giving inspirational speeches all over the world, I've also told off every boy who has broken my heart from sixth grade on and listened as they've all begged for forgiveness before my last swing of the bat, stride on the track, leap off the ice.

Yet upon Lora's demand that I lose my athletic body, it was as if my kickball field melted away and I could no longer see the little kid, the inviting bases, or the roll of the ball that had set it all in motion.

We'll let you know when you can stop. But after two months of extreme dieting, and still no word from management, what stopped first was my period. My desire to skate soon followed, and the artistry I had worked so hard for turned into listlessness. All that was left of grace was the question of how many calories it burned.

We sat in the trailer, undressed, and waited our turn for the scale, covering our breasts with our arms if there was a chill in the air. Otherwise, we had no need for modesty. We were used to seeing one another naked, hurrying from one scanty costume into another. The bodies of these women seemed so odd, so skinny yet so flabby that when they pulled on their fishnets, their skin jiggled as if their limbs were filled with water. Cellulite does not show up beneath fishnets and spotlights, but it did in the trailer. There were no visible muscles left in these women's legs, perhaps only enough to carry their bodies through the most basic motions: walking, sitting, gliding over the ice, and waving. Peripherally we glanced at one another, each of us silently comparing her body with the woman's next to her. We never looked at the one who stood naked on the cold little metal judgment podium.

From atop the scale we watched Pegi, the kindhearted Mexican seamstress, record our weight in kilograms in the little black book that eventually made its way back to Lora's office. No one ever dismounted the scale without overseeing exactly what number Pegi inscribed. She wrote slowly and neatly, and watched our faces. If she saw our eyes become moist with worry, sometimes she subtracted a quarter kilo. We never asked her to do so, for her job was at stake as well as ours if the numbers in the book didn't match our appearance on the ice. "*Muy flaca, demasiada flaca,*" Pegi would whisper under her breath. So skinny, too skinny. How I wanted to believe her.

When I climbed on the scale the second Sunday of weigh-ins, Pegi looked at the contraption's numbers and flipped back to my first weigh-in. *¿De veras?* She asked me, wondering if she had made a mistake the week before. Was it possible to lose seven pounds in a week? The look on my face answered that it was possible, but not easy. *Relax, Captain Graceful, I've got this one covered. I can do it again next week, and the week after that.* Hurt, anger, loneliness, and frustration proved fantastic motivators.

Coming off the scale, skaters ran to their handbags and pulled out whatever food they had brought with them to the trailer. Fruit, crackers, little cereal boxes, bread, candy, chocolate—they shoved these small, broken pieces of denied sustenance into their mouths, not caring about the twenty-five-dollar fine that accompanied eating inside the dressing room. They ate naked, dressing afterward, carefully wiping their fingers before touching the costumes.

Then we sat half dressed and watched the men enter the trailer for weigh-in. None of them were asked to strip down. They came in fully clothed, hopped on the scale, paused, and hopped off without looking at the numbers that came up. The men were never fined; they had no target weight to keep below. The men did not diet, and their hunger was for ob-

sessions other than food. Five out of the six were skinny men who preferred alcohol and drugs to ample meals. Lenny was the only skater with
chunky legs and a potbelly that protruded beneath his spandex costumes.

Len was the cast's funny guy, the charmer, and he had an "in" with
management. His weight was giggled at, not scolded. *¡Ay Len!
¿Demasiado bistec argentinos, no?* Too many Argentinean steaks, huh,
Len? For the men, Sundays were just another day in the undifferentiating
week that never really ended. For me, Sunday became judgment day, so
different from the Sundays of my past, when skating competitions, road
races, or softball tournaments had celebrated the capabilities of athletic
bodies.

Felicia, my roommate and confidante, was the only one with whom
I discussed my weight as it fell from my body week by week. Although
quiet and shy in the presence of others, and often known to turn beet-red
in the presence of friendly men, Felicia had an unsurpassable confidence
in her solid, muscular body and did not give a "bloody 'ell" what Lora
and the rest of the lot thought about her shape. They could take their
bloomin' scales and bugger off, as far as she was concerned. She was my
hero of body image, and I was proud and jealous of the fact that she ate
whatever and wherever she wanted and didn't care if parts of her body
were formed differently than Lora wanted them to be. Felicia was issued
warnings three or four times but never actually received a reduced paycheck. I couldn't understand how it was so easy for my roommate to just
laugh away the very problems that were beating me up on a daily basis.
Why wasn't she worried about getting fat and what others might think?
How did she escape that pressure? Where did that kind of strength come
from? Every now and then I caught a hint, usually in overhearing phone
conversations. "Yes, yes, I'm eating enough, Mum. I'm fine. Love to you
and Dad."

Sometimes I ate food just for Felicia, when she asked quietly and
gently if I would have a little snack at midnight because my stomach rum-
bles were keeping her awake.

I fed myself no magic foods. The portions of bread, vegetables,
beans, or tuna simply began to get a little smaller at each meal, until my
plate looked as if it had already been eaten from, the leftover scraps of my
dinner-to-be. There were a few things I ate, some substances I put into

my body that dropped my weight more quickly than others, things that came from local pharmacies or on the recommendation of other skaters — things I will not name, schemes I would rather leave untold and unlearned, as I now wish others had done for me. I scrounged for tips on starvation and purgatives that were unfortunately all too easy to find. I did not realize it would take me so much longer to erase them from my memory.

For every pound of weight I lost, my mind began to lose the equivalent in perspective. The years of strength it took to build my body meant nothing anymore, not here anyway, not to the people of Hollywood on Ice. I was to deprive myself until the curves of my thighs became narrow and linear, and my prominent rower's shoulders softened into skeletal boniness. Captain Graceful was about to be sacrificed, her cape would become her shroud, her spirit transformed to memory. I was reverting to the body structure of a little girl, when only long braids and heart-shaped earrings had revealed the gender of my fragile frame.

Hollywood on Ice had originally been a U.S.-based show. Sometime in the eighties, the owner sold it to his Mexican business partner and the tour relocated south of the border, eventually moving on to South America. We never saw the mysterious owner, Ernesto, for he was said to be an elderly man with health problems who lived back in Mexico. The laws and regulations usually required by American businesses were simply nonissues in Hollywood on Ice. Passport detainment, weight-related pay cuts, sexual harassment of employees, no days off or vacation time, paychecks that arrived up to three weeks late (and weren't paychecks at all but wads of wrinkled currency from whatever country we were in) were all part of the Hollywood way. At first the situation was quite laughable, as Felicia and I shook our heads and dismissed all the surrounding absurdity with exclamations of disbelief. *We have to get on the scale in our panties every freaking week? Whatever! Shit, man. This place is nuts.*

Lora kept her distance from the dressing rooms. She did the hiring and judged the fat factor, too. She looked at our bodies and pulled a number from her head, which became the target weight we were required to keep below. There were no scientific ratios based on height, bone density, or body mass index, just a number Lora dreamt up. She was a forty-year-old woman who represented the exact opposite of what she wanted her skaters to look like. We were mere carrot sticks to her Thanksgiving-like girth. She smiled at us in person, but when we weren't looking, she contacted the line captain to complain about our appearance. I got my first compliment from Lora after the first twenty pounds dropped from my already slender frame, my body transforming to gaunt proportions. She sent word that I was to swap finale costumes with Olga #1, as my bare midriff was now more attractive, she decided. Olga was five-four. I was five inches taller. Olga threw the turquoise ensemble at me, and began a rigorous sit-up routine in the trailer that night. Lora refused to have the costume altered to fit me, and the sharp edges of the sequins dug deeply into my skin, chafing areas of a private nature to a rawness unfit for torture.

Things like costume swapping happened all the time and created a rift between some skaters, although the root of the problem was usually a rift within ourselves. What we couldn't take anymore about our own bodies, we took out on others. When I was hungry, which was always, it was hard to be anything but negative and abominable. When a fellow skater grew edgy and irritable and stomped about the trailer, it was all too easy to take things personally and vent our frustrations by asking the malicious little bitch if she would kindly shut the fuck up. Sometimes we said it under our breath, sometimes out loud, sometimes in a foreign language. Yet I didn't resent any of my castmates, just their bodies.

Although I knew deep down that skinniness was not right for any athletic body, strange impulses coursed through my veins when I looked at the über-petite, long-starved women of Hollywood on Ice. When I correctly identified such feelings inside me, I was devastated to discover that I was jealous. One hundred percent jealous. Jealous to the core. Jealous that they were thin and I was "fat." Jealous that thin was loved and muscle was loathed here. I was just plain jealous, envious, covetous, desirous, invidious, and green-eyed monstrous. The feeling sickened me. What was going on here? I had been a promising runner, a collegiate rower, a senior-level skater—and here I was, jealous of the bodies belonging to chain-smoking, pill-popping, self-shrinking women who were the very opposite of all I had ever striven to achieve. But self-confidence requires energy, and I simply had none left. Why bother eating every day? My jealousy was a python: it could take a big swallow of something and then stay full for weeks, slithering around in quiet solitude.

Sundays were horrendous from a mental standpoint, too, as weigh-ins came at 6:00 P.M. and left all day open for obsessing about food and body image until scale time. The idea of eating before standing on a scale horrified me and filled me with guilt, so the only option my thoughts conjured up was to go all day without food. Passing the time by running, sleeping, reading, and snapping at Felicia whenever she offered me food got me through Sundays. Once I had built up the stamina of Sunday starvation, I'd tackle Saturdays, then Fridays, working my way back. After a few months it mattered little that I could not remember what I was starving myself for, as by then the routine of deprivation took on a life of its own. As each day of the week loomed closer to the weigh-in night, my anxiety grew in inverse proportion to my diet.

If Sundays were the days when mental anguish was at its worst, Mondays were set aside for an hour or two of mental rest even as the body experienced the physical consequences of starvation. On Mondays I forgot about the muscle cramps, the shortness of breath, the dizziness, the eyelid twitches, the weird heart palpitations, the strange amounts of hair accumulating in my brush. Tuesday through Sunday I ate one "meal" a day that was not really a meal at all but a puny menu of instant powder-food or other tasty water-based gunk. Monday was the day my mind allowed me to eat freely. Monday was Permission Day, but it was short-lived. *Eat up,* I told myself, *this has to last you all week.* Though my mind and body were caught in a ruthless civil war, both sides fighting for control, Mondays began with what I mistook for a truce.

In Mar del Plata there was a Chinese buffet restaurant on the boardwalk overlooking the Atlantic Ocean. I once stayed there for over an hour on a Monday afternoon, eating alone, until I decided I was done. "Deciding" to be finished with a meal replaced my natural feeling of satiety, for I no longer understood what being full felt like. I was either empty in both the physical and mental senses of the word, or physically ill from the discomfort of food in my stomach. In that Chinese restaurant, I could have eaten all day if my mind had let me and if my body had been able to accommodate such plentiful quantities on a starvation-shrunken stomach.

I recall two other skaters passing by the window of the restaurant, and although certain they could not see inside, I hid myself as best I could behind the laminated wine list, avoiding eye contact with the teary reflection of Captain Graceful who was constantly trying to get my attention. Eating had become a shameful and lonely ordeal. Only in the short time it took to chew the food did I feel a slight relief, a freedom that reminded me of the days when skating was untainted by food and weight. When there was only ice.

Those had been the days when I had simply *needed* to skate for no other reason than to feel the slick surface usher my body around the rink. Somewhere in the physics, aerodynamics, power, and agility of figure skating I had found my niche in the world when I held my arms out, put my head back, and let the breeze of my own speed whisk past my face, through my ears, into my hair, and out over the ice behind me. I loved going fast. I loved spinning faster. I loved flying, weightless, through the air. I loved falling, weighted, to the ice. Spread eagles, Ina Bauers, spirals; the stillness of a held position, traveling over the ice for what seemed like eternity, the breathless feeling created by those postures were strong enough to fleetingly erase the concept of all physical perimeters and boundaries of skating, so that it felt as if the ice went on forever, without walls or borders. Jumping took only a fraction of a second, spinning required a few whole ones, but grace seemed to last the entire light-year of a moment.

As a skater, the only true control I had over my body was to let it go, trusting my limbs as they experimented with grace and gravity. There was a loving, symbiotic relationship between my mind and body back then. I depended on my body to be where I needed it, just as it asked the same of me. To soar, spin, fly, and fall—my mind and body had to learn them all and love this education. Speed, revolution, elation, completion—each built a wall of the house where my passion for skating lived untouched but hidden by the throes of the tour. During the tour, when there was true digested energy in my body, even for a moment, the reality of Hollywood on Ice faded away, staved off by the memories of my love of skating.

✦

Chapter Eleven

The Love of Something

"Love is like a fever," Pam announced to me one day in the trailer, "it comes and goes without the will having any part in the process." Just as I was about to commend her for the most profound statement ever uttered by someone wearing spandex, I realized that our line captain was quoting from the worn-out textbook in her lap. Pam spent her hour between shows studying for the correspondence course in philosophy she was taking through a university back in Ontario. "What do you think?" she asked me, referring to Stendhal's feverish simile. I was weary of those who compared love to symptoms of the flu but was intrigued by the analogy.

"Okay, I'll buy that. What else ya got?" I put down the list of calorie consumption I was working on: short stacks of numbers adding up what I had eaten that day and what I planned to consume later on, if at all. *Coffee, half a banana, water with ⅓ teaspoon lemonade mix . . . 300 calories of this, 125 of that, don't forget about the skim milk in your coffee and the sugar-free jam on your toast, Fatso.* I kept a running tab on my starvation, scribbling numerical lists in the margins of books and on the backs of magazines. Love seemed like a better topic to discuss, something more fulfilling to concentrate my evaporating energy on. I was always up for insights into the elusive emotion anyway, as love eternally duped me. I had tried to give my love to various people plenty of times but seemed to have a talent for choosing those who had no desire to accept it. If timing was everything, then my alarm clock was seemingly close but completely off, mistakenly set for P.M. instead of A.M. Maybe now I could learn something from Stendhal, Aristotle, de Beauvoir, Ortega, and the rest of the experts who cogitated from the pages of Pam's book.

The hour between shows offered just enough time to sit down and relax but not enough time to return to the hotel or venture into the city. Most skaters hung around outside the trailer, smoking or stretching, while a few stayed inside reading beneath their lightbulbs or napping on the bench that ran below our costume rack. Felicia and Jody wrote letters as the Olgai did crunches and Bella stared at herself in the mirror, retouching makeup that did not need it. When she was done, Bella just sat and stared at the wall. At first, I thought my trailer neighbor was forever lost in thought, but later it became obvious she was just rather vacant. I have known slices of dry wheat toast with more personality than Bella, but in the grand scheme of things she seemed like a nice person. Besides, it was better to be a bland slice of bread than the neurotic packet of Sweet'N Low I was becoming. I began to see how Hollywood on Ice could turn people into wall-staring zombies after a while. Sometimes during the break our little visitors, Stefanie and Cathi, would come in with their crayons and ask if we wanted to color with them. Cathi, the nine-year-old daughter of the seamstress, always came to me first. *Katarín, ¿puedes dibujar?* But that day the trailer was quieter than usual, and perhaps more lonely. It was Valentine's Day, and I had been with Hollywood for almost two months.

Dressed in our fishnets, Pam and I sat with our gold lamé opening number costumes drooping in a pile of spandex and rhinestones around our waists and T-shirts with makeup smudges covering the rest of our bodies. For that hour and the short intermissions laced throughout the show, we debated whether the idea of love was the love of something or the love of nothing, whatever that meant, citing examples and metaphors from our own beliefs to give weight to Plato's query as we laced our skates and sprayed our hair.

"You have to love *something,* so therefore love is the love of something."

"Isn't 'nothing' something?"

"Ah."

"Ah, indeed. Can I borrow your eyelash glue?"

Deep thoughts were scarce in the trailer, and it mattered little that we had no idea what we were saying — it just felt wonderful to partake in conversation that had nothing to do with food or skating. As we discussed the philosophy and poetry of love, we observed how odd it was that poets and writers were always metaphorically flinging themselves off cliffs or swimming shark-infested oceans to prove their worthiness and that love might last longer and inflict less bodily harm if the suitors went to Blockbuster, brought home a movie, or struck up a nice conversation in a landlocked coffee shop. If love was the love of something, then spending time together might prove more productive than saying, "Honey, I love you so much I'm gonna go hide out in a big fake horse and start a war. See you later." I suppose the latter provided more literary inspiration than movie rental, but nonetheless, Pam and I debated and exhausted all possibilities.

Hollywood on Ice was not a safe haven for romantic love. The choices boiled down to Pedro with the inverted eyeball or the vampiric alcoholic Russians, most of whom had severe orthodontic issues that made Dracula look about as dangerous as Eddie Munster and were already paired with their appropriate, soulless mates. The Russian men spent their days asleep in the hotel and rose just before the show. Groggy, pale, and sometimes still drunk, they performed with the listlessness of too much experience and too little desire. Afterward, they took off into the night, searching for endless bottles of vodka that they exsanguinated with a disturbing passion. Leosha, one of the sketchiest Russians, was let go from the tour after missing a show because he and his prostitute overslept.

None of the couples in Hollywood on Ice appeared happy except for Alexei and Olga #3, who tied the knot after a couple of months of dating. I found it painful yet amusing that during my time with both Holiday and Hollywood on Ice, nine out of ten times my bed was in direct alignment with the headboard of the cast nymphomaniac on the opposite side of the wall. In Holiday, it was the Romanian pairs team who could not get enough of each other in Switzerland. In France, Ingrid and Alexei put in some late-night undress rehearsals of their own, before

Alexei returned to Hollywood on Ice and married Olga #3 a few weeks down the road. Between the steady couples, the constant swapping of significant others, and the groupies the male skaters brought back from the audience of Hollywood on Ice, there was always an active headboard tapping out its frantic Morse code somewhere in our hotel. My straight-arrow background and mostly prudish existence finally started to come in handy. No matter how much my own personal needs pulsed, just imagining the disease factor was enough to quell all desire for physical contact.

After Pedro and the vampires, the third option for seeking companionship was to venture outside the circus tent and browse among the citizens of the villages we visited. All three alternatives made a strong argument for celibacy, and my fragile sense of self was unable to relate to matters of the heart anyway. Despite being an enthusiastic fan of physical intimacy, neither my body nor my mind was up for exploring the options. The only relationship I had time for was with food, though it rarely returned my calls these days. And there was also Steven.

Steven telephoned from the States every few days to track me down in whatever far-off land Hollywood on Ice had dragged us to. When the phone rang in our room five thousand miles down the Atlantic coast from New York City, Felicia always let me answer. Steven was a college buddy with whom I crossed the platonic boundary now and then, though we always denied any physical activity to our friends, who already believed otherwise. Steven had a girlfriend and I got to be the extremely insecure other woman who, like a jackass, believed that all would work out for us in the long run and we would eventually be together forever. Relationships were not Captain Graceful's field at all. At the first pang of male trouble, she simply grabbed a chair, bought some popcorn, and sat down to laugh her cape off at my pathetic attempts in the love arena. Given my mostly uneventful high school social life and the fact that I was an English major in college, boyfriends were something of a confusing prospect that I tended to fictionalize into a back-of-the-shelf supertrashy romance drama. Steven was no exception.

Both of us kept quiet about the late-night visits to each other's dorm room and off-campus apartments. Our timing for a normal relationship never aligned during the Colgate years, our status never matching up at the right place or time, although our feelings for each other kept blazing lustily onward. The core of the problem was that I was simply way too intense, not in a needy way but just in the only way I knew how to be: passionate and committed right off the bat. Why stick your big toe in the water instead of jumping in headfirst? Oh, right, the shallow end. Always forgot about that. Many, many concussions later, I still hadn't learned a thing.

Whatever it was that I held dear—relationships or skating—I wanted more of it and as often as possible. Men were my triple lutzes: complicated, awkward, difficult, and something I'd probably never land. Still, every time I fell on the ice or head over heels, some inner voice screamed, *Get back on it!* She likely meant the skating jump, not the actual man. My bad. Regardless, I was devoted to skating and sports, and this approach of "give it all ya got and don't hold back" just trickled over into my intimate relationships and irreversibly scared the gadzooks out of anyone who paid me the slightest bit of attention.

"Uh, Kathryn, you wanna go to dinner, uh, sometime?"

"Sure! Tonight will work. And what about tomorrow? The following Thursday? Do you have any plans for Christmas? We should strategize ASAP. It's almost April. Are you hungry right now? Can I bake you some cookies? No? Make you a mixed tape of love songs so that you can correctly decipher my true feelings, perhaps?"

"I'll, uh, call you."

Adding to the dramatic element of our affair was the fact that Steven's current girlfriend was a rather grumpy woman who gave me (and any other female who came within a hundred yards of her man) the evil eye whenever possible. Jealous and lonely, I completely dismissed the likelihood that I was acting downright trampy when Steven came by for middle-of-the-night relations. Alas, the nonsmoking, nondrinking, nonpartying straight arrow had found her downfall! I was trampy! I was trampy! Finally! It's always the quiet ones.

Although I found it inexcusable to cheat on anyone I happened to be dating, I seemed to be just fine with bedding someone else's catch when I was single. But the situation left me with more heartache than happiness, and I never got used to that feeling of denial, secrecy, and being completely ignored when the legitimate girlfriend was anywhere in sight. Nontrampy seemed a better way to go, damn it. Ultimately, my morals caught up with me, but while on tour the loneliness for all things familiar still made my heart leap when the phone rang in El Gatex's habitación #3.

Steven's job with a corporate bank in New York allowed him unrestricted phone privileges, which meant he could safely call me from work without the Girlfriend knowing. Steven called day in and day out because she was cruel and I was kind and he was confused and we were all safely distant from one another. We spoke of what-ifs and homecomings and how things would be different when I returned, how everything would be right and we would be together at last. This much I knew of love at twenty-two: that it was far away and I was second-best, and that long-distance longing and the ache of being runner-up was enough to tear me down and keep me going at the same time. As perspective and rationality were bullied by my desire and loneliness, I listened to Steven's stories of her misdoings, and he listened as I told him of the calf cramps that woke me up at night as my leg muscles ate away at themselves. *Eat,* he said gently, *you have to eat, Kathryn.* I longed for such permission, and his words felt like just that. If only concern were enough to subsist on, then we would have fed each other well. *Break up,* I nourished back, *break up with her, I'll be home soon.* When I went home that summer, Steven finally proposed. But I didn't go to their wedding.

"Love is blind," Pam read from Plato's *Eros.* I insisted that it was also deaf, mute, and probably quadriplegic, a good argument for why it had not yet gotten around to me even though I kept a steady vigil for it. Pam had a boyfriend of seven years back in Canada whom she lived with when not on tour, whereas I pined for seven different boys and had trouble living alone with myself on any continent. If love had not yet found me, there was no way it was going to breeze into the trailer and discover me beneath purple feather boas and gold sea-horse skin. If love was truly blind, there was nothing in Braille lying around to welcome it into this stage of my life. There was, however, an unspoken connection with skating and love, a relationship between the two that quietly grew as I did.

Corny as it may sound coming from a goofball tomboy who once despised slow music and pink spandex, love was always something that bolstered my skating. Through my war of emotions and battles of the heart, my skating was my armor, my blades my weaponry. Whether someone had touched or crushed my heart, I saw his face when I skated, heard his voice through the instrumental music, and felt his eyes on my body as it expressed what I was too timid, shy, angry, or hurt to say in person. On the ice, I was at once so free from my body and so connected to it that every confusing thing about love made sense after the psychotherapy of a good, athletic skate.

Lonesomeness and thoughts of what might have been subsided once my muscles grew warm and adrenaline heated up. Then it was easier to let go of his face and touch, his smell and taste, the sound of his voice and the feel of his skin. It was in the rhapsody of a solid jump and a fast spin that I would finally realize what my body had already known: his loss, his loss, *his* loss. And yet the desire to skate also intensified when love was something new, still fragile, wavering between the possibilities of nothingness and everything. Only the height of a jump came close to the sensation of falling in love: speed, power, elevation, and the euphoric certainty of a perfect landing. And the layback spin — bending the body backward, retracting the spine and exposing the heart — is the position contrary to all protective instincts, the inverse of fetal and the excess of courage, the body itself a lingering question mark at the mercy of the relationship between strength and revolution.

Love, grace, and ice. This was my confidence — to move my body just beyond the perimeters it felt on land, to stretch out where it was impossible to reach without balance and velocity holding me steady. Toe picks were also a great help, as kicking the shit out of a piece of ice could always be counted on to release whatever remnants of grace and love got stuck in the works.

"Eudaemonia," Pam exclaimed, flipping through the pages in her book. "Ever heard that before? This Abraham Maslow guy says it means living at peace with one's true self, that happiness shouldn't be a goal, but a 'right here, right now' kind of thing."

Just then, Cathi appeared in the trailer doorway to hand me a drawing she had made and to help me with my Flintstones bikini. With intermission nearly over, Cathi never failed to emerge just as I needed help buckling the back of a suede bra top. I tied the purple-and-black skirt around my waist as her little fingers hooked the three tiny clasps in back of the halter. We then went through the ritual that kept her coming back to help me show after show. As soon as the costume was in place, I put on the saber-tooth necklace with the clasp in the front and the faux claws all cockeyed along my protruding clavicle.

"¿Listo?" I'd ask Cathi.

"¡Ay, no!" she responded each time, adjusting my necklace, fixing the claws and re-routing the clasp. "Aquí . . ."

I told her over and over that I didn't know what I'd do without her help—"muchísimas gracias, cariña"—while I taped her drawings to my mirror. If there was anything I loved about Hollywood on Ice, this was it, the small glimpse of unselfish help and a brush of human touch so innocent that for a fleeting moment my body did not feel so awful and ugly. There is love in touch, even in the faintest hint of contact, and there was something eudaemonic in the notion that a little kid thought me worthy of drawing pictures for and of. I dismissed that all her portraits of me were stick figures.

Pam, still contemplating love according to others, had just turned to the concept of "know thyself" when the theme song to the second half of the show rang forth its Yabbadabbadoooooo. We began shuffling out of the trailer, saber-tooth jewelry clanking on collarbones, dinosaur paraphernalia pinned to our ponytails, suede skirts swishing, as Pam put everything having to do with love back into the splintered drawer from which it came.

❧

Chapter Twelve

A World of Ice and Water

Love was nothing like the fever I came down with a few months into the tour. I fell ill partly because of a cold going around but mostly because my immune system was unable to perform its duty on my measly energy supply. The tour had set up shop in Bahía Blanca, a small city south of Buenos Aires tucked into eastern Argentina's coastline. Feeling weaker and dizzier than usual after the first show of the night, I collapsed into my folding chair, unlaced my skates, and crawled beneath the feather boas to rest for a while. Sweats and chills relayed through my body, and when it was obvious that skating was not physically possible that night, Pam sent me back to the hotel in a taxi. My whopping weekly salary of three hundred smackers was docked accordingly—$25 per missed show—but that was of little concern to my ailing body and delirious mind. I slept for two days straight, waking only once so a house-calling doctor could look at me, surmise that I had the flu, and tell me to get some rest.

When Dr. Sherlock Holmes left, I slept even more, fevered thoughts running through my head. On the one hand, being sick was horrendous—I was unable to eat anything, my exhaustion was overwhelming, and my body aches were excruciating. Between bouts of delirium, lying in a foreign hotel room with the flu gave me plenty of time to think "poor me" thoughts. *Poor me, I don't have a solo. Poor me, this skating show sucks, what the hell am I doing here? Poor me, I think I'll starve myself be-*

cause some really stupid lady thinks I'm fat. Poor me, I think I killed Captain Graceful. I miss her. Poor me, why did the Ice Capades have to shut down? On the other hand, an illogical feeling of happiness gave me misplaced comfort: my weight had been steadily dropping every week, but the illness took off ten more pounds in three days. When I arrived back at the trailer, even the tightest costumes felt loose around my back and hips. The windows of fishnet stocking were narrower than usual when pulled across my thighs. My muscles had shrunk even more, and caught up in this web of disordered thinking, I was pleased at their retraction. Hey, all right! Less is more! Thanks, flu. Good job.

Of course, my health continued to deteriorate. Colds and lethargy came so easily, and each day brought new muscle cramps and strange spasms. My eyelids spastically pulsated like wind-up toys while other small earthquakes shook through my system, and I paid no attention to the fact that it was all due to my self-created protein deficiency.

Sitting before my mirror and pulling on the leotard for the opening number while dabbing makeup over my pale, fluey face, I studied the picture of my college rowing team taped to the corner of the glass. Nine altogether: eight rowers, one coxswain. Five of us were the seniors who remained from a group that had started out forty strong our freshman year, the less dedicated dropping off one by one along the way. How strong we had been, how powerful our bodies and our friendships had grown. Tara and Lisa in the bow pair, Heather in six seat and me right behind in five, our beloved underclassmen Valley, Martha, Megan, and Beth filling in the rest of the order while Danielle shouted the commands that had steered us to victory in nearly every race that season. Even the photo itself, with its steely gray winter background and the intense shock of yellow boat cruising through the foreground, looked strong and indestructible. My arms were the slightest of the bunch and I was not the tallest, but I could pull that shell wherever it needed to go. My legs, built up from years of skating and running, were my propulsion. They were not the same legs or the same body that now sat before this photo. Everything I knew of athleticism was gone; my body was someone else's entirely. Rowing, figure skating, college . . . . it all seemed so long ago, as if it had happened to a different person.

*   *   *

I arrived at Colgate University as a freshman with a chip on my shoulder and a transfer application to Williams College packed in the top of my suitcase. My father and grandfather were Williams alumni, but my legacy was stopped at the wait list, which I'm apparently still on. Never did get a final letter. I wanted what I could not have, and Williams seemed like something my shortsightedness couldn't live without.

Not long after my Ice Capades audition, the college selection process had begun. Since Williams was out, I had to choose someplace fast. Colgate recruited me to run cross-country, and I had visited the campus the previous summer when it was quiet and empty of students. *Perfect,* I thought. *It's got a rink and no people. I could do well here.*

Colgate had a reputation as an elite educational institution that was typecast in the eighties as a "work hard, party hard" school. The first part I could handle; it was the second half that scared the bejeezus out of me.

"*You're* going to Colgate?!" my fellow Bronxville classmates exclaimed upon hearing my decision.

Needless to say, I had no evidence that college was going to be any different from high school. Just a bunch of older people saying, "College is going to be the best four years of your life." I wanted nothing more than to put my fingers in my ears and la-la-la away their postgrad wisdom. Had I known they were right, I might have been a little more accepting of my first days at Colgate, which I eventually came to love with the greatest passion one can have for an intangible experience. Only after I matriculated did I find out that Colgate was the exact opposite of my high school: it was a place where students respected individuality and only the judgmental kids were inevitably ostracized.

My initial plan for university life was to keep to the same athletic schedule that had worked for me in high school, as far as running and skating were concerned. Why fix what wasn't broken? *I'll skate in the morning, go to class, run in the afternoon, go back to the rink, and then study. What's so tough about college?* I hadn't even arrived on campus yet, but apparently Captain Ignoramus was already feeling very well settled. I did not allow for the element of change, which turned around and bit me in the ass when I tried to put it on a restrictive leash.

My relationship with running was turbulent, as I had held a sort of love/hate passion for the sport since I first began to compete in junior high school. I loved the cross-country season with its outdoor races and off-road courses. I despised track, especially during the indoor months, with its monotonous circle of boredom. My running evolved slowly, creeping into the spaces around the time I spent in the rink, my passion for athleticism quietly developing without my conscious knowledge. What drew me to running was the simplicity of it all, that all I had to do was put on a pair of sneakers and go forward. There was no complex rotation of the body, no elaborate equipment or costumes, my feet rarely got cold, my body always grew warm, and falling was not a common side effect. So I kept on running.

Toward the end of high school, a few recruitments began to trickle in. Colgate, Bucknell, Boston College, and a smattering of other schools in the Northeast and Midwest gave a nod to my career standings. Princeton and Brown expressed interest in my running and then took it back after seeing my standardized test scores. Math did me in every time. I was very talented at addition and subtraction, even with double digits, but it was all downhill after that. Did anyone honestly care how fast one train was going and when it would pass by another one? As far as I was concerned, that was more about geography, anyway. If the question had been based on whether it was possible to outrun Train A or Train B, then perhaps I would have put forth a little more effort. My mind always wondered where the trains were headed, who was on board, why they were there, and what they served in the dining car. Actually, there was one area of mathematics that I understood: geometric proofs — that whole deal where the object was to figure out that if A equals B and C, but not B and D, then what the heck was up with D? *If Anne is friends with Betty and Chuck, but not Betty and Donald . . .* Yeah, I was good at that because the examples in the book always gave little bitty stories or turned the letters into people, and suddenly math became very clear, and I developed feelings for Donald and wanted to help the poor, unpopular, misunderstood consonant find its niche in the world. Now *that* was practical math.

Good grades and not-so-bad essays got me into a few kind schools that were able to look beyond my mathematical retardation, and Colgate track and cross-country wanted me; and being wanted felt beautiful, so I went to run for the Red Raiders and left the Ivies to ponder their theoretic Amtrak schedules. But the first month at Colgate immediately threw me for a loop, as I got my butt kicked off the varsity cross-country team for missing a practice that I thought was cleared with the coach. She thought otherwise, put big red X's through BERTINE on the bulletin board, cleared out my locker, and left me a note, *Turn in your uniform tomorrow.* Welcome to the world of Division I athletics. Maybe if the conference had been called Addition I, I would have had a better general understanding. Hurt and angry that I would not be able to run for Colgate, I let my adrenaline autopilot take over and started searching for another athletic outlet.

Skating alone was not enough. Even if I skated twenty-three hours a day, I still needed two sports to keep me balanced. That was how it always had been, another sport helping to strengthen my muscles for skating and provide a little perspective. No rink-bubble existence for me, nooo thank you. I'd seen too much of that suffocating, end-all-be-all complex that lures athletes straight down Burnout Alley.

Yet the fall sports season had been under way for three weeks, and trying to walk on to a Division I sports team was not going to be an easy task. I headed back up the hill to my dorm room, wearing my unsweaty running clothes, cursing the cross-country program, and wondering in which drawer I had stashed the Williams transfer application. My roommate, Danielle, lay on the bottom bunk, looking at flash cards.

"What are you studying for?" I asked.

"Rowing," she said.

The coach of the crew team had recruited Danielle, all of five feet and ninety pounds, to be a coxswain for the women's squad as she walked across campus earlier that morning. Danielle was going over a list of coxswain jargon: easy on port, hard on starboard, weigh enough, feather on two, power ten . . . She saw that I was upset from the cross-country debacle and offered, "Why don't you try rowing?"

I remembered all those mornings my father chauffeured me to the rink and then drove himself to the boathouse to put in his own workout. In all those years, I never saw him practice, I never saw him race. I knew only the shape of his boat on top of the car in the dark mornings as it sailed along with us to Murray's rink and then floated out of the parking lot en route to the docks at the New York Athletic Club.

"You have a rower's build," my dad used to tell me. "Strong legs, limber back. You should try it sometime." Those words came back to me in the dorm room, mixing with Danielle's suggestion. I walked back down the hill to Huntington Gym to seek out the coach of the crew team.

"We've already started the season," said Sean, the novice women's coach.

"I learn very quickly," I lied. He took me over to an ergometer and sat me down on the spiffy-looking rowing machine. I knew this contraption well; my father had one in our basement. I used to stand on the sliding seat on one leg, hold my other leg out behind me, and practice my spirals for skating.

"Sit down," Sean said. I kept the spiral information to myself and put my rear end on the seat. He gave me some brief instructions about pushing off with the legs, swinging the upper body slightly backward, and finally bringing the arms into the body. "Pull for twenty minutes." I did, and when Sean came back he looked at the numbers that ticked by on the mini–computer screen. "Come to the boathouse tomorrow morning, five forty-five."

In addition to watching my father's boat float away from Murray's parking lot every morning, I was not a complete stranger to the watery sport. I learned to row many years before I set foot in the Colgate boathouse, at my family's lakeside cabin in the Adirondack Mountains (if you were from Bronxville, you either had a beach house, a ski condo, or a camp in the woods somewhere. It's all part of the package deal of being born there, along with the family golden retriever and the SUV you'll get for your sixteenth birthday). There were two ways to get to camp, either by walking the quarter-mile trail through the woods that circumnavigated the edge of the lake or by rowing. Option two necessitated taking an old tin contraption of rickety charm that we filled with our luggage and pets and rowed squeakily from one side of the lake to the other.

The old aluminum tub of a rowboat, with its hee-hawing oarlocks and rusty bolts held in place by nothing more than rugged tradition, was distorted and misshapen and looked as though Paul Bunyan had used it in a heated game of kick the can. After dinner, my father trolled a fly line from the stern while I rowed a semistraight course down the lake.

"Fish bite best at dusk and dawn," he promised, though the fish in our lake apparently adhered to some other time zone. I pulled the oars as my father cast an arch of fishing line across the Adirondack twilight. *Ten o'clock, two o'clock, ten o'clock, two o'clock . . . release.* I watched as the rings of impact circled out from the unseen landing of the fly, and if no fish struck instantaneously, I started rowing to a new location.

"Be patient," my father whispered. But I wanted to row, not wait. I wanted to race the fish, not catch them. Nor to eventually skate dressed up as one.

Pete and I held races to see who could make it to the dock first as one of us rowed across the water while the other ran around it on the lake trail. The short distances were so even in length that it made our competitions close and exciting, for a slippery rock or a rough headwind varied the factor of the game so that it never had the same outcome. Gender was of little importance in calculating the winner, as my brother's strength and my quickness created an equal playing field. The boat also came in handy by providing an escape route from his violent bipolar mood shifts. *Here comes the big scary monster Pete! Quick, Captain Graceful, to the center of the lake!*

My competitiveness with Peter was easy to channel into later races. When other crews did their best to pass Colgate's varsity women, I saw not the bow ball of Syracuse or the approach of William Smith's green-and-white jail-striped blades, but the stride of my brother running through the woods out of the corner of my eye, over the outlet bridge, around the edge of the lake where the roots of the enormous pine tree bulged from the soil like hurdles in our made-up steeplechase. Little sisters who can beat their older brothers know that every other source of competition pales in comparison.

Rediscovering rowing at Colgate was like landing my first axel, like passing a runner on the steepest of hills, like coming home to my body in its most comfortable state, where everything just felt right, good, and strong. Trailers, scales, Olgai, and anorexia were an inconceivable prophecy, and standing inside that university boathouse, I would have laughed in the face of anyone who attempted to unveil such future truths. In all its athletic power, rowing was an embodiment of grace so different from my world of skating that each sport filled the void left by the other. All the rivers, lakes, and ponds I drove past and subconsciously assessed for wintertime skating potential also became possible summer race venues after rowing had worked itself into my thoughts, as if each sport just naturally melted or froze into the other. The independence of skating craved the gregariousness of crew life. The commanding, monotonous repetition of strokes coveted the fact that later in the day the very same limbs would be liberated in lithe, graceful movements on the ice. On the lake there was silence in the air and the music of waves beneath our boat, while in the rink there was music overhead and the silence of ice beneath my blades. Between a boatful of teammates and a rink I shared with no one else, Colgate allowed me to live in a world of ice and water where very few athletes have been.

Rowing led me to understand that all sports are truly interconnected at their core, not only in spirit but also in physical power. Skating, rowing, and running all shared the common bond of movement but dispensed their momentum in separate ways. And then there are the moments before all athletic frenzy begins. At our sprint regattas, as our boat aligned at the start of the race, the pent-up adrenaline was so intense that the energy itself could have visibly combusted by the end of the starter's countdown. *"Five, four, three, two, one . . . Are you ready? Row!"* There is a slight pause after "one" that lasts just long enough for the mental opponents of doubt and reaffirmation to go head to head for nine rounds at warp speed.

If there is an athletic equivalent of having your life flash before your eyes, it happens there, defining an athlete's state of composure to the hundredth of a second, giving some a chance to focus and others an opportunity to crumble. Silence is a ruthless opponent.

Skating has its own pause, which lingers in the air of an arena before it erupts with music. Once the toe picks have settled into the starting stance, the arms are wrapped gracefully into position, the head in its pose of drama and balance, there is a moment so thick with silence that only the most seasoned skater can feel at ease. I reveled in this instant that so many feared, when all eyes were on me, feeding into the power and energy of the moment. In this silence, only I could hear the current of adrenaline that rushed through me, and could see the immediate future—for this is the pause when an athlete decides what will happen, *before* the game begins.

Beneath the Hollywood on Ice tent, Grígor, one of the favorites among the Olgai, with his come-hither stare, bad-boy reputation, and rather direct manner of flirtation—*"We have sex now, yes?"*—would "row" by me on a daily basis. Grígor liked the photograph of my teammates taped to my mirror and would come by often and try to pick out which one was me. I'm not sure why this posed an ongoing challenge for him, as the photo held up its end of the bargain and kept me in the same place every day. *You? Yes, Grígor, still me.* The lanky blond Russian, with his Dorothy Hamill haircut, pale manila skin, and longitudinal abundance of nose, ran his hand over the boat and the bodies of my teammates. It was the same hand that left bruises on his girlfriend, Olga #2.

"Grígor show them real rowing," he claimed, gripping some imaginary oars in the trailer and launching his body into a rhythm of chest and pelvic thrusts, repeating, "Stroke, stroke . . . ," until he crossed some finish line that I was grateful not to see. This never failed to garner a few laughs from the others in the trailer, especially the three out of four Olgai beneath his spell, but what I found most amusing about the situation was that Grígor was holding his make-believe oars the wrong way. Underhand. Had he actually tried this while in a boat at race speed, the oar, upon contact with the water, would have flown out of his grip, caught him in the stomach, and literally launched him out of the boat, prematurely ejecting him before the real finish line. In rowing, this blunder is called catching a crab, I explained to the oar-happy Russian. "No, no, no," Grígor insisted, "we use condom."

When the show was in progress and there was no talking allowed backstage, Grígor rowed mutedly by with his most seductive stare. Dressed in his white spandex and rhinestone unitard, he wove his one-man boat between Little Mermaids, Michael Jacksons, and Barney Rubbles, thrusting away into the South American night.

When Grígor was out for a row, I could always count on Coach Rosario swinging by the trailer to give me a pep talk and instill a little athletic pride in my day.

"¡*Gordita!*" the wiry stagehand would address me. "¡*Comes de-*

masiado!" Fatso, you eat too much. Even with an eating disorder and a shriveled sense of self-esteem, I thoroughly believe I could have landed one decent right hook on this trollish man, and I still repent that I never gave it a try. Having found some sort of soul comfort in the consumption of grapes, I brought small clusters to the trailer and ate "dinner" between shows, sitting on the ramp outside. I could be found there at about nine o'clock every night with my pitiful little handful of globular sustenance. Rosario caught on to this habit and would surface from the conglomeration of props and costumes to call me a fatso and tell me I ate too much, then disappear into the scenery once again, like some sort of fruit-sensing boogeyman. *Ka-pung!*

At first I thought Rosario was being sarcastic. The argument that maybe he liked me but just didn't know how to express it might have worked if we were both seven. Yet as time pressed on, I realized that the mean little man was really quite serious and rather despicable. Katarina Gordita, Hollywood on Ice's fat figure skater, overdosing on a handful of raisiny fruitlets. It seemed less comical at the time. I was already uncomfortable enough eating in public and now grapes were banished from my diminishing list of viands. How I wished Grígor could have rowed by right then, impaling Coach Rosario on his imaginary bow ball and skewering him off into the sunset forever.

With a spot on Colgate's rowing team, all that was left to figure out was my skating schedule. With the goal of taking my senior free-skating test, the highest level in skating, at the end of the year, I needed a coach to help me train. And of course there was the Ice Capades contract waiting for me that was the driving force of all my skating motivation. Thirty minutes away from Colgate, the Clinton Figure Skating Club stood on the outskirts of Clinton, New York. I made the trip at least three times a week in the evenings after crew practice, working with a wonderful coach named Jason.

In my car I played my short and long programs over and over, skating along in my mind through the frozen farmlands of central New York. Sometimes the commute was tedious and the journey was frigid, as my 1989 Wrangler was like Murray's on wheels, letting in more than a comfortable amount of snow and rain through cracks in the soft top. The heater usually worked, but only on my feet, and was scalding if it functioned at all. The trip took exactly thirty-two minutes, for if I attempted anything over sixty-five miles per hour, the Jeep's two rear Velcroenforced windows flew off in protest, no matter how much duct tape I used. With freezing hands, sweating toes, and snowy hair, I arrived at the Clinton Figure Skating Club half warmed up and half numb (Captain Not-So-Graceful) until the temperature of the rink and the movement of my body eventually brought everything into balance.

The rink in Clinton was nearly eighty years old. The concrete structure was not much to look at from the outside, but the rink itself was beautiful in its old-school charm. The CFSC surrounded me with a family of skaters not unlike the community I had known at Murray's: warm people, good coaching, and an atmosphere of kids doing what they loved to do. But three days a week? There was no way six hours of ice time was going to satiate my skating addiction. I needed more, not because I felt the pressure to sustain fitness and skill levels but because I was head over heels in love with skating.

When Starr Rink, Colgate's campus arena, opened for the season in October, I set up a meeting with the assistant athletic director to ask for ice time. This seemed more polite than breaking down his door and panting with glazed, unblinking eyes, *must have ice . . . must have ice now.* Although a major hockey school, Colgate did not have a figure skating program, and it never occurred to me that I might not even be *allowed* to use the ice. The men's hockey team took precedence over all other rink sports, but I figured that surely there would be some free time when I could fit in to the schedule. Varsity hockey couldn't possibly practice more than a few hours a day, with a few games per weekend. I felt confident about ice time until the assistant AD began to ramble off a list of other scheduled practices. I listened in fear, as the days seemed completely booked with ice-related activities: women's club hockey, phys ed classes, youth hockey programs, high school team practices, intramural tournaments, club games, broomball, weekend public sessions. Hearing my assurances that I'd take any time I could get, whether it was midnight or beyond, the patient man took me seriously enough to look at the schedule again as I rambled on about my contract with the Ice Capades.

There was a slot of time between 1:45 P.M. and 3:00 P.M., just before the varsity men got on the ice. He sent me over to the Zamboni pit to ask the drivers if they would resurface the ice after I skated (to cover my tracks of toe pick divots and deep-edge ruts so that the hockey players would not trip in my battlefield of edges); if they agreed, the ice was mine.

The Zamboni guys and I found some common ground. They would clean the ice as long as I kept the rink's radio station tuned to their favorite: Big Frog Country 104.3 FM. Could I play my skating programs during the commercials? Yes. Okay, then. Deal.

Thinking that the price for such ice time would be astronomical, I braced myself. The AD laughed. The rink was there for the students; the price was included in everyone's lofty tuition.

"But," he added, "maybe you could give us a performance or two in return for the ice time." He may have been kidding, or perhaps just being polite, but as soon as he mentioned the possibility of performing, I was looking through the men's hockey schedule to find an exhibition date. The exhibition was to be a one-time thing, but it turned out to be a well-received enterprise and for the next four years I skated five times a season between the second and third periods of the ECAC Division I hockey games at Colgate University.

Starr Rink was not a luxurious piece of architecture, to say the least, but it was a palace compared with Murray's aviary. Fully enclosed and birdless, Colgate's rink sits on the south wing of Reid Athletic Center and its bubbled dome is the first recognizable feature upon arriving at campus from the southern part of New York State. Starr Rink has enough seats to accommodate Colgate's students and at least a third of the townspeople of Hamilton's population of 3,800, with bleachers surrounding three sides, a lofted press box, and locker rooms embedded in the western wall.

The rink had a grayish feel to it: cold but not unwelcoming. A small rainbow of colors dangled down from the ceiling, as the banners of the Red Raiders' ECAC opponents hung from the eaves above the bleachers. The royal blue of Yale, the fierce orange of Princeton, the bold green of Dartmouth, the obvious hue of Brown, the lemon-lime combinations of UVM and Clarkson, the reds of Cornell and RPI, dropped vertically from the rafters, while maroon Colgate in its horizontal contrast hovered with pride above the student section.

Inside the tent of Hollywood on Ice, cheap red-and-yellow triangle flags like those of used-car lots angled down from the high point of the insta-rink to the spectator entrances. There was no breeze to give life to the pointy banners, and the triangles hung in unmoving lines, like rows of sharp teeth hovering over our heads. The seats in Hollywood's audience were royal blue, the underbelly of the big top was painted with white stars, and the frame around the stage was decked out with shiny portraits of Fred, Wilma, Barney, Betty, and Dino. Bright colors everywhere promoted the vibe of an energetic show that I could see only as dismal black, while in the gray drabness of Starr Rink I was nearly blinded by the vibrancy of a building that allowed me to do what I loved.

There was no locker room for figure skaters in Colgate's Reid Athletic Center. I carted my clunky red skating bag with two pairs of leaden skates on my shoulder across campus every day. Winters in Hamilton are unforgiving, and my years of walking through Colgate in blizzards involved falling on hidden ice patches many, many times and spilling my skates down the steps behind my dorm. Despite its exterior decrepitude, the old Kendrick-Eaton-Dodge Hall felt like a palace to me. It was the most anti-museum structure I had ever seen, and I was calling it home by the end of my first week.

Eventually one of the maintenance men at Starr Rink found an old trio of broken lockers and set them up for me in the boiler room between the furnace and the floor-washing buckets. I was the orphan of Division I athletics, the individual achiever among a family of well-funded teams. Thankful that I had any place at all to keep my own equipment, I was in no position to question the location of my lockers. They had no locks and only a slam would secure the tinny door. Prying one open sent the whole structure into spasms of vibration, the trilogy of lockers laughing like metal hyenas. In ratty sweats and with bandaged limbs, the varsity hockey players loafed down the hall to their clean, carpeted locker room while, dressed in spandex tights and skating dresses, I turned left into the dingy boiler room after hunting down the elusive custodian with the halo-size key ring to open the door.

Near the door of the men's locker room a small set of stairs led up to the bleachers. I claimed this as my skate-lacing zone, as it was the easiest point of access to the ice from my boiler room locker. It also provided a nice opportunity to talk to guys. Big sweaty athletic ones! But more than trying to flirt, which I was terrible at anyway, I just liked being around the hockey players because they, like me, were skaters, and that just felt comfortable. The guys on the team tolerated my presence, a few of them became good friends, a few of them remained indifferent to a figure skater, but most accepted my desire to skate. I was there every day, as they were. Sometimes a few of them got on the ice early and we'd share the rink, my peripheral vision sharpening with an acute sense of puck detection as I flying-cameled over rebounded shots and double-lutzed between incomplete passes. Every now and then as the guys passed through the rink, a hockey player paused for a few seconds to watch me skate. Or, as they later clarified, "to watch my skirt fly up." Oblivious to the latter reasoning, the momentary attention helped remind me of my love of audience, as the small, empty rink grew into a packed arena of imaginary thousands.

For at least an hour and a half every day Starr Rink was all mine. Although grateful for the time I was allotted for practice, I wanted more. *Get back on it!* Showing up on the mornings when I had no classes and in the evenings when the local Pee Wee hockey programs finished early, I took the ice until the Zamboni engine rumbled in its pit and the corner doors of the rink swung open to let the mechanical beast out for a run. Joining Colgate's skating class for phys ed credit gave me a few extra hours each week, and I enjoyed giving pointers, helping my classmates learn to skate.

Down the hall, in the lavish physical therapy room, kind therapists and student trainers crossed the varsity lines by sympathetically giving me Band-Aids for blisters and ice bags for triple salchows. In all my previous years of amateur skating, there had been no such things as physical therapists and free medical swag. I carried moleskin, blister ointment, and instant ice packs in my skate bag, administered them myself, and winced through the discomfort of everything from boo-boos to bursitis. The small offerings from Colgate's sports med guys — Baggies filled with melting ice cubes, little plastic bandages, and the most therapeutic of questions—*How was practice, Kate?*—was all it took to make me believe that these people were actually great deistic healers posing as humans in their spiffy collared maroon-and-white shirts.

Giving performances during the hockey games, I became somewhat recognizable in the small town of Hamilton. People at Colgate knew about my contract with the Ice Capades and offered support and encouragement, always asking how my training was going, and would I be nervous about performing in front of so many people? Not a week went by when someone—student, professor, local townsperson—did not inquire about my skating. Every comment solidified my dream and made the Ice Capades seem even greater than I had ever imagined. No longer was I the only one who wanted me to skate professionally. I was *the* skater, the one who was going places, the one who had a plan, a dream, a passion. Without the Ice Capades, I might have just been *a* skater, some kid without goals, an alter ego without a cape.

"There seems to be a girl in a funky bathing suit circling the ice, and we're not sure why," came the voice of Colgate's hockey announcer over the radio. When I stepped on the ice after the Zamboni finished its course following the second period of the Colgate-Harvard hockey game on November 20, 1993, no one was sure just what they were witnessing. This was supposed to be a hockey game, and all of a sudden a woman wearing a short spandex dress was doing waltz jumps, stretching her quads, taking off her warm-up sweater, and laying it over the boards near the penalty box. There was laughter and shushing and a new energy circulating through Starr Rink's full-house crowd. Colgate was down, 5–2, going into the third period, and those of little faith were starting to trickle out of the building. Yet the presence of a scantily clad person wearing figure skates kept some from leaving quite so soon.

Joe Caprio, the voice of Colgate hockey, bellowed into his PA system, explaining the exhibition about to take place, mentioning something about the Ice Capades and a student who was headed there. In my mind I imagined Dick Button somewhere in the audience, commenting on my performance, tearing me apart for my triple-less repertoire of jumps but paying homage to the Captain. *Well, ladies and gentlemen, she's got about one-eighth the talent of Michelle Kwan, but, boy, does she look like she's having a good time out there. That's a wonderful layback position, but Maria Butyrskaya and Tara Lipinski are still to skate, so Kathryn will inevitably have her ass handed to her. Over to you, Peggy.* It didn't matter that I wasn't Michelle Kwan or Dorothy Hamill, nor would I ever skate with a tour of Olympic champions. I was happy just being Skatie from Murray's, slowly morphing into Kate the Skate from Colgate.

The crowd gave a very welcoming round of applause for someone who was delaying their sacred hockey game, and I took my starting position at center ice and performed a routine to Celine Dion's very sappy yet graceful "Power of Love" (not to be confused with the Huey Lewis song of the same title). I remember nothing of my performance that night except that I landed all my jumps, each spin was precise, and the applause ripped though me like lightning. I wanted more of everything. The crowd, expecting hockey and getting sequins, actually responded well to the exhibition and when the players skated out for the third period I went into the stands and watched the rest of the game. Within a few minutes Colgate began to rebound from its deficit, scoring a third goal, then a fourth, and in the final seconds a fifth to tie it up. Overtime came, and Colgate found itself ready to beat the nationally ranked Harvard University. The crowd erupted when we sank the puck first, and on the way out of the game, people kidded me that my skating performance had brought good luck that night. Aw, shucks. I had nothing to do with it. All I did was put more holes in the ice, how lucky could that have been? In fact, from that performance on, I had to cover my divots with slushy snow from the Zamboni bucket while the hockey players circled the ice warming up.

That first skate so invigorated me that I practiced harder for Colgate exhibitions than I did for regional competitions and collegiate championships. Constantly looking for music that would be hockey-crowd-appreciated, I cut numerous programs on my old stereo, playing songs again and again until I drove my hallmates nuts and ended up with a perfectly spliced, shorter rendition of the original piece. From James Brown's "I Feel Good" to Jerry Lee Lewis's "Great Balls of Fire" to Mitch Ryder's "Devil with a Blue Dress," I dressed the parts and skated the emotions, and the people of Starr Rink responded. The ladies who ran the concession stand told me that the hot dog sales in the lobby slowed down whenever I skated, and I took it as a great compliment that someone would choose to watch me skate instead of buying a corn dog.

I had one rule when I skated for Colgate. There would be no falls during my shows, period. It wasn't uncommon for me to fall during a competition — skaters always do — but I never fell during a show. There was something about those Starr Rink performances that made me fall in love with my sport all over again, with twice the earlier passion, something that instilled a sense of pride in my body that I never thought could be destroyed. Starr Rink was like my second Murray's, and Colgate my first true sense of home. Of course, most of my male college buddies amicably hoped I'd wipe out in the middle of my routine because, like, dude, it's funny to see chicks bite it, especially, like, when they're all dressed up and stuff.

There was a movie in the late seventies, a cult favorite of the figure skating world called *Ice Castles*. The star of the fiction-based movie is a very good teenage skater who has a freak accident on her quest for Olympic greatness. The actress launches herself into a double axel while skating on a wall-less outdoor rink. She misses the landing and falls headlong into an entourage of patio furniture at the far end of the ice and knocks herself blind on the leg of the wrought-iron dinner table. While most viewers let go a gasp of frightened sympathy, I simply couldn't empathize. I'd rewind the movie over and over, wondering how the heck she managed to slide herself across the ice and entwine herself in a lawn chair — and on top of all that, go blind — without messing up her ponytail. Now that deserves a medal.

My first of countless spills in competition happened at the age of thirteen, at the annual Low Tor Competition in Nyack, New York, a two-sheet rink just west of the Hudson River that has since been turned into an iceless array of condominiums. The competition was sanctioned by the ISIA (Ice Skating Institute of America, now renamed the more inclusive International Skating Institute), and I skated in level Freestyle Five, in which one of the required moves was a camel spin. Normally this maneuver posed little threat, which made the fall that much more of a shock. The camel was just one of those spins that felt like second nature, so I was not quite prepared for nature to backfire so suddenly. As soon as my right leg reached back to form a ninetyish-degree angle with the left, my body pitched forward onto the toe pick and down I went like a fly beneath gravity's swatter. Kids sometimes get stitches in their chin from this particular fall, but my face didn't make contact with the ice that day. My chest hit first, absorbing all the impact at a very tender stage in life. Whatever had been doing its best to develop there on the barren plane of my body was quickly pushed back in, discouraged into hibernation for at least another year.

Falling was not as rare in Hollywood on Ice. There was a week on tour when the ice beneath the tent refused to congeal with its typical smoothness. A faulty compressor left the stage warm and watery with small icebergs of solidity floating about. Management in all its brilliance came up with the plan to buy bags of ice from the local *supermercado* and scatter the cubes into the surface of the stage to hurry the freezing process. This idea is somewhat akin to buying a really big umbrella and Mary Poppinsing oneself out a second-story window. Half optimism, half stupidity. The ice cubes froze themselves into the surface of the lakish stage and formed an expanse of bumpy ridges like miniature icebergs floating across the rink. There was no possible way to skate on such angular ice, so of course management required that we do exactly that. Canceling the show just because the ice was vertically hemorrhaging was not a valid option in their eyes. When the opening number began that night, the showgirls took to the Andean rink and immediately went down one after another in a big pile of limbs, feathers, and jewels. After the audience wiped away their tears of laughter and filtered out of the tent to demand their money back, we finally got the night off to ice our bruises and curse Lora.

Everything about my skating developed while I was in college, from artistic expression to jump combinations. My confidence doubled, my emotion matured, my body strengthened not only from the twice-a-day practices but also from the new muscles that rowing added to my figure. With hockey exhibitions on either Friday or Saturday night, and most regattas being held on Sundays, I rarely had to choose between the two sports. I could do them both, and from that grew the feeling that I could do anything in the world. The best days at skating were the practices that followed two-hour rowing sessions, when the pushoff of the foot stretchers in the boat carried over onto the ice and seemed to launch my jumps higher into the air than I was normally capable of. I could spin forever on the axis of my strength, and I held camels, death drops, and laybacks longer than on the days when I did not row beforehand. Solid quads and defined hamstrings, flat stomach and strong back, rowing embellished my features without adding bulk. Or so I believed. Not everyone saw it that way. There was a foreshadowing of my future struggles with Hollywood on Ice, one that came in the guise of a different ice show and pulled up the shades of naïveté that were hanging over my window of professional skating.

In the middle of my senior year at Colgate, Disney on Ice came through the nearby city of Syracuse. Disney was the main rival of the Ice Capades, enticing young audiences with their on-ice version of whatever animated movie was either hot that year or a perennial classic. When *Snow White* came to upstate New York, I decided to audition. A few of their soloists, usually men, had high-level triple jumps, but otherwise there was nothing in the repertoire I could not do. What the hell, I already had the contract with the Ice Capades, so why not see what Disney had to offer? I did not want to replace the Ice Capades but rather to display my improved skating and see how these casting agents responded.

The Sunday-night audition was extremely similar to that of the Ice Capades, the main difference being that one producer, not three, observed and evaluated. A few members of the cast also sat in the audience to watch. Just what Captain Graceful wanted. *Go ahead, ladies. Bring on the pressure. Aww, a few little stares and narrowed glances? That all you got?* Actually, the cast members were quite friendly and supportive-looking, but the Captain had to do a little mental manipulating to get her edge going.

I ran through my spins and jumps and then an assortment of artistic movements: spread eagles, spirals, Ina Bauers, footwork patterns. Everything was solid, more than it had been four years beforehand, as confidence and maturity pushed the envelope further than I could have back at the Nassau Coliseum at age seventeen. I wore a black halter-top skating dress and smooth, tan tights, my hair in a tidy bun. I even looked more professional than four years before. The director was pleased and commented on my graceful arm positions and artistic quality. Score one for the Captain. He even had me skip some of the basic maneuvers, dismissing their triviality with remarks of "Oh, let's not waste time, that'll be easy for you." I stepped off the ice at the Syracuse Oncenter feeling proud of my performance, and headed backstage for "one last little thing."

There was a scale in the dressing room and I was instructed to stand on it. My weight was recorded and sent along with a written evaluation of my performance to Disney's director, Judy Thomas. I got on and off the scale, and the man in black looked at the number and said, "Oh," and then, "Hmm."

"Is something wrong?" I asked. "You don't have to worry, it's muscle, not fat. I'm a varsity athlete, I row *and* skate." Why was he looking at me differently now? Couldn't he see my strength through the sheer tights and the open back of my skating dress? Just the other day, I was doing pull-ups in the gym when a friend gave me the ultimate compliment an athlete can get. "Damn, Kate, you're strooooong, girl!" Adonal said in his booming Grenadine accent. Adonal Foyle was Colgate's first basketball phenom destined for the NBA, and a writing classmate of mine. When Adonal spoke, people listened. He was six feet ten inches of raw athleticism, and if he said I was strong, then so I was, and no one could dispute the matter. Especially not this comparatively small skating man now *hmmm*ing with doubt.

"Oh, no, you're fine," he said, though his tone of voice indicated otherwise. I grew nervous. What if I did not "look" the same on paper? Couldn't they have videotaped me? What if Judy Thomas cared only about the number on the scale instead of a skater's abilities and proportions? What, exactly, was I feeling? *Ka-pung, ka-pung, ka-pung.*

"Don't worry," the director said, "I'll be sure to tell her how well you skated."

Three weeks after the audition, a letter from Disney arrived in my Colgate mailbox. It was thin. I tore open the envelope and read what I was not expecting.

Dear Ms. Bertine,

Thank you for auditioning with Disney on Ice. We have no available spots for you at the moment, but we would like to see you perform again in the future. In the meantime, please consult a dietitian and nutritionist about maintaining a healthy body weight. Should your appearance change in the near future, please send photographs. Happy training!

Sincerely,
Judy Thomas
Disney on Ice

I read the third sentence over and over until the words made it clear that they were not going anywhere. There must be some mistake, I thought. Had Disney just told me I was too fat for them? Back in my dorm room I called Judy Thomas herself for clarification, forming my defense. The number on the scale is not indicative of my appearance, I rehearsed.

"Hello, Kathryn," she said. "Yes, I was told you had a lovely audition for *Snow White*." I told her about the letter I received, and was it a mix-up? Judy explained that I was not what they were looking for in body type. What?! I looked like a figure skater, and in comparison I was even taller and leaner than I had been at my Ice Capades audition. Could she explain what kind of body type she was after?

"Your weight is more than we're looking for," she said gently but with stern matter-of-factness. I could find no immediate words to respond, but when they finally came from my mouth they sounded foreign to me.

"How much would you need me to lose?" I asked. In the background, Judy Thomas ruffled through my files.

"About fifteen pounds."

"All right. I'll get back to you soon."

In the full-length mirror in my room, I looked at my body as I changed for crew practice. Turning myself around in self-conscious circles, I searched for what it was Disney despised so much. Was it the rounded bulge of groin muscle that brushed one inner thigh against the other? The plateau of quadriceps? The curve of the glutes? Were my shoulders too much, the embankment of my back too large on either side of the river of spine? Surely they liked my arms: spindly and unbulkable, they dangled down no thicker than cooked linguini. At practice, I set the ergometer computer on caloric countdown while my teammates rowed alongside, hammering out watt percentages and metered distances. As their numbers rose, mine ticked away, the exertion all looking the same from the outside.

"Kater, your computer is set on calories, silly."

"Oops. I'll change it over at the break. Thanks!"

By the end of the week I was sick, the kind of sick that would return in an Argentinean hotel room a year later. In a mad frenzy to drop fifteen pounds for a woman judging me from the other end of a telephone line, I ate very little, had no energy, and got the flu. After a week of flu-related barfing, night sweats, and general dehydration, I stood on the scale and saw that ten pounds had slipped from my body while I lay sleeping and sweating. The athlete that would have seen this as a devastating loss of power was replaced with a rejected girl who saw happiness in the lower number. I knew the weight was mostly a water-related loss, but ten pounds was ten pounds to Judy Thomas. And she said "about" fifteen pounds. Maybe this was close enough.

Putting on my skating tights and a black leotard, I tracked down a dormmate to grab his camera and shoot a roll of film. *Please send photos,* Disney said. In an impromptu modeling session I faced the camera from all angles, sucking in my stomach, holding my breath, sticking out my neck, pushing up on the balls of my feet, and, finally, putting my hands behind my back, I secretly lifted up my butt so that my legs would appear longer and thinner without the weight of my muscles affecting their appearance. Nice one, Fix-it Woman.

The film went to one-hour developing and in that time I called Judy again.

"I've lost ten pounds," I told her.

"So soon?"

"Yes. I can get rid of the last five by next week."

"Send us your photos."

The photos were mailed and in a few weeks' time, I got another form letter from Disney. I tore into it, awaiting validation of what I thought was worthiness and talent, awaiting the acceptance that would serve as an apology for the first mishap, awaiting the restoration of my now wavering self-confidence. The letter was an exact duplicate of the first one. Only the date at the top had changed. And so it seemed that no longer was my body a tool with which to carve my dreams, but now it was a far-off dream for which I had no tools to carve. After dinner that night, I put my fingers down my throat and wiggled them around, but the only thing that came up was deep sobs of disappointment.

The next day, rowing practice started out as usual. We did five-minute repeats of anaerobic threshold sets on the ergs, a typical day of winter training. Between the fourth and fifth sets, when the adrenaline and energy and sweat came to their athletic boil, something inside me broke down. It was all too much, nothing felt good. *Pull yourself together,* I snarled. Torn between loving and hating rowing for what I believed it did to my body rather than appropriately opting to loathe Disney instead, I broke down in confusion. Strength had been so good for so long, and now according to a scale and a person who never saw me skate, strength was something unworthy and ugly. One of my teammates found me in tears by the water fountain. Valley was of a take-no-prisoners mentality, a good friend who rowed with passion and strength and expected just that from all her crew. With more embarrassment than I ever felt, I told Valley that Disney had rejected me because I was too fat and that I pretty much felt like a worthless piece of bacon.

"Kater, look at your body. Look!" she instructed, and when Valley instructed, one complied. "You have lines all over the place . . . muscle," she said, pointing to the indentations where three separate sports had carved themselves into my body through years of pride and dedication. "There is no fat there," she added with an unexpected softness.

"Lines aren't a good thing anymore," I whimpered.

"Disney isn't a good thing," Valley countered.

Valley was right, and although I knew it inside, hearing it from an outside source did wonders in counteracting Judy Thomas and her evil letter. I should have known that Disney had an issue with weight and wickedness: Cruella De Vil, Cinderella's nasty stepsisters, Lady Tremaine, the Wicked Queen, even Jafar from *Aladdin*—the evil nemeses were always depicted as underweight caricatures. It figured that I'd try out for the

Disney show whose villain was an anorexic old hag armed with her trusty poisoned apple. Then again, the heroines didn't pack much weight (or muscle), either. Belle, Jasmine, and Sleeping Beauty all had a waist the size of a peanut; Ariel's seashell bra was clearly an A-size conch and even skilled canoe paddler Pocahontas had rather emaciated features jutting from her risqué loincloth. Only Disney animals — and males, at that — could pass for talented despite their weight: Dumbo, Baloo, a certain Mouse with a noticeable spare tire. Over the next few weeks I regained the confidence I'd lost in the experience with Disney. I spent extra time with my teammates; eating meals with the girls and just hanging out reminded me of my worth as a person, not a body. Forget Disney and all their Cinderella requirements. I refocused on the Ice Capades. They wanted me, they had no weight shenanigans, and they were the original plan from which I had stupidly strayed. There were two more skating events left during my days at Colgate, and there would be no more thoughts of Disney, no more energy wasted or focus lost. With a renewed faith in my body, I rowed and skated with more determination than before, awaiting graduation and my tour with the Ice Capades that lay ahead.

When I stepped onto the ice in Starr Rink on February 28, 1997, it was no different than it had been four years before. Now, in my final exhibition before graduating, I was feeling sappily sentimental. I had decided a few weeks before that I would skate to the same routine I had started with my freshman year, the croony "Power of Love" song. Until that point every exhibition had been different, from the music to the choreography to the outfit I wore. That night I circled the ice in my warm-up routine, weaving around the Zamboni as it meandered through its spiral pattern, erasing the evidence of the game's second period. Colgate was playing St. Lawrence University, and we needed the crucial win to get into the ECAC playoff round. The score was not in our favor, with St. Lawrence up by three going into the last twenty minutes of play. A thought occurred to me as I took off my warm-up sweater and stood in the same red dress I had worn four years ago on the night of my first exhibition. Same dress, same routine, same music . . . same hockey score, Colgate down, 5–2, going into the third. The same fair-weather fans migrating out of the rink, all hope of winning lost. Huh. Weird.

Joe Caprio announced that this was my final exhibition and handed me the mike so that I could say a quick thank-you to the 1,700 people who had been so very kind to tolerate me over the past four years. Then, out of nowhere, Captain Graceful proclaimed over the loudspeaker: "Colgate is going to come back, tie it up, and win, six to five, in overtime. It happened four years ago, and it is going to happen tonight." This garnered a few kind war whoops from the audience.

"Don't ever give up," I tacked on with cheesy giddiness. Then all grew quiet and the hush of the arena echoed my music for the final time. The routine was exactly the same and completely different. I was stronger now, my speed greater, my jumps higher, my spins faster. From my limbs poured more grace than I knew I had in store, and that night I skated with a love of the sport that moved me to tears at the end of my program. Dick Button broke down in a fountain of emotion and had nothing to say but *graceful* and *good-bye,* then handed the microphone over to the weeping Peggy Fleming, who nodded before they both disappeared forever. I gave a small encore to a shortened rendition of the Colgate "Alma Mater." The crowd stood, and for the first time in my life, a few flowers were thrown to the ice. Three boys from my class of 1997 held up small white cardboard squares with a 6 painted on one and 0 painted on the other. Two of the guys got a little confused and gave me 0.6s, but that was still a huge step up from my Bronxville days and I waved a heartfelt thank-you to them. To Colgate. This was my moment, and I lingered to take it all in, then curtsied, accepted some roses from the athletic department, and went into the stands to watch the score change.

And it began to do just that. After five minutes, Colgate put in its third goal. A few people turned to look at me. The fourth goal came almost immediately after the third. We had to wait a while for the tying goal, but sure enough it came just before the buzzer. "No shit, Bertine," someone said. When Colgate put away the winning goal, the crowd erupted with energy. Not only did we win, but Colgate also had a berth in the playoffs. On the way out of the building people teased me affectionately, asking me to predict lottery numbers, telling me they'd miss my skating performances. Someone told me the karma of the rink had shifted when I skated, and though it seemed a little over the top at the time, maybe they were right. Maybe some unseen cosmic powers align when desires are pure and the timing is right, jumps are landed, games are won, and everything happens the way it is supposed to. Sounds pretty neat. Either that, or hard work, long practices, constant dedication, and personal aspiration come together like the gravitational component of binary star rotation to whoop up on anything that threatens its bad-ass vortex. Science, fate, and feng shui aside, all I knew was that we were going to win that game, 6–5, in overtime. If there is magic in athleticism, it showed itself that night in a small, snowy upstate hockey town where for four years people welcomed slapshots and spandex with equal regard, and in doing so brought my skating to a higher level.

In Starr Rink I had always lingered after skating, talking to children, students, and other hockey enthusiasts, but on tour I was in a frenzy to escape the grounds of Hollywood on Ice. The atmosphere felt claustrophobic, as if my dream had become a small room and I was locked inside. *Must! Get! Out! Quick!*

On stayed the makeup that I would lather away in the hotel room, off came the skates, the fishnets were peeled, the sweatpants put on, the feet rejoiced in their sneakers, the wristwatch was refastened, the hair got de-bunned and de-crisped with a yank or two of a boar-bristle brush, and out the trailer's brown bedsheet curtain door I walked with a brisk pace, prostitute face, and Felicia in tow back to the iceless hotel. I strove to leave the tent first because it was my only source of beloved competition, though no one else knew they were playing my game. Sometimes I found a worthy opponent, if one of the girls had a date waiting for her in the vestibule alongside the T-shirt stands and popcorn machines. Then there was someone to race, our desires for leaving the tent as strong as they were different.

Rare were the nights when the cast did something together after the show, but it happened from time to time. Birthdays were a reason for such gatherings, often planned weeks in advance. The day before the flu came to get me (or I willed it to come), Krystal, the only other American with Hollywood on Ice, celebrated her twenty-eighth birthday. In the hotel's private courtyard we set up shop for the party with the three base ingredients of every celebration: vodka, chocolate, and a stereo. Krystal was one of the more temperamental skaters and went through roommates faster than the boxes of candy she regurgitated. Hollywood's weight policies affected everyone differently, and even more rare than birthday celebrations was the skater who was not affected at all.

Knowing a week ahead of time when and where Krystal's party was taking place, I made the appropriate starvation schedule so I could allow myself a sliver of cake that night in hopes of looking like a normal guest. Arriving at the party with a long-empty stomach and an angry Captain Graceful, I moped around while everyone had a good time and began to dance. When the cake came out I had my wispy slice, wandered around the room, and found that I had wandered in a big circle right back to the cake. I had another piece. Wandered. Then another. The cycle went on until half the cake mysteriously disappeared. Then the sugar rush came on with such might that I began to behave in a manner that made the Trix rabbit look tranquil and the Cocoa Puffs bird look as if it had eaten a bowl of Quaaludes. The cake hit my fasting stomach first and then moved on to my central nervous system, completely bypassing my brain. I began to dance. First alone, and then with anyone who would let me near them. Grígor didn't seem like such a bad guy! Hey, Lenny, put down that pork chop and get over here! Where's Ruslan? Let's see how flexible he really is! *¡Dónde está mi guapo Pedro?* Valeri, Leosha, quit obsessing with your mullets, leave the Olgai alone—I *said* I *want* to *dance. NOW!*

"Keeeaaatrin, how much drink?"

"No drink, Grígor. Cake."

"Keek? What is?

"*¡Azúcar, azúcar!*" Sugar, sugar!

After that night, Grígor rowed by me with a bit more gusto in his stroke and commented, "Bad Girl Keeeaaatrin. Grígor like bad girl." With my body one step ahead of the rest of me, everything seemed very far away for the next few hours. Felicia asked Krystal if there was something in the cake.

"Just chocolate. Look. Everyone else is fine." But it wasn't just chocolate in there. There were eggs, flour, oil, sugar, and water—foods my body had been without for way too long. The cake wasn't made of chocolate, it was made of energy and I was on the verge of a sweet and wonderful overdose. I danced from song to song, and when they turned off the radio I kept going, aware that sound had ceased but unaware that

I had to as well. Up to that point I had barely spoken to any of the skaters beyond the daily salutations and occasional tour-life banter, so everyone assumed I was high as a kite and had a good time laughing at me as I flew around the room, chattering, dancing, touching. I was like a Laker girl with no basketball game in sight, and yet I felt more like an athlete than I had for the past three months.

For those two confection-tripping hours, I loved Hollywood on Ice and everything about it. Ice Capades? Ha! Who gave a rat's ass about that show? Hollywood was the place to be. The people were fantastic, the work conditions were fabulous, the nightlife was incredible, and the show was the most amazing work of theatrical genius to hit the stage since *Les Misérables* took to Broadway. That night, everything was less miserable. Everything was right.

I danced my way back to my room, drenched from the sweaty efforts of my sugary happiness, not thinking clearly enough to change clothes. I collapsed on the bed, where I woke up with the flu and a stomachache that brought me right back to all that my life with Hollywood on Ice had been before cake, before energy. How did I get here? Oh, that's right. I chose this. This was my dream, my third take of the original version, my remake of the master plan. The deferred one. The one that was supposed to be, and I just could not let go of its ghost. But no use crying over the what-might-have-beens, right? Not like that does anyone any good.

And there was the root of every problem, every emotion, the source of the hunger that manifested itself in my anorexia. I *should* have cried, mourned the original dream I'd lost, moped around the house, muttering, "Aww shit, this sucks, this really, really sucks." Not forever, just for a cathartic little while. I should have spent time healing the wound instead of slapping a flesh-toned Band-Aid over the crack running through my broken goals, and saying, *Back on the horse, Captain. Get back on it!* Quick thinking and snap judgments had never failed me in athletic situations, but dreams and goals do not work that way. That's only how they're born, but not how they are nurtured. Only time can do that. Time and grace. I had only physically moved on from the disappointment of the Ice Capades but remained stagnant in a memory of what was supposed to be.

‑‑ʌʮ‑‑

Dream Deferred

I graduated from Colgate University in May 1997 and re-signed with the Ice Capades in July after a brief panic attack. The Ice Capades had changed management during my college years, and although my name was still on file from 1993, I now had to send in a recent audition video to verify my ability. Selecting one Colgate exhibition and a performance from one of my Clinton figure skating shows, I sent the videotape and waited with trepidation, wondering if it was going to be Disney all over again. The Ice Capades had enjoyed my talent four years before, but what if they put my body before my skills and now found my muscles too unappealing? What if they sent Captain Graceful a form letter asking her to keep saving the world, but only on celery sticks and carrot nubbins? The situation left me a bit high-strung. I spent my time stalking the mailman, calling the operator to double-check the working status of my phone line, and calculating the speed of every passing postal train in the Northern Hemisphere. Within a few agonizing weeks, the Ice Capades called and said all was well—my spot was secure, ready, and waiting at the end of the summer, September 8.

For two months I again lived in Lake Placid, where I had once spent my summers training as an amateur. Now, I practiced on the verge of professionalism, skating and waitressing until the start of the tour. At night I pulled out the FedEx envelope and re-read the Ice Capades' contract with a level of passion usually reserved for *Sports Illustrated for*

Women and Ralph Waldo Emerson. Every sentence was a beautiful, well-crafted work of art, and the salutation just below the dignified letterhead delivered an instant goose-bump-inducing gratification: *Hello and Welcome to the Ice Capades!*

This information packet was the tangible blueprint of my achieved goal. There was a calendar listing all the shows, dates, and venues. Even the W-4 form and proof of U.S. citizenship pages held my interest. A sheet for costume design required the specific measurements of everything from my wrist to the width of my calf. There were no more weigh-ins, manager Julie Patterson told me over the phone. They had been done away with in the eighties, after problems with eating disorders jeopardized the health of too many skaters on the tour. The Ice Capades changed their body-judging outlook, and skaters were now required to be healthy, as opposed to weighing a certain amount. There was pride on both sides of the contract, more so than I could have understood right then.

A biographical chart for publicity events and a skating background sheet were also included. Questions ran from basic to thoughtful, asking about birth dates, Social Security numbers, and *What was the most outrageous thing that ever happened in your amateur skating career?* I wrote of the time my long program music and its backup copy mysteriously disappeared from my skate bag at a regional competition far away from home. Not wanting to withdraw, I went into the local town and bought a tape of instrumental music at a bookshop, returned to the rink, turned in the tape to registration, got on the ice, and asked the skating referee to shut off the tape after four minutes passed. I ended up coming in fourth with a program neither the judges, audience, nor I had ever seen before. That was the day I learned that choreography and manipulation were not so different from each other, that confidence was the sole factor needed to carry out either one successfully, and that Captain Graceful was the best sidekick ever.

Another question asked us to describe our skating style to someone who had never seen us skate. *I have the strength of a hockey player, the endurance of a speed skater, the grace of an ice dancer, and the ability to captivate an audience like a Zamboni driver. My style is my own.* Who is your hero? Ice Capades wanted to know. *My dad.* Why? *He is an athlete still.*

The contract offered detailed paragraphs of rules and regulations that were both humorous and professional. Ice Capades figure skaters were not allowed to bring ferrets on skating tours. Paragraph 3, page 7, also stated that fish and mice were not acceptable travel companions. Rule 25 demanded that my armpits be shaved every show day, specifically in the midmorning. Rule 41 declared that wedding rings must be covered with flesh-toned tape during performances. Having no pet rodents, spouse, or desire for hairy pits, I was ready for the Ice Capades in every respect that the contract stipulated.

In early September I packed two bulky Eddie Bauer duffel bags, attached the ICE CAPADES luggage tags to the clackety zippers, set them by the back door, and waited. The flight to Las Vegas — rehearsal home of the Ice Capades — was two days away, but my excitement was on its own schedule. Even the clothes I planned to wear on the plane were already picked out. A yellow sundress with a blooming-flower print was hooked to the back of the bathroom door, dewrinkling, while an old pair of tan sandals flopped in waiting beneath the hem. The airy dress was an easy outfit, in case I had to change right away into skating clothes upon arrival. A spare set of tights and a leotard were packed in the zippered pocket of my shabby, well-worn skate bag.

Physically, everything was in place and ahead of schedule by a few days. Emotionally, all luggage had been packed long ago, back when grace was just a new acquaintance. The years of training and competing as an amateur figure skater — all those mornings of breathless cold, all those evenings of bypassed opportunities, all the errant falls and fragile landings, the devotion to sport — had finally resulted in a real-life, twenty-one-page, ferretless contract, and in two days I was to be a member of the cast, a professional skater after a decade of preparation.

I do not remember much about the phone call that came later in the afternoon of September 6, except for the part where I asked the manager of the Ice Capades, John Warren, to repeat himself. "Yes, the show went bankrupt. I'm very sorry. Good luck with your skating." Bankrupt? No, that only happened to small businesses in small towns, or big stores in big cities that already had too many big stores. Not the Ice Capades. Not the very Ice Capades that Dorothy Hamill owned, where audiences left no seat vacant and Donald Trump himself was at the show the very night I auditioned. John Warren had no time to explain the intricacies of bankruptcy, and at the moment it was the last thing I wished to have explained.

"Okay, fine. But we start in two days," I argued. I had proof that things would be okay. *Go ahead and tell him, Captain Graceful. The light-up visor in the back of my closet still works, Mr. John Warren. It still works. Bankrupt? It's not possible.*

Anger was setting in and growing inside me as he began to apologize not for the bankruptcy but for his error in timing. According to Warren, the Ice Capades had actually gone under three weeks beforehand, right after I had had my last contact with them about plane tickets. Everyone else in the show had been told weeks ago, with the exception of the three or four new skaters joining the cast.

"You just fell through the cracks, Kathryn. I'm very sorry. You should have been called earlier," Warren said, placing the blame somewhere else. I asked for phone numbers, contacts, anything that might help me get into another show somewhere, until the Ice Capades got back on its feet. He gave me numbers for some cruise ships and casinos that had twenty-minute skating shows performed on plastic, synthetic "ice." Oh, and I could try Busch Gardens. They might have an opening between their giraffe shows and elephant parodies.

There were three immediate impulses that followed hanging up the phone with the Ice Capades. The first was to crawl under the kitchen table, get into the fetal position, and rock back and forth for a few months. The second, and the one I eventually went with, was to start looking for another tour. But the third, a happy medium between the other two, was to just sit and stare vacantly for a while—and it led me into the family room, where I watched TV for about eighteen hours before remembering to turn it on.

That night I sat in a chair in the living room with the atlas that Captain Graceful had meekly pulled off a shelf and placed in my lap, flipping through the pages until the sun came up. There would be no Thanksgiving weekend in South Bend, Indiana, no Christmas shows in Montreal; my New Year's Eve was not going to be spent in Minot, North Dakota, and I wouldn't turn twenty-three in Portland. I had memorized the tour schedule back in July, when I had signed the Ice Capades contract. On the large layout of the United States, I mapped out the bus route that we seemed most likely to follow from show to show, thinking of college friends who lived along the way. I had already written letters and sent schedules to friends who resided in the cities where the Ice Capades would play, my audience arranged and waiting, letters and post-cards already coming in to wish me luck. *All those mornings of breathless cold, all those evenings of bypassed opportunities, all the errant falls and fragile landings, the devotion to sport . . .* Now there was nothing except the excruciating possibility that I would have to settle for being an ordinary has-been athlete who came so close to personal greatness, then slipped off her own charts and into obscurity. Later on I came to find out that it wasn't exactly bankruptcy that had ended the Ice Capades, but rather lack of interest. To avoid bankruptcy for her company, Dorothy Hamill sold it to the media conglomerate International Family Entertainment, which in turn was bought by a division of Rupert Murdoch's News Corp. News Corp., which decided not to fund the show. And just like that, there was no more Ice Capades.

Sometime the next morning, in a sudden surge of who knows what, the vacant staring phase ended. I began to scour the atlas again and settled on the shapely expanse of Europe. There *had* to be other tours, other shows, and I would find them. There was no time to con-template why this urgency to skate professionally took over my thoughts and actions; the autopilot of my athletic nature was in full swing, kickball-style. An athlete does not concede defeat without giving it everything she has, so I began a monthlong process of phoning skat-ing tours in other countries and sending audition videotapes all over the world: Europe, Asia, the Caribbean. I started with the numbers John Warren gave me but gave up on cruise ships that had openings for only a month or two and hung up on the casinos that asked if skating topless would be a problem. Every phone call began with hope and ended with disappointment. No employment vacancies, no Americans wanted (visas too expensive), no clothes above the waist. A few of the managers laughed at me, saying they had already cast the "remnants of Ice Capades" and wasn't I a little late to be calling for work when everyone else had called three weeks ago? Falling through management's cracks now worsened my chances of finding work in any professional skating arena. Every few days I called the Ice Capades again, just to feel hope for the one and a half seconds before the monotonous beeps of a disconnected dial tone. There was nothing now to do but wait, leaving me with plenty of time to figure out what for.

If there was a time to think about new goals, about redreaming, this should have been it. But completely changing goals meant letting go of old ones, and there was no time for that. I equated letting go of the Ice Capades with failing, and even though it was the company that had failed, I felt as if I had. There is always a "why?" that comes with disappointment, unfairly questioning irreversible circumstances, dramatically overtaking blank thoughts and peaceful moments. My "why?" ran through my head like a scrolling marquee, *Why didn't you go with Ice Capades before you went to college, dumbass?* Unbearably unanswerable, the words looped through my mind, perplexity leading cruelty, logic following denial. I never had an off switch for that thing, just a reprogrammable control panel that was too tough to find and a real bitch to rewire. Instead of punching the buttons to display a nicer, more patient mental massage, such as *Coming soon! Kathryn's brand-new goals and bankruptcy-free dreams!* I skipped the mourning stage and went right for the first headline that caught my eye. *Now Playing: Holiday on Ice!*

With the Ice Capades leaving a gaping void in my immediate future, there was only one other way to cope with the loss of my goal. Between overseas phone calls and sending out audition tapes, the waiting grew insufferable and the only thing that left me with a feeling of accomplishment was engaging in something athletic. Athleticism, my great healer of broken hearts. I kept up my skating with daily trips to a rink in New Rochelle (Murray's being not yet open for the season), but there was frustration interlaced with every workout. There had always been something to work toward, but now that my professional skating dreams seemed dashed, it was harder to focus on my love of the sport. I needed something else to remind me that ice was not the only thing important in life. Water seemed the appropriate substitute.

The New York Athletic Club, where my father rowed, was fifteen minutes away from Bronxville. Its rowing program was just beginning the fall racing season, and I signed on with the hope of making it into one of NYAC's prestigious boats. Vinny Ventura, the coach for the men's and women's squads, took me on despite the possibility that I might have to up and leave in the middle of the season if one of the skating tours ever took pity and hired me. Such an allowance is highly contradictory to the philosophy of rowing, in which the team comes first and any self-ish, individualistic thoughts (like quitting to join a professional skating show) are not usually welcome. In return for this understanding, I promised hard work and as much dedication as my devotion to skating permitted. Vinny did me a tremendous favor in getting me out of the house and away from my turned-off-TV telethon, overbearing atlases, and un-ringing phone. Not only that, he broke the mold of all nonskating coaches I had ever known and was actually supportive of my skating. It would be this coach who, nearly a year later upon my return from Hollywood on Ice, would not allow me to row for him until I gained weight and looked healthy again.

The women's team began practice at 5:30 each morning, and we sat on the cold concrete floor of the John J. Sulger Boathouse, waiting for our lineups and workouts. We tallied up the drills and sprint pieces that Vinny assigned, counting in our head how many meters we'd row that day. Most of the women were in their mid-twenties to early thirties and had real-life jobs to go to after crew practice that did not necessitate fig-ure skates. I worked in my father's office, answering phones and artisti-cally enhancing the margins of pink memo pads every afternoon, but my mornings were wide-open and I wished we could row forever up and down that 2,000-meter stretch of murky water in Pelham Bay.

Some mornings we rowed on the erg machines, Vinny taking down our times for 5,000-meter pieces. These tests were long and painful, and I absolutely loved them. The little computer kept time and distance of its own accord, and it made me quite angry. These were the very elements I wanted to control. Erg tests provided just the right outlet for my frus-trations with skating, as I pulled on the handle with more aggression that fall than during my entire college rowing career. My split times dropped well under twenty minutes, which was not too shabby for a figure skater. It was just enough time to melt and sweat away everything from the world of ice that seemed to be freezing up on me outside the boathouse. Vinny liked my erg scores because I could outpull a bunch of the bigger girls, and he let me row with the heavyweights (the category now called a more ambiguous "open" weight) instead of the lightweight squad. Within the NYAC, our sense of team was solid and these women befriended me in the weeks we practiced together before stuffed elephants and thrusting Grígor became my immediate family.

One rower, Jen, did not have to leave for work directly after practice, so we prolonged the mornings by going to Bruegger's Bagels. We shared stories and procrastinated, flicking the stray grains of whole wheat bagels at each other—usually eating two, since the previous workouts left us ravenous. We were athletes, it would have been fine to eat half a dozen and think nothing of it. Once, forgetting to bring my wallet to the boathouse, I swung by the house after practice en route to meeting Jen for breakfast.

"Helloooooo?" my mother sang from upstairs, hearing the front door open at 7:30.

"Just me. Going to get a bagel with Jen."

"Bagels are faaaaaaaattening."

Ka—$#@%&—pung. Apparently someone's bionic ear could hear the *ka-pung*ing cabinets across town. With my pretour jitters and general disdain for corporeal judgment, comments like this often left me holding back bagel-size tears, despite the fact I knew that Crouches With Radar had no idea what she was talking about.

Ever since I had begun rowing four years before, my body weight, shape, and size were of even greater importance to my mother, more so than during my teenage years. Coming home from Colgate on holiday breaks, I was met with questions of how much did I weigh, was I still a size six, had I lost any weight that semester? My father never made comments about such things, but neither did he defend me from my mother's judgmental inquiries. But when she wasn't paying attention, my dad still scooped some of his food onto my plate, winked, and then got up for his uncriticized second helping. Still, the entire act of borrowing food just didn't taste very good, and Home Sweet'N Low Home was not upholding its reputation as a comfortable place.

But Bruegger's and boathouses were, so I lingered as long as possible where my body and I did not feel like separate entities. Some days, when Captain Graceful was off-duty, or far away, and I felt a void in my confidence. What I would have given then to know how to live within myself, to haunt the house of my body with a spirit so beautifully strong that it could scare away all disparaging intruders.

In mid-October I finally received the phone call from Holiday on Ice in Europe. They accepted me into their Christmas tour, which ran through Switzerland and France, and then I would be signed on to one of their three permanent year-round world tours. Was I still interested? Interested, yes. I signed with them immediately. Informed, no. Rooster suits, angry ducks, the slow death of athleticism . . . the next year was not going to be like anything I had expected from the world of professional figure skating.

Holiday on Ice started in November, less than two weeks after the last regatta of NYAC's fall rowing season. Perfect. The best of both worlds. With the weight of my skating future lifted off my chest and a new scrolling marquee up and running through my head, I enjoyed rowing even more. On Sundays we raced at the Head of the Connecticut, the Head of the Charles, and the Head of the Schuylkill, and each weekend away from home was a celebration of athleticism. As we rowed toward our finish lines in the boat, I sailed toward bigger things in my mind. *How did I get here?* Skating videotapes, résumés, and recommendation letters got me onto the tour, but rowing, focus, and physical strength pulled me through the entire process. When the NYAC women's open-weight eight stepped off the dock on the banks of Philadelphia's boathouse row that Sunday afternoon, I knew it would be a while until I felt the hull of a boat around my body, but it would not be forever. What took place in the interim was the slow realization that not all goals were worth hanging on to and that skating or rowing would never again feel the same.

Chapter Fourteen

✦

In Search of Greatness

In the trailer, Felicia and I did not receive our makeup mirrors right away. We waited for weeks until Pam or Sunny or someone who knew the whereabouts of Hollywood on Ice's storage unit had time to go there and dig up a few giant rectangles of the warped reflective glass. In the meantime, we bought small, plastic handheld mirrors at the supermarket and propped them against the wall. This bothered me more than I expected. Never before had I felt the need to own a large mirror for any reason, but now I was a professional skater and all the other professional skaters had one, so I wanted one, too, the righteous preschooler in me whined. Not to mention that it was rather uncomfortable contorting into Igor-like proportions while putting on my makeup and costume in the little makeshift compact. After I played the squeaky wheel for a few weeks, someone shut me up and found me a mirror. In blocky sticker letters the name LIZZI ran across the bottom of the glass. Jody said that the previous girl had been a wild-child troublemaker who had run away from Hollywood on Ice a few months ago, and no one had heard from her since. I picked at the stubborn stickers, peeling them off with impatient yanks, rubbing at the streaks of sticky gunk until they balled up and dropped off, leaving a comet of smudge on the mirror.

"*¿Tienen pegatinas?*" I asked some of the skaters, who passed me a few leftover letters. Vowels were a hot commodity and Lizzi hadn't left me much to work with, so the best I could do was KTHRN but Cpn Grcfl was fine with that. The mirror was all mine now, a place where I could hang my photos, put up some silly decorations, and look not so much at myself as at the backdrop of my surroundings and all those who shared the scenery.

My chair was in the front end of the trailer and the only three reasons to go to the far end were fan readjustment, weigh-ins, and lodging a complaint with Sunny, who was not the most pro-active line captain. The large circular upright fan sat right in front of the broken air conditioner and looked just like the ones Bronxville High School dragged into the gymnasium, where we took our final exams. In the trailer someone — usually Olga #1, with the princess complex, glass-breaking shriek, and general disdain for monogamy — was constantly repositioning the contraption to get the most breeze possible. In her mirror she glued on black eyelashes as the fan blew her blondish, half-permed mane away from her face, the gust turning her into something that might inspire the cover of a romance novel. A very seedy one with a handful of female co-stars on the cover.

Krystal's mirror was the most decorated, with various photos of guys, supersparkly stickers that came from the plastic eggs of twenty-five-cent machines, and small Disney characters holding up the block letters of her name. A magazine article titled "Pre-Bikini Belly Blasters," which showed an unsweaty woman folding herself into perceived perfection, was taped to one side of the glass while right above it was another cutout that listed one hundred things to do before you die. Krystal had slash marks through a number of the wishes, things such as learn a new language, tell your first kiss that he was just that, rent every Audrey Hepburn movie, do something that scares you, and so forth. I read through the goofy proverbs but could not find one that said skating for Hollywood on Ice would bring inner fulfillment. Still, it was definitely covered by the "do something that scares you" clause.

All our mirrors angled downward just enough to see the drawers that lay beneath the costume rack behind us. The drawer opposite Krystal's mirror had the scale. Nasty little apparatus. I was way too familiar with Krystal's seat, sitting in it when she was not around, digging the scale out from its hiding place, standing before her mirror, and challenging the crunched-up Miss Pre-Bikini Belly Blaster to a blast-off. I'll see your fifty crunches and raise you two hundred and fifty, you designer-sports-bra-wearing sweatless dingbat.

The trailer floor was warped in some areas, so it was common to see someone pull out the scale, stand on it, curse, take it three feet to the left of that spot, stand on it again, swear again, and repeat the process until she found a part of the floor that tipped the mechanism in her favor, finally exhaling with relieved victory. The spot just to the right of Krystal's mirror worked best.

One thing I could see all too clearly in my new mirror was my hair. At Lora's request, the darker brunettes were summoned to go lighter, which her value system ranked more attractive. My hair was a dark mix of brown with reddish tones, and not one strand of lightness could be found anywhere. Krystal's original hair was a similar color to mine, but she pleased Lora by adding a few light streaks of blond. A streak here and there — that I could handle. Krystal pointed out the salon on the way back from the show one night and said to ask Emilita, the hairdresser, for *mechitas*. Highlights.

Emilita gave me highlights all right. In fact, she gave every hair on my head its own personal *mechita*. I should have known that something was amiss when the stench of peroxide cleared out my sinuses and murdered all my nasal nerve endings. Panting like a dog, I breathed my way through an hour beneath the vicious heat lamp, thinking it was a much too complicated procedure for a streak or two of blondeness.

"Confíame," Emilita sang — trust me — when she saw my frumpled forehead. I wasn't in the habit of doling out instantaneous trust to strangers, but there was little I could do about the situation already brewing inside my holey, goo-covered skullcap. By the end of the day I was yellowed into a new head of hair, which my denial actually enjoyed until the next shower proved that my newfound Barbieness was not going away anytime soon.

"Felicia! I'm in the shower, my head is under the water, and it is not getting wet. The drops are bouncing off my hair. What the fuck?!"

"No worries, Kathryn, your hair has just lost all its absorption ability from the bleach, that's all. It'll be back."

"When?!"

"Next year, at least."

Every glance in my trailer mirror reminded me that I was getting further away from who I wanted to be. Sunny and Donna, two of the Canadians at the opposite end of the trailer, were the quiet, nearly invisible cast members who had been on tour for quite some time and didn't appear to have future plans to lead them elsewhere. They were both in their early thirties, with long hair and sad, indifferent faces that I cannot recall smiling except for the mandatory on-ice grin. Though there wasn't much to smile about in the trailer, there was certainly a lot of opportunity for laughter, whether directed at one another or at oneself. I ran the gamut of emotions, from sugar high to tearful low, but rarely was there a moment reserved for apathy. Sunny and Donna were two of the palest women I ever saw, not sun-cautious pale, but Wonder-bread white. Felicia and I referred to them as the Vegan Vampires, as they slept away the day and went out at night with their boyfriends, Valeri and Ruslan, until the sun began its threat of ascension. We did not know the girls' actual dietary preference, but their lackluster attitude toward life and noticeably frail physiques made it hard for us to picture Donna and Sunny in the same category as some of the more devilishly carnivorous bloodsuckers on tour. Their pale reflections always showed up in all the trailer's mirrors, so our vampire analogy was slightly flawed. The girls' mirrors reflected the end of the trailer's costume bar, where their prehistoric polyester Betty and Wilma costumes hung below the famous orange and black bouffant wigs, always in the exact same place, facing the same way, secure in their location.

A few seats over, Pam kept her mirror plain. The stickers on hers were leftovers from someone else, a few Olympic mascot decals here and there. For two weeks in February, Pam brought us news from North America. Her Canadian boyfriend sent newspaper clippings and occasional e-mails about the Olympic Games taking place in Nagano, Japan. The Argentinean media weren't into winter sports and our hotel rooms in Mar del Plata had no television, so what little we heard through the grapevine came from Pam. She posted the figure skating results on her mirror, the Russians scoffing at Tara Lipinski's gold medal victory at the age of fifteen, beating out their veteran stateswomen Maria Butyrskaya and Irina Slutskaya. Pam's mirror was something of a congregation point for those two weeks, as those of us who wondered about the outside world stopped by to see who was now considered skating's greatest. When the Olympics were over, down came the articles and results, turning the mirror from a bulletin board of achieved goals back to a reflection of reality.

The one skater who did not have a mirror was Pedro. Bella, Pedro's mostly consistent girlfriend, did his makeup for him. The men were only required to wear a base foundation for an even-complexioned, brighter skin tone and were spared the details of false eyelashes, lip liner, and the like. When done with the makeup process, Pedro sat on his chair facing the door and the costumes instead of the mirrored wall, singing Chilean songs and making small talk with Jody, Felicia, and anyone else near our end of the trailer. His personality was always bubbly, but just to the right level of carbonation that always fizzled down right before it spilled into annoyance, a skill I personally longed to master.

What I learned quickly was that the images staring back at us from our mirrors were not the same people we saw up close in the trailer or away from the dressing room. The makeup made us look physically brighter, more alive, and when we took it off, our natural selves looked drab and unhappy. Which most of us were. When I was without a mirror in the beginning, it was not clear to me why I was so intent on having one, but once I had a glass of my own, I understood. Before Hollywood on Ice and Holiday on Ice, or any sort of professional skating, I was just a kid with a crazy dream who was part of the background of figure skating, a face in the crowd of all those who aspired to greatness. I wanted to be in the front, just for a little while, so I could see what it was like to be the one people came to watch. Until the mirrors began to show too much reality, these cheap squares of reflection allowed me to see that I was finally there in the world of pro skating, right where I always thought I wanted to be.

I have shared the ice with greatness: Scott Hamilton, Elaine Zayak, JoJo Starbuck, Jill Trenary, Debi Thomas, Christopher Bowman, Paul Wylie, Scott Davis, Aren Nielsen, Lisa Ervin, Yuka Sato, Sarah Hughes, and Dorothy Hamill. I've been on the ice with champion skaters who never knew I was there, a kid in the background dodging their triples with sharp awareness and staring at their programs in trancelike admiration. No one wants to offset greatness and force it to reroute around mediocrity.

During practice sessions in Lake Placid or Colorado Springs, New York City or Atlanta, either these skaters were just passing through the area or I was. How it boosted my confidence to be in their proximity, how I prayed for some osmosis of agility to work its way through the ice from their skates into mine. Honing in on their techniques, I copied their movements and borrowed what I could from greatness.

Sarah Hughes, America's 2002 Olympic gold medalist, was six years old when I skated with her on a practice session in Lake Placid, ten years before her history-making upset of Michelle Kwan and Irina Slutskaya, coming all the way from fourth place to capture the gold medal after the long program. Working as an announcer for Lake Placid's annual competition that summer of 1992, I called her name in the Olympic Center's 1932 Rink during the Juvenile Ladies Free Skate. "And now, from the Skating Club of New York, please welcome Sarah Hughes." I watched the future of figure skating unfold before she could even grasp such a concept. In the same building three years later, down in the USA Rink, I watched the body of two-time Olympic gold medalist pairs skater Sergei Grinkov roll lifelessly by on a stretcher when a heart attack took him at the age of twenty-eight. I was a ghost to the elite, a lingering presence whom they might have acknowledged for a graceful spin or a solid jump, yet I forever remained a mortal athlete in contrast to their deistic echelon of figure skating. I passed for greatness once, but even then it was not in person.

"I don't know, who do you think it is?" 1992 Olympic silver medalist Paul Wylie asked Olympic gold medalist Scott Hamilton, staring at a photograph in the office of the Lake Placid Olympic Center. The 20-by-24-inch poster they were looking at was a professional photograph taken by a local company. The profile of a girl in a sparkling pink dress above a shock of white ice in the foreground and turquoise wallboards in the back was eye-catching in both color and form. Her body is captured in a catch-foot layback spin with her free leg raised up to her head and her posture perfectly angled toward the camera. The leg she spins on is a skater's leg, the great wave of quadriceps rising over the knee while a defined hill of hamstring ascends from the leg brought back to her head. The other arm is outstretched yet supple. The hand has not finished its journey upward and the photograph suggests the existence of movement. It is her fingers; they are cupped and hidden in the hand, still rising against the pull of gravity and the speed of the shutter. Those who know skating know that soon the fingers would have appeared as the final extensions of grace, the last bloom before the wilt of the spin.

The photo hangs alongside action shots of famous skaters from Discover Card's Stars on Ice tour of Olympic champions, which practices in Lake Placid from time to time. With the vibrant colors, the lighting of the rink, and the angle captured, the camera has made something more of this pink-dress skater in still life than she is in the real one. I am the girl in the photo.

"I don't know, but I think it might be Kristi Yamaguchi," Scott Hamilton says.

A jet-black stream of ponytail trails from my head. In the throes of velocity and the curve of the spin, my ponytail is parallel to the ice, reaching out like a fifth limb of womanhood. The camera, in too much of a hurry to differentiate brown from black, decides the latter will do just fine. Kristi Yamaguchi has black hair, an Olympic gold medal, and a few world and national titles. My hair is brown and I have a certificate of participation from this regional competition in which I failed to advance, but neither the camera nor I am aware of that yet.

"It is not Kristi Yamaguchi," Paul Wylie asserts. He points to my figure skate, noting a smudge along the outer heel of the otherwise white boot. "Kristi's mother would never let her get on the ice with unpolished skates." He thinks for a moment. "Maybe it's Katarina Witt?" They rule out a few givens: Tonya Harding, Surya Bonaly, and Nancy Kerrigan as I'm not blond, French-African, or dressed in Vera Wang.

"Hmm," says Hamilton.

"Hmm," says Wylie. They leave the office, but not before one of the gentlemen comments on the graceful position of the spin. *Graceful? Me?* If only I had been there to hear it in person. Greatness had spoken, giving me grace, but I never knew it, until years later when the compliment (and the story of the Olympians' conversation) was finally relayed to me by the office secretary. I was fifteen in the photograph, seven years before I went in search of grace on the professional tour, trying to find the very thing I did not know I already had. The secretary never told the Olympian observers my name and I appreciated the anonymity, as "Who?" would not have sounded quite as good as "Hmm."

Despite the possibility of being immortalized on film with grimy footwear, polishing my skates didn't make sense to me. My equipment worked well just as it was, and I wasn't up for constantly repainting it. My skates and I always kept the positive chi flowing, I dried the blades and made sure the soles were waterproofed as often as needed, and in return the boots stayed strong for nine months — until we had to say our farewells and part ways on good terms, leaving me to begin again with a new pair.

I practiced hard and found comfort in the fact that it showed on my skates. There were nicks from the toe pick, where one foot stabbed the other unintentionally, and slashes from the close-call landings of blade on boot instead of blade on ice. Well-worn hickey-shaped splotches up near the toe exposed the gray underleather of the boot at the point where ice and other rink elements sucked at the skate with too much force and friction. Yet judges preferred cleanliness, so I debutanted my skates with a dressy layer of white paint once or twice a year for regional or national competitions but left the marks of dedication visible for the local contests and shows. I knew there were strict rules about unkempt skates in the professional world, and I had no problem with the policy that everyone's skates had to match and that most ice shows went with tan skates to create a longer-legged look. I wasn't argumentative about everything in Hollywood on Ice.

Before I could take the Hollywood on Ice stage, my skates had to be painted tan. My latest skates were already tan, but the makers of SP-Teri figure skates do not use the same shade as Hollywood on Ice. A southwestern color of pinkish brown dripped from the bucket of house paint backstage, and two coats later my skates were a brighter shade of skin tone that looked nearly orange under the spotlights. All my smudges were gone and my feet were now the color of adobe, but the darker hue of my fishnet stockings draped over the boot muted the brightness. The new skates and blades I ordered before starting the tour proved a poor investment for both Holiday and Hollywood; my old blades and worn-out boots would have sufficed just fine for tromping around the gritty backstage areas.

There was no greatness here, no headliner of Olympic credentials, no up-and-coming skater sure to take the world by storm. We had Ruslan and Olga, who hung from the ceiling cables with intertwined flexibility, and we had Alexei and his parents rolling around over the ice, but there was no trace of a great champion who came from the true background of figure skating. Then in March we got a call that greatness was on its way from Russia.

Pam announced that soon Viktor would be coming back to Hollywood on Ice. Felicia and I looked at each other, excitedly. Viktor Petrenko, the multiple Olympic medalist and world champion?! "No, not Petrenko. Viktor *and Elizabeta*," Pam corrected. A pairs team? Wonderful! Felicia and I racked our stumped brains, trying to recall an Elizabeta of world-class stature. None of the other skaters in the trailer received the news with enthusiasm. *"Vanyuchiya,"* Olga #1 said, sending the skaters into laughter. *Stinks.* That figures — Olga was just jealous that another pairs team was going to steal attention from her. Besides, Elizabeth was my own middle name, so I had a positive preconceived notion about the newcomers. I knew four Elizabeths growing up and shared similar personality traits with each of them, so I was truly looking forward to meeting the great Russian skater Elizabeta.

What I did not realize was that Viktor and Elizabeta — but more so Elizabeta — would literally stink. Elizabeta was a cow. An honest-to-God, udders and all, cow. That could skate. I was right about one thing, Elizabeta and I did share one trait other than our name. According to Hollywood on Ice, we were both ice skating cows.

Greatness arrived the first week of March as Viktor brought not only his skating milk factory but his poodles, duck, and chicken, all of which skated as well. They wore figure skates Viktor himself hand-crafted to the webs, claws, hooves, and paws of his trainees. These animals flapped about the ice to a medley of circus music while Viktor, who was no less than 300 pounds, sat on a stool and conducted from center ice. The scene sent a shiver through my spine, as if Holiday on Ice's

Christmas Parade of Animals had sprung to life and come back to haunt me. But this batch of barnyard creatures was really alive, not just temporarily possessed of plush costumes with sewn-on faces. Would there be a headless elephant, too, and would it come after me for cutting the buckle out of its neck?

Something about seeing a hen with tiny hen-size skates was not normal and just freaky enough to threaten Mrs. Butterworth's position on the scale of creepiness. The skating animals were surreal at best. Enough to provoke dreams about the pigeons of Murray's coming down from the rafters, lacing up their custom-made SP-Teris, and joining the other skaters for morning practice. It was all too much to bear, and for once Olga #1 was right — backstage turned into a stockyard that reeked of animals in captivity, with clipped wings and bladed feet. The dogs and fowl let out howls of discontent every time a human skater walked past their cages, crying out from cramped quarters of wire and mesh that made the trailer look like a castle by comparison.

Elizabeta was the only animal permitted to live outside the tent, and she stood tethered to the rink with a piece of cruelly short twine and a bucket of hay and water at her disposal. She was the one female in the cast that did not have to attend weigh-ins and could eat as much as she wanted without guilt or other repercussions. The cow, unlike her barnyard buddies, gave little acknowledgment to onlookers and failed to find humor in the salchow jokes that someone always threw her way. There was something snooty about Elizabeta. The way she held her nose high and turned her head away from us gave her an air of pretentiousness, a bit of a dairy princess complex. She wore a necklace of red beads, too, perhaps as an indication to passersby that she was indeed a special heifer and not just awaiting a destiny with the Argentinean grill.

As echoes of greatness mooed, quacked, and squawked through our trailer, I wrote letters home about the other acts in the show. No longer did the cheeseball *Flashdance* routine seem so embarrassing, nor did the sea-horse costume I was promoted to after putting in my time as a backup fish feel quite as insignificant. Even the ridiculous number in which the rag dolls and pretty Barbies flopped and pranced around with self-esteem issues was now information I was happy to relay back home, rather than confess that Hollywood had more or less turned into Mr.

Viktor's Future Entrées on Ice. The display of skating poultry was something I decided to keep secret, as I was too ashamed to admit that all my years of hard work found me a bit part in the chorus while a plethora of four-legged mammals received solo numbers in a professional skating show.

Everything around me screamed (clucked, etc.) that this was not what I wanted, that this was not the place my dreams agreed on, and yet I still continued searching for acceptance. Animals that could skate and humans who could not; everything was backward and unfair, but I wanted the chance to solo—and how could that be so far-fetched if Hollywood on Ice willingly gave the spotlight to a cow every night? When Old MacViktor's farm began to moo moo here and quack quack there and everywhere I went went there was a duck duck on skates skates, I relied on my fantasies of greatness to take me out of that place. The daydream went like this, and I lived it at least ten times a day:

"*Katarín, teléfono en la oficina, Gordita.*"

"*Gracias, Rosario.*" *¡Pendejo!*

I made my way to Lora's office and took the receiver. On the other end of the long-distance line was Tom Collins, the owner of Champions on Ice.

"Kathryn, we've been keeping tabs on your skating career. We had a secret agent planted in the Murray's bleachers and the Colgate audiences, and he's been tracking you for years now. Sorry to hear about the Ice Capades, those Disney bastards, Holiday, and now Hollywood. . . . Darling, what an ordeal! So listen, we've got an opening we need to fill ASAP. How soon can you get here?"

"I'm on the next plane, Tom."

"Fabulous, darling." Then I walked away from the trailer the way they do in the movies, not needing to retrieve anything from the past or tell anyone where I was headed. I looked completely normal strutting down the sidewalk in my opening-number outfit, my skates, and feather headdress (sometimes I threw in backup dancers and a big parade with a steel drum band). I got into the first cab I hailed, it whisked me off to the closest South American airport, and then all of a sudden—scene change—there I was, performing with Champions on Ice before a packed house full of friends, family, personal heroes, and extremely attractive single men devoid of commitment issues, all holding signs and clapping and crying tears of joy. I was teary myself, waving and trying not to trip over the flowers that people were thro—

"Moooooooooooooooooooooooooooooooo." Fantasy over. Delusion dissolved. No big deal, I rewound it and started again. This hallucination often came sandwiched between the one in which Bruce Springsteen calls me to be his backup drummer and the one where my mother makes hamburgers and milkshakes for dinner.

Elizabeta, Elizabeta, Elizabeta . . . in the back of my mind the fact that I felt competitive with skaters outside my own species was worrisome, but such thoughts were just about as irrepressible as the rest of my funhouse surroundings. The only thing I was able to control in this bizarre place of uncontrollability was my weight, and that became everything to me. Counting out bran flakes and rationing halved grapes was not any more bizarre than constantly watching a Russian stroke his imaginary boat or a flightless duck flap by on figure skates. I would not stop until my goal was finally acknowledged, until pride replaced the feeling of worthlessness that grew every time Hollywood called an unscheduled intermission because their honorary quadruped soloist took a crap in the middle of the rink, the heat of which left an indentation for the human, potty-trained skaters to contend with.

Yet the thought of quitting was barely a blip on my radar screen. If I could survive all those mornings at Murray's filled with bitter temperatures and bird droppings, then nearly everything else in the world was easy to endure. I could tough this out and reach my dreams, as persisting was the one true thing I knew best.

Strangely enough, I gave no credit to the idea that I had indeed achieved my goal. I was technically a professional skater and had been since receiving my first paycheck back in Switzerland with Holiday on Ice. But money was never the motive of the dream. I wanted only to continue skating at the highest level of my capabilities. My dream scored 6.0s for technical merit but could not rise above a 1.3 in the artistic impression, and the combined total was even more pathetic than my inability to calculate it. My body, however, began to understand just how low the score really was.

✲

Chapter Fifteen

Walking with the Plankton

I kept two journals on tour. The small, square, spiral-bound blue notebook with a globe on the front was inscribed with G-rated stories for my friends and family to read. My college rowing teammate, Tara, sent it to me along with a stale pancake wrapped in a plastic Baggie (she was concerned about my weight loss), which I ate piece by piece over the course of a week. Little vignettes and travel narratives were recorded in the blue book, humorous drivel complete with my best stick-figure artistry depicting foreign customs. Knowing that other people would read this travel log, my writing was relatively neat and punctuation was even considered. The other journal was a red flower-print lockless book with important-looking lined paper bound between the cloth covers. This one became something of a literary spleen, a dumping ground for all my self-imposed mental problems. Without the red diary, there would have been so much goo swimming around in my head that a new life form—some kind of psychoplankton—could have easily come to life and snacked on what little was left of my eating-disordered brain.

So the goo and plankton went into the red journal while the puns and parodies went into the blue as the two books contrasted each other like Laurel and Hardy, thick thoughts and skinny realities operating separately but seemingly sharing one brain. The blue book included passages such as "Great day to be in South America!" while the red one shared a same-day entry that began, "The ½ banana peel I ate for breakfast just isn't sitting right. Will try rest for lunch . . ." Pure goo. The red diary raised some questions that the dying athlete inside me was unable to answer. First and foremost, how does one suddenly wake up with the idea to peel a banana, throw out the innards, and then chow down on the wrapper? Though obviously disturbed and losing IQ points at an alarming rate, I was not a literal idiot about my behavior. I *knew* wrappers weren't technically edible, I *knew* peels didn't taste particularly good, and I even *knew* that chewing on cardboard, digesting plastic, and swallowing rinds was certifiably weird. But wrappers didn't have calories. Something about that felt comforting.

I didn't know how hard starving was going to be—not in terms of the actual fasting, but the slow passage of time and its wicked torment. I thought that anorexia happened overnight and to other people; one day Girl is healthy and happy and the next day Girl is a sixty-pounder in the hospital bed, whining about her enormous hips. That wasn't me, so I must be fine. Magazines and movies of the week never focused on the beginnings, just the dramatic outcomes of eating disorders. Moms spoon-feeding their daughters with weepy tears of love. Promises. Funerals. My anorexia seemed the opposite of all that, as if I had all the answers and none of the questions. Where did this come from, why had it begun, and who was gonna do what about it? All I ever remembered hearing about eating disorders was that experts said goal-oriented women tended to struggle with eating problems more than their less-focused contemporaries. Not fair. Why can't the lazy people be the at-risk group, have their own sort of slackerexia? They've got plenty of time to get sick and then figure out how to get better; they're not on a tight schedule to be the best, best, best. There is something dreadfully tragic about the notion that dreams of greatness can simultaneously harbor nightmares of physical inadequacy.

Although it is terribly heartbreaking to see someone consume a single kernel of corn in multiple bites, one cannot deny that anorexia is an odd and perplexing sight. Eating disorders are very funny. Not ha-ha funny. *Strange* funny. Sad funny. Well, maybe a little ha-ha. The plankton, with its dark and complicated sense of humor, makes smart people do weird, weird things that would border on humorous if death wasn't part of the punch line. *Chew the pea nice and sloooooow, ten little chomps, okay, swallow. Rest a few minutes. And again now . . . go get that baby carrot!*

Canned vegetable humor aside, the hunger was nothing compared to the loneliness. Even in my most obvious moments of moronic philosophy, I had a pretty strong feeling that this whole starvation mind trip didn't have all that much to do with actual food. There was something deeper going on, something at the root of all this famine, and I knew what it was. I was lonely in the worst way—for company, friendship, intimacy, and love—loneliness burrowing its hollow, hungry path from one to the next, the kind of lonely that spared no genre of emotion. I hungered for someone who could understand—or at least try to understand—everything happening to my body and brain. I craved nothing more than being understood by someone. Anyone. Myself, especially. But I didn't know how to fix that, so it made more sense to stack Wheat Thins into little towers, smash them with my fist, and eat only every eleventh shard. Didn't most people do that when they were lonely?

So my stomach rumbled for food, my body rumbled for acceptance, my heart rumbled for attention, and my mind rumbled for the energy to think of something other than Food and Weight, the two Neuron Police arresting any regular idea going through my head and throwing it into the slammer with the plankton, which made every normal thought its prison bitch.

Yet there was no one except myself I could rely on for nourishment, and no one who I wanted to risk letting inside my goo-filled mind. Captain Graceful was in constant battle with her newfound adversary, Darth Plankton, so I was on my own most of the time. Even my posture changed. As if to comfort my forlorn body and provide what little sense of company I could, I began standing with my arms wrapped one around my waist, holding the opposite shoulder, or sitting on my trailer chair with my legs drawn up in the fetal position, encircling myself with touch. I slept balled up like an animal in hiding, just trying to keep warm alone. The positions were not as strange as how often I crouched into their angles. Being upright, tall, proud—I had lost this confident poise, now replaced by the slouch of lonesomeness. There was no one around to tell me that my body looked better strong, healthy, or athletic, and for me to concentrate on such positive thoughts I needed energy I did not have.

As an athlete I knew that what I was doing to my body was wrong. Starvation did nothing but damage my muscles, mind, and soul. Not only was this deprivation physically unhealthy, it was sacrilege to the code of athleticism, whereby strength is greatness and weakness is avoided at all cost. Food is energy to every person, athlete or not, but for the athlete, food is the base layer of persistence, the energy required to persevere through the most harrowing physical demands. Athletes don't *skip* meals, they *add* them. Before races, regattas, and competitions I ate heartily and fatigue was never an issue when the gun went off or the music began. Pancakes before 5k runs, bagels before regattas, PowerBars before long programs — food was fuel. No true athlete goes into a performance with only half a tank, and definitely not with an empty one.

In the moments spent off the ice and away from the trailer, I occupied myself with wasting away and how to do it best. Trying to keep the mind-set of an athlete in the body of a waif was proving a challenge, one that needed a goal of its own, a false verification that what I was doing to myself was okay, natural, and normal . . . something that justified my daily intake of canned vegetables and eight-mile walks to far-off Diet Coke machines on the opposite side of whatever city we were in.

As the days passed, there was no shred of evidence that Hollywood on Ice would let me skate a solo, especially since the arrival of Viktor and Elizabeta. My once strong and solid dream was now nothing more than a festering hunger, but still I could not let go. So I added on instead. Just in case there would be no skating, there had to be something else I could do with my skinny body — a second goal, a backup plan to this universe of backward skating.

Mail was rare, but correspondence came now and then from my rowing teammates back in the States. I read their letters and looked at the photos on my mirror, thinking how food and friendships had been strong and plentiful before this tour. *Come back soon, row with us,* a few letters concluded and, without meaning to do so, began to give life to Plan B. After the tour ended, I could row as a *lightweight,* not just recreationally but as a serious endeavor! My body was light enough, far beneath the 125-pound requirement for international racing, and height was on my side, a rare combination for a five-nine rower. That was it, that was the backup goal! No solo? Then row-o! But this ideal was not symbolic of a new beginning, nor a re-dream of athletic greatness . . . it was a goal formed on the basis of staying thin, a plan to keep my body within the planktonic boundaries set by Hollywood on Ice. All I had to do was switch the setting from the trailer to the boathouse.

The new plan expanded a little more each day, gaining momentum each time I passed by a skating chicken or refastened the feather boas to the hook above my tailbone in the opening-number bodysuit. Rowing spandex was slightly more practical attire, and any ducks we passed on rivers were naturally bladeless. With the times I had once pulled as a heavyweight, my erg scores would be incredibly fast as a lightweight, I thought to myself. There was even a possibility of making the national team. I knew those results, I could make the top ten for sure. No sweat. Just stay thin, that was all I needed to do. Never once did it dawn on me that the muscle with which I had pulled those times was lost, long gone in stale bread crusts and empty cans of peas. But, hell, good news! I wasn't anorexic anymore—I had *goals,* justifications for my rapidly decreasing body weight. Doing sit-ups beneath the makeup counter and tricep dips along the bench of drawers beneath the costumes, I believed I was helping my body stay strong, while my body cursed me for forcing it to burn calories it could not spare. Staying thin was the misleading answer to the question still running through my mind, *How do I get to greatness?*

Henry David Thoreau's essay "Walking," which I brought with me on tour, taught me that the camel is supposedly the only animal that ruminates while walking. Yes, well, camels and anorexics. Camels, though, probably reflect on more meaningful topics than self-starvation. Although it is a safe bet that Thoreau did not suffer from an eating disorder, he describes his desire to walk with a passion any anorexia sufferer can relate to: "I think that I cannot preserve my health and spirits unless I spend four hours a day at least—and it is commonly more than that—sauntering through the woods and over the hills and fields, absolutely free from all worldly engagements."

I never saw the hills and valleys or the woods and fields on my long walks through the city streets of Argentina. Nor did I see very obvious buildings and pedestrians, the hustle and bustle of city life. I saw only the visions in my head and the mental pictures of paranoia that accompany such persistent obsessions of weight loss; I saw miles of roads that needed to be walked or run, I saw my body shrinking smaller and smaller through the journey. My "sauntering" began with a goal, often in the form of a diet soda or a small bunch of grapes that I set out to purchase from a store five or six miles away. Walking was a justification, a calorie burner, an allowance, a forgiveness, a confusion so manipulative that it made perfect sense. Walking granted permission to eat and the false sense that I was indeed "free from all worldly engagements," when in reality I was a prisoner in my self-created world.

Argentina is a nation famous for its beef, legendary for having the most incredible steaks in the world. I was never much of a red-meat fanatic before the tour, so the temptation of steak did little for my appetite. Eating disorders, however, sometimes create cravings beyond comprehension. While I was subsisting on pale-colored canned vegetables that were more anemic than I was, one day the idea of meat slammed into my unwilling brain with such force that an absurd bargain was eventually reached. I limited my already ridiculously low calorie count for three weeks and in doing so permitted myself to try a steak at the end of the twenty-one days before immediately returning to the canned nastiness I clung to as safety food. For three weeks I ate almost nothing and burned that off by walking the streets in search of the perfect restaurant where I could enjoy my forbidden meat. I paced all of Mar del Plata, hunting for some place small and inconspicuous, a place where guilt might have a hard time tracking me down for an hour or so while I picked at my impermissible food. Eventually I settled on a small parrilla six or seven blocks south of the city center, hidden on a quiet tree-lined street that housed old apartment buildings and fruit vendors and amiable pedestrians. Argentinean parrillas often have spectacularly vulgar yet deliciously artistic window displays of the meat they cook. Large fire pits glow from the window, and the beef sails around a vertical, rotating spit, where it is not cut up into slabs but is still attached to the skeletal system of the animal. Each carcass is sliced down the middle, pried open like a book, legs outstretched, body beheaded, and fitted onto the grill so that each slab of meat looks as if the animal was doing "the wave" at its time of execution. Disgusting, yet strangely inviting.

I walked by this restaurant five times in three weeks, checking up on its menu, choosing a table from the window I peeked in, looking to see if they served bread with the meal and how I might deal with such an obstacle. The bargain was for steak. Bread would throw everything off. Walking would keep it all in line.

Three weeks passed in the painful time warp of hunger, and the morning of the steak adventure was spent in eagerness and fear as I set out from the hotel, six miles away. I don't remember much about the beginning of the walk, as my mind was too weak to ruminate on anything but the greatness of steak. Along the coast of Mar del Plata, on the city sidewalks that snaked in from the beachfront boardwalks to the hotels and financial district, my body knew exactly where it was headed and which path took me to the restaurant fastest. Everything felt good that morning, the sun was bright, the air was warm, and the hunger subsided in anticipation.

The two-mile stretch of walkway along the beachfront was coned off and closed to traffic, and I thought it was nothing more than routine construction work until a pack of cyclists rode by, wearing bathing suits, water cascading off their bodies, legs churning with the speed of competition. There had been posters lining shopwindows for weeks, advertising an annual triathlon event. It was Sunday, and the advertised race was now in progress, the athletic competition directly corresponding with my starvation plans. We had been weighed that Saturday in a "sneak attack" by Lora, which happened from time to time, so my usual feeding day came a day early and matched up perfectly with the multisport race that Sunday morning.

As I slowed my own pace to watch the triathletes careening by, an impulse to be out there with them flickered through my body but then died out when I mulled over how much food they probably ate to sustain such energy. The thought was unendurable. I could not fathom eating enough food to provide that kind of power. Eating as an athlete was a thing of the past, a feat way too difficult to consider ever doing again. The guilt of consumption and the threat of weight gain was too powerful. Yet for a moment I imagined myself among the triathletes, how it must feel to emerge from the ocean, fly through the streets on a bicycle, and then run past all physical expectations . . . absolutely free from all worldly engagements. Swimming, biking, running—that would have been the easy part of the race. Eating was the tough event, the one discipline I'd never be able to master.

A block from the restaurant, there came a small elderly-sounding scream that did not fit with the peaceful surroundings of the day. I looked to see an old woman standing in the middle of the calm street, hurriedly laying down a blanket. She was chattering something, but I was too far away to hear anything but the sad, moaning inflection of her words. It was then I noticed that the thin quilt in the street had a shape beneath it. A small breeze picked up an edge of the bedcover to reveal an unmoving shoulder. A man approached the woman, and the two of them pointed up to an open window, three stories above. I went into the restaurant and sat at a table facing the window and prepared to order my food while death took care of its business on the other side of the pane.

A police car arrived first and then an ambulance, the sirens silent but the lights rotating with their red-and-blue half-moons of soundless emergency. May I have a *bistec lomo, por favor?* It took about forty-five minutes to clear the suicide from the quiet street, where a small handful of onlookers gathered. Bread? Yes, please. The crowd pointed from the window to the body and shook their heads in sadness. Would there be potatoes? I forgot to ask. I sat there, eating my steak through the entire scene of the suicide aftermath, feeling nothing of the meat's texture and tasting little of its flavor as I rushed each guilty bite into my mouth as if it were a task that needed completion. While I watched the body being loaded onto the gurney, a lifeless arm slipped to dangle from the edge, my first true sighting of death. There *were* potatoes, giant wedge-cut french fries. I moved them into my napkin, squishing them all into a huge wad of carbohydrate glop that I could not bear to look at. The ambulance slowly pulled away and the people dispersed. The old woman took her blanket from the street, folded it hand over hand, and shook her head as the police asked her what I assumed to be unanswerable questions. Could I please have a Diet Coke? *Gracias.* I wanted another steak, the first one had disappeared so quickly, I wasn't even sure I remembered eating it. No, nothing else, just the check.

I went across the street and looked at the ground where the body had been. There was no blood, no mark of impact, no sign that life or death had ever visited the little street across from my steak restaurant. I still had the ball of french-fried napkin in my purse, too ashamed to put it on the plate or leave it on the table. It was a greasy lump of paper and potato and I craved all of it, putting the thing to my lips as if to take a bite, just one bite, then fighting back tears as I threw it away. Threw it all away.

✦

Chapter Sixteen

Dinosaurs and Aneurysms
on the Drive to Nigeria

As the days passed in the trailer, undifferentiated and eternal, the show became routine and memory took over all the details that had once felt so overwhelming to understand. Certain cues in the music now automatically triggered arm positions and ignited footwork sequences that no longer required me to pay attention; everything coasted on the autopilot of rehearsed repetition. The latter half of the show was entirely devoted to the Flintstones theme and there were only two costume changes, so the pace slowed down significantly from the first hour. A few numbers within the Flintstones act weren't too bad, as the rock 'n' roll music we skated to provided an upbeat tempo that helped chase away the piddly circus music Viktor's skating farm had previously waddled to.

In Spanish, Flintstones on Ice is *Los picapiedros sobre hielo*. In the trailer, it translated to How Drunk Is Dino Tonight *Sobre Hielo*. Leosha, also referred to as Crackhead by most of the English-speaking skaters, played the part of Dino until he was fired for repeatedly oversleeping with prostitutes. In need of a quick replacement for Fred Flintstone's much-loved attention-deficit dinosaur-dog, Lora crowned her fifteen-year-old son, Miguel, as Leosha's makeshift successor. The Dino suit was an enormous outfit of neon violet foam material painted with black splotches that enveloped all humanness and required, like the rest of

Hollywood on Ice, very little skating. Dino had two scenes. One involved adoringly tackling his master at center ice, and the other required Dino to catch the end of a pinwheel formation, in which the skaters stood side by side, hooked arms, and glided around in a momentum-gaining circle. The dinosaur was to latch on and enjoy a free ride for a few seconds. After that, Dino was supposed to let go of the windmilling skaters and fake a big collision with the tent post at the end of the rink. Not a difficult task, if one is willing to perform the role. Miguel was not.

When the number was done right, the children in the audience screamed with hysterical delight at the antics of the goofy, klutzy, purple half-breed. Yet in How Drunk Is Dino Tonight *Sobre Hielo,* there was no telling just what the half-baked dinosaur would do. Miguel was in his teenage rebellion stage and found an outlet for his angst by piloting Dino through a post-*cerveza* haze of staggered movements. Instead of grabbing on to the end of the pinwheel, Dino often headed out to center ice to dance lewdly. Sometimes a skater would improvise and pat Dino on the head, a playful affection that he returned by grabbing a pawful of the skater's behind.

The naughty dinosaur also enjoyed random belly dives and triple axel attempts, the former often a result of the latter, as Miguel was not technically a figure skater. As for his calculated crash with the end of the rink, well, sometimes he missed the tent pole altogether and fell halfway into the audience. Other times the collision looked anything but deliberate as Dino hit the pole so hard, the whole stage wobbled and the dinosaur's recovery time did not match up with the musical cues. The dino-dog sat there on the ice, unmoving, as the background soundtrack of puppy barks, hurried paws, and Fred's lovingly ferocious yell of "Dino, get back here!" continued on, leaving Fred to chase an imaginary dog while the real one sobered up from his self-inflicted impact. Keeping the mandatory professional skater smile was always a little easier during the second half of the show.

Dressed in suede, prehistoric belly-and-bottom-revealing bikinis, the showgirls and skater-dancers bebopped between the Fred and Wilma antics to a medley of oldies such as "Rock Around the Clock," "Angel Eyes," and then the randomly selected "Travelin' Band" by Creedence Clearwater Revival, one of Argentina's "current" favorite American groups that brought the audience to a craze of syncopated clapping. When we were on the ice, Felicia and I engaged in an ongoing competition to see who could make the other break character and stray from the statuesque attentiveness we were required to exude at all times. Felicia had little of the restraint needed for keeping a straight showgirl face. All I had to do was look at her and she would begin laughing. If silly glances didn't get us to crack, then the wigs of the male skaters did. The boys for this number wore disheveled-looking punk wigs in addition to their caveman loincloths, and the weak elastic chinstrap that held their hairpieces in place didn't do such a good job. The wigs flew to the ice, slid over their eyes, hung down the back of their neck, or relocated to goatee position. With laughter on my personal list of endangered emotions, these few minutes of cavegirl prancing were my high point of the show.

Even Captain Graceful enjoyed the final dance pose that "Travelin' Band" called for: legs planted shoulder-width apart, arms outstretched over head, head thrown back—the body poised victory-style, as if I had just set some sort of showgirl world record. The finger-waving "jazz hands" took away a bit of the stoic nature of the stance. That part I would have replaced with fist pumps. But in that moment of physical extension, the show, lights, makeup, audience, and inebriated dinosaurs all vanished for a fraction of a second and I went someplace else in my mind, somewhere victorious but unfamiliar, where I might use that pose appropriately. I thought of the triathletes I saw racing through the streets of Mar del Plata, and wondered if they raised their fists in proud accomplishment at the end of their grueling races.

While we were on the ice everything moved so quickly and looked so bright 'n' shiny that there was no need to be serious or sad, no need to acknowledge any problems that lay waiting backstage, outside the circus tent, or away from the trailer. For some people, life beyond the confines of Hollywood was an abyss of forgotten territory.

Lenny never really stepped off the ice and away from the mentality of the tour. At thirty-five, he was one of the oldest skaters with Hollywood on Ice. Having signed on shortly after his eighteenth birthday, he had not left the trailer since. His citizenship was Canadian but he had not been back to his homeland in years, and it was quite possible that half the reason he stayed with Hollywood was that he could not remember where Canada was. Len was not the sharpest spoon in the drawer and often bragged that the last time he had read a newspaper was in the mid-eighties. Because the ice show altered everyone's sense of time and place, it was not uncommon for skaters to ask one another what day it was or even what month, but only Lenny asked the year every few weeks or so.

Lenny had an ever joking, lighthearted manner that in small doses no one could dislike. His stage presence and confidence on the ice were enough to mask the fact that his abilities were slipping as fast as his waistline. Len was a big boy, maybe six feet tall and nearly two hundred pounds, and the ongoing years of partying his way through tour life had physically caught up with him. The shoulder-length blond feathered hair reminiscent of glam rockers framed his widening face and doubling chin, and all his skating outfits snugly announced bulges Len enjoyed making sexual references to. *I gotta cut back on the steaks but, man, does this spandex make my package look good!* While he waited for his dates to meet him at the hotel after the show, Lenny told us stories about his girl-friend back in Colombia who made G-strings for a living and how he would marry her someday after he decided he had had enough of the tour. After three months, the tour was getting to be enough for me, and the thought that Lenny had spent half his life with the show was both in-triguing and repulsive.

Since he never appeared anything but ignorant and jovial, it was unusual to see Len with a worried look on his face one day as we sat in the trailer, waiting our turn at the scale. He was talking to Pam when I overheard him say that his mother just had a brain aneurysm but was still alive in a hospital back home. Unsure of what to do, he asked Pam if he should catch the next flight to Canada.

"Yes," I found myself interrupting, the impulse taking me by sur-prise. "You probably should." Normally I stayed out of people's private lives, especially those of my fellow trailermates, but this was a subject I knew well. Aneurysms that left people on this side of consciousness were rare indeed. If ever there was a time to take a break from Hollywood on Ice, this was Lenny's moment to brave the outside world and cross the abyss of trailerless reality.

"Why?" Lenny asked. "This aneurysm thing serious or something?"

"Yeah. Sorta."

An aneurysm had found its way into my family years before the epic tour began and lingered long afterward as a constant reminder to me of the brevity of life, the resilience of the mind, the strength of the body, and the realization that deferring a dream is a tragedy far greater than any physical ailment.

They stretched from behind her right ear clear across to the center of her forehead, to the point where the hairline frames the face. The doctors called them staples, and that's exactly what they were, twenty-five metal slivers holding life and gray matter in place within their miniature grasp. The staples marching across her scalp looked strong and invincible, nothing like the flimsy strands of opposable steel that bound sheets of loose leaf to one another. Shifting my gaze elsewhere was of no use, the image of the train-track scar traversing her head was permanently ingrained and gripping me so tightly that my heart began to pound faster and faster and a chill sprinted through my body, as if trying to cool down my racing pulse.

Her mouth was open, her slack-jawed chin drooping slightly. Her tongue rested on her bottom teeth, the way an infant sleeps. Her chest rose and fell, rose and fell . . . at its own lethargic pace. Each breath nudged the rubber tube that circled her neck and ran up her nostrils. Little clouds of breath whitened the tube with each halfhearted, almost lifeless exhale. My eyes, magnetized to her forehead, could not let go of that horribly inhuman scar. Was survival even a possibility? The hair that once grew in that space was now shaved or matted to her scalp—no longer the vibrant blond she used to spend so long fussing with each morning.

A small slit gave way between her pale, gray eyelids. She put all her effort into this action, even her fingers began to bend with determination. Her head tilted gently, swaying slowly as her eyes began to open. A thousand questions ran through my mind, crowding out any room for emotions. Could she see me? Could she hear me? Would she remember? Would she remember *me?* "Mom?" I whispered.

An aneurysm is a blood clot that forms in veins or arteries in the brain or heart. Neither genetic nor hereditary in any way and with no

physical hints to their existence, aneurysms lie dormant of their own unfair accord, hibernating like neurological grizzly bears awaiting an unknown springtime. And like various species of bears, there are different
breeds of aneurysms. Three to be exact: two specific to the heart and one
to the brain, each as fatal as another. The saccular aneurysm grows in the
heart, forming on the middle of the aorta's three layers. As it develops,
only one side of the aorta will swell up until it resembles a hunchback
cowering beneath the burden of his bulging lump. This was not my
mother's aneurysm. Neither was the one known as fusiform, which
weakens the artery all the way around like the body of a snake that has
recently eaten a hearty mouse.

What grew inside my mother's brain is called a berry aneurysm.
Apparently named for its clustered appearance, a berry aneurysm grows
only on the point where a larger vein branches into separate, skinnier
paths. Caused by an unknown congenital defect, the festering growth
sits there quietly, sometimes alone, sometimes in a small bunch, waiting
until it decides it is ripe. Then the berry aneurysm harvests itself, spilling
its messy juice all over the place, drowning the nearby tissue in blood,
depriving the brain of the oxygen it needs and bringing about outcomes
like death or staples.

An aneurysm, as the doctors told my father, is like a land mine or a
time bomb, ticking away hidden under a shadow of human biology. Only
a CT scan can detect the location of such a clot, but it is rare that the average healthy person decides to have one performed for no apparent reason. Why search for something you do not want to find? Most aneurysm
eruptions are labeled as freak biological accidents, as they claim lives
without warning, but actually they have been there all along, just waiting
in the wings of consciousness. My mother's aneurysm perched itself on
one of the veins near the top of her skull just off her hairline. On May 1,
1994, it decided to explode, bursting the vein that it grew upon, embed-
ding its unexpected shrapnel into the soul of my family and into my
mind.

I arrived at the hospital two and a half days after the "incident," as
my father's reassuring tone had convinced me to stay at Colgate and finish my freshman year final exams. Like Lenny, I did not fully understand
what an aneurysm meant, just that it must not be all that bad since she

was still alive. Besides, I had seen her three days before. She had been fine on Sunday.

Only a few days before the cerebral explosion, my parents decided to drive up to West Point to watch my team race in the Patriot League rowing championship. My mother's hair was perfectly in place despite the wind, and in a sea of spandex-clad rowers, my mother stood out in a Donna Karan outfit that screamed loudly for attention. The sweater was a combination of orange, brown, pink, and red wool all forced together in a plaid pattern of hideous sophistication. Somewhere on the inside tag the initials DKNY justified its visual candor. There was no tag on the inside of my gray grease-stained sweatshirt.

The skyline along the Hudson was cloudy and gray, but she still wore her bulky, tortoiseshell sunglasses that were much too big for her narrow face. The lenses were the size of Lender's bagels and although I have shared this comparison with her many times, she assures me that these jumbo glasses are still very much in style, just as they had been in the days of Jackie O. I inherited her light-sensitive eyes. My glasses were small and narrow.

"Hands on, ready to lift, and LIFT!" our coxswain said, commanding us to pick up the four-man boat. We lifted the hull to our shoulders and carried it down toward the docks. After we returned to the dock with silver medals, my parents left. I hugged my father good-bye and put my arms around my mother and released a flutter of superficial little pats, as if drying my hands on the back of her beach-towelish sweater. They hurried off to watch the New Jersey Devils play hockey that night.

Oddly enough, my mother is a die-hard Devils fan, a taste she acquired in the late eighties when she decorated the house of the team's owner. Although it does not appear to go with her exterior character, ruffled chintz and hat tricks are two of her favorite things, while a close runner-up was picking out young, eligible Devils and seeing if the owner's wife, Mrs. McMullen, might arrange an introduction for me at the next game. During my later teenage years, I met a plethora of mostly Russian, toothless Devils as the injured or bench-riding players stopped by the McMullens' box and my mother dragged me over for their approval. Not the most comfortable of situations. "My daughter is a *figure skater,*" she'd say slowly and loudly, raising her voice to the level that she believed transcended the international borders of language. The given Devil would usually smile or nod as I prayed that a goal might be scored and attention diverted from the matchmaking ceremony back to the hockey game.

Late in the night my mother woke up my father.

"Peter, I have a headache."

My father suggested aspirin, but my mother told him that she had already taken so many throughout the day. A few minutes later she was semiconscious, barely able to sigh, "Peter, call an ambulance." Then she collapsed. The hibernating bear in her brain was awake, provoked by time and agitated by aspirin.

For eight hours, five doctors operated on my mother's brain. Eight hours for one little berry. The veins were dangerously thin from the numerous aspirin she had taken, and her chances for surviving the aneurysm were already less than 10 percent. With the condition of her veins, those chances were cut in half . . . 5 percent, life. Ninety-five percent, death.

The steel folding hospital chair squeaked as I shifted my weight from thigh to thigh, the same noise the trailer chairs would make beneath my body five years down the unseen road. I was glad that the chair did not squeak when I shifted my eyes. White . . . clear, clear, clear. White . . . clear, clear, clear. White . . . clear, clear, clear. Tubes slithered all over my mother's face, changing color with her breathing pattern, the forehead scar still unbearable to look at.

"Mom?" I whispered again, not sure which would scare me more, the answer or the silence. Oblivious to my presence, her eyeballs thumped against the inside of their vein-mapped lids. Nothing else stirred. To escape looking at the labyrinth of tubes running all around her head and face and the Frankenstein scar, I lowered my eyes to her limp hands. Her fingers were naked and I wondered where all the rings were. My mother's fingers are always encircled by bands of sparkling stones. She likes to wear ring upon ring, little skyscrapers of gems towering toward her knuckles.

I looked at my hands. There were two small gold bands. One was my high school class ring, in which an unassuming jeweler spelled both of my names wrong. KATHRIN BERTIG, the immortal inscription reads. My mother is appalled by this atrocity. I think it is funny. On my right hand, another ring sat quietly at the base of my index finger, plain and slight and not even a fraction of the shimmer and shine in which Hollywood on Ice would dress me. I closed my eyes, as memories came and went without being invited to do so.

I am standing in the middle of the shop. Everything is very shiny.

"Don't touch, your hands are filthy!" my mother says. "Just *look*."

Craning my neck, I stare into the displays. I peer into each case, at the rings and bracelets and earrings formed into a wealthy arrangement. *Boring,* I think to myself. I wonder how long I'll be held captive in this place. This is my mother's favorite store. I have been here many times, a hostage of her shopping sprees. But today is my tenth birthday, and I am supposed to pick out something "nice and pretty." My mother believes that jewelry will be the antidote for my terminal case of chronic tomboyitis. I look into case after shiny case, wondering where they keep all the silver trinkets. I am ten, and I like the way silver shines.

"*Gold,*" my mother says. "Pick out something *gold.*" I trudge around to the back of the store. The old lady behind the counter monitors my actions carefully. She is afraid that I will suddenly lose all bodily control and crash through all her precious glass towers. She cannot hide this paranoia from me. I can read it in her wrinkly face and jittery hands as she fiddles with some keys behind her back.

I am tempted, so tempted, to knock something over just to see if I can get away with it. But I don't. I know better. Instead, I pick up my pace and strut around the store just a little too fast, as the display cases become my slalom course.

"Katie, did you find something yet?" My mother asks, not looking up. She is putting more rings on her already jeweled fingers. She takes them off and asks to see others. She calls the store lady by her first name. I know the names of all semi- and fully precious gems. I know the types of settings that these rocks rest in, and how to distinguish the cheapest stones

from the most expensive treasures. I know rubies from garnets, and tour-
maline from the quartz that tries to pass for it. I can tell diamonds from
cubic zirconia, or impostors, as my mother says. I do not know how I
know all of this stuff. I do not like rings; they hurt my fingers when base-
balls land in my glove, the steely prongs stabbing into my tiny hands. I love
bracelets but they do not sell the macramé ones here. It doesn't matter, because I can make my own. I want to get my ears pierced because the boys
I skateboard with think it's cool to have holes in your ears.

"Yeah, okay . . . found something. It's over here," I call back toward my mother. She comes over to inspect the ring I've selected. A gold
band no thicker than a dime sits toward the back of the display case, a
sparkly runt among all the other jewels. The top of the ring is slightly
square, and a tiny purple stone, one-third the size of an ice-cream sprin-
kle, is resting on one squarish corner. That's it.

"Dear, that's so . . . plain," my mother begins. "Wouldn't you
like—"

"No," I state firmly. "I like this. Can we go?"

"Well, if that is what you really want."

I don't, but I say that I do and she is happy. I wear the ring under
my glove and smile wickedly at the weary saleslady.

"See you next week, Lynn," my mother says. "Call me if the cabo-
chon ruby can be downsized." Lynn agrees. We leave, twice. Something
in the window drags my mother back in, but it's only peridot and not
emerald, so we leave again.

Time loses itself in the hospital. My mother's body was enough to
trigger flashbacks over which I had little control. Like a lightning storm
they struck quickly, powerfully, and I was the metal pole in a barren field
through which these bolts of remembrance channeled, then left me alone
to understand their meaning. The memories were strong and detailed,
but far from tender and personal, and I had no tears to cry except for the
tears that came from this very realization. I was sad that I was not sad.
We simply were not close, but maybe this thing that exploded in her
brain could fix that. It was too soon to tell. Shopping and skating competitions and car trips to the Adirondacks flooded back to me, but
nowhere could I see my mother and me conversing softly, snuggling on

the sofa watching TV, hanging out making pancakes, or going for a hike together. That was Dad.

Wait . . . Fridays, we used to go out to lunch on Fridays, to Scarborough Fair, just down the street from my school. She ordered ladyfingers, six skinny snippets of a cut-up sandwich, and iced coffee. Sometimes she let me pour in the milk and watch it swirl into liquid clouds storming through the dark, dark coffee. Usually she poured. Then she nibbled on a few of the crustless sandwich strips before going out to smoke while I finished my lunch and wandered around the gift shop. I forgot about Fridays. I could be sad about that. I could be sad about Fridays and I could be sad about death.

Looking at the clock, I kept count of the little dots and dashes that move us from day to day and wondered how it was that such small movements were responsible for creating our existence. Sitting next to my mother, I could feel death. I could hear her breathe a collection of sickly breaths: gurgling inhales, short gasps, jaw twitches, and the long-awaited exhales that were far too weak to promise repetition.

Away from the hospital, there was only one other place to think of spending time, a place that could erase all visions of surgery scars, whirring machines, whitening tubes, and other reminders of a life in the balance. A place where time was measured by physical movements instead of linear minutes, and the airborne crest of a jump let me literally leave the world behind, even if only for a moment.

Slipping my feet into their skates, my pinky fingers hooked into the slack nylon laces, pulling the strings that snapped tight at my command, zigzagging the remaining string around the ankle hooks, bow-tying and double-knotting the final surplus. By the time the second skate was laced, I noticed the blood in the crease of my pinkies and the throb in my too-tight skates and started all over again, asking Captain Graceful to think about something other than death while relacing. As I stepped onto the ice, the rest of the world melted away, time dissolving dots and dashes and pulsating berries. I understood this clock. There were no hospitals, no brain dysfunctions, no dying mothers . . . only a clean, clear sheet of ice where I was free to inscribe my thoughts with an indelible blade. I had a story to carve, a masterpiece to complete, with a due date fast approaching. My senior free-skating test — the big kahuna of the ranking system, the black belt pinnacle of amateur figure skating — was scheduled for the following week at a rink in northern Westchester County.

The other girls and I circled one another in our patterns of practice, orbiting one another like a solar system in private harmony, understanding the erratic movements and spatial relations that guide skaters around collision. In a symphony of athleticism, I conducted my movements differently from the other skaters on the session. As they skated to the music that poured from the loudspeakers overhead, I moved my body to the soft speakings in my head. Nothing — jumps, spins — seemed as difficult as it did a few days before. I would pass this test. There would be no nerves of doubt. Perspective had paid me a visit in the hospital. Death drops and double axels were easy, aneurysms were hard. I would bring the aneurysm with me to the rink, and kick its ass. A new focus was born, as though what had burst from my mother's brain brought a better outlook on everything, some sort of life explosion in the midst of impending death.

Other than the panel of judges, there was no one I knew at the rink in Katonah, New York, to watch my senior free-skate test. Usually, passing the test brings parties and gifts and suffocating hugs from all those who have witnessed the skater's lengthy personal evolution from waltz jumps to double axels, pigtails to buns, inelegance to grace. Failing the senior rank brings sympathetic pats on the back and heartfelt reassurances of "next time" with bitter comments about the judges' mental stability lovingly whispered to the downcast skater. With one parent in a hospital bed, the other by her side, a brother too much in the thrall of his own brain, a coach away on her family vacation, and the contingent of Murray's skaters disbanded for the summer, I drove myself to the unfamiliar rink and took the ice alone, thriving on the independence of the moment and calmed by the fresh realization of what a human body can endure.

The only thing there with me on the ice was my mother's aneurysm, and we battled head-to-head for four minutes — sequins versus death duking it out to a background melody of Broadway show tunes — until the music stopped, the judges deliberated, and all three test sheets came back with a penciled circle around the word *pass*. Cold buildings with icy floors — strange are the places where life flourishes and grows in unexpected plenty.

*   *   *

"Kathryn?"

"Yes . . . Mom, I'm here." A week after the aneurysm, the eyes of the woman in the hospital cot had become partially open slits. My mother named me Kathryn—I love the name, with its two powerful syllables and seven pretty letters—but I have never heard her call me it before. She tried to focus on me and then shut her eyes, the effort too intense.

"How was swimming today?" she asked.

"It was good," I lied, slightly startled by both her question and my answer. I was not a swimmer, but my mother had been a long time ago. Her mother was a diver; her daughter is a figure skater. Three generations of women excelling in different sports, each necessitating the use of water. That day, I decided to be a swimmer. She fell asleep for another few days.

On the hospital window ledge, there was a picture of me. The doctors said it would be a good idea to bring familiar items from home that might spark her memory as well as trigger a positive healing process, even though we all knew that survival was the current objective.

In the photo, I am skating. It is my mother's favorite picture of me, and I have never understood why but can assume that it is partly because she took the snapshot. I am in the middle of a layback spin during one of Murray's seasonal shows, and her camera has immortalized my body in a most contorted position. In a violet outfit, my torso is arched backward and my head dangles from my neck, down toward my lower back as if I have just passed under a not-too-low limbo bar. The photo is not a profile shot but a head-on view, and because my neck is bent backward, I appear to be a headless body. I am thirteen in the picture, and the only clue to my age is that the purple spandex hugs my upper torso the same way in the front as it does in the back. This is my mother's favorite picture, and you cannot see my face. Just sequins, spandex, legs, chest.

"Here," my mother says, "this one. You look just like this one." She holds the fashion magazine open and points with three sharp finger wags to the woman on the bed, draped in luxurious jewels and leather handbags. I don't bother to read the ad but recognize the interlocking symbol of Gucci at the bottom of the page. I am fifteenish. Last week she found me wearing Prada in *Vanity Fair,* next month she'll discover me in

Vogue, sporting the pearls of Mikimoto or portraying the flowy essence of Versace. I am no fashion model. These pictures are of women my mother wishes me to resemble.

"Uh-huh," I say.

The woman lounging in the magazine has long, straight brown hair and dark eyes. They all do, though occasionally my mother points out a feature that some blonde or redhead and I share in common. Lips, nose, eyes, ears; I have been shown parts of myself in the faces of others since I was a child. Legs, bottom, breasts, and shoulders, my body repeatedly subjected to comparison with the airbrushed figures on glossy pages. I think I look like me, but my mother enjoys finding my twins in the world of glamour magazines, searching for hints of what I might become.

Returning home from school, I would find dog-eared newspapers and women's magazines laid out on the table, some poor model — or worse, a single feature of her body — circled with pen and a *looks just like you!* scribbled beneath in my mother's perfect cursive. I interpreted these women not as a compliment but as a goal to be reached, a standard of beauty I needed to achieve to be seen as attractive or worthy. She never found my look-alikes in McDonald's advertisements or Vagisil commercials, only the finest and most sophisticated products featured the images my mother mistook for her daughter.

The height of the magazine comparisons came during my teenage years, when my slow metamorphosis to womanhood was a confusing time marked by the awkwardness of befuddling growth spurts and mysterious undergarments. I had lanky limbs and a face I was only beginning to grow into. I was indeed a model, a walking billboard for puberty.

Peter dealt with cloning issues as well, finding Polo and Armani models, or my mother's perennial favorite — JFK Jr. cut from the socialite pages of *Vogue* — on display in his bedroom with the same, circled inscriptions of awe at the resemblance. *Pete, it's YOU!* He would laugh and toss his twins into the garbage, but it was years before I was able to bid good riddance to these strange women who stared out at me from their perches of grandeur, glamour, and physical haughtiness.

After my mother had been in the ICU a month, the staples were removed, a shunt was permanently inserted into her brain to drain any residual berry goo, and she returned to life without a physical trace of brain trauma and with a new head of hair beginning its quest to hide the past. Only my family sees the post-aneurysm difference, small instances of strangeness surfacing now and again that are harder for outsiders to catch. She treats the matter of a lost sock with the same level of intensity that one might reserve for a burning house filled with children, and the threat of biological warfare and running out of milk are of equal concern. But mostly my mother has stayed the same, which is not always for the best. Between her pack-a-day smoking habit and minimal physical activity, her second shot at life remains an unacknowledged gift.

The aneurysm became a taboo topic in my family. The word creates an uncomfortable atmosphere, much like publicly saying words like *rape* or *suicide,* acceptable and correct when used in an appropriate manner but still fostering an unease that we mask well with feigned maturity. For me, *aneurysm* is one of those disquieting words that, much like *professional skating,* sends shivers down my spine.

My mother does not remember much of the incident or of her time in the hospital. My father does not want to remember it. It was too much stress for him then, and I know that it still is at times. He keeps it inside. My mother likes to discuss her aneurysm in medical terms, just the way the doctors explained it to her.

"Aneurysms, yes, I survived one of those . . . not many people do, you know. It kept me out for some time. It's interesting, really, an aneurysm is a tiny blood clot inside . . ."

She never saw the ordeal from the outside. The vicious aneurysm exploded inside her, but she did not have to clean it up. My father and I did that, by sweeping it under the Great Carpet, where things like brain dysfunction, manic depression, and eating disorders all ended up. *Welcome to Bronxville: Home of the Psychotic Dust Bunnies.* Even years later, I still want to pull out the gritty aneurysm and ask the family to wallow in its dust for a while, dirtying our consciences in the purity of truth. I want to ask my mother what it felt like to face a 95 percent chance of death and what it is like to be given a second shot at life. I wonder if her wrist still hurts from punching the Grim Reaper in the face and which one of them bears the bruise of the impact. Instead, I turn my questions into personal interrogations and feast on the answers: how high can I jump, how fast can I run, how strong can I pull, how far till the finish?

Although my mother was the one to live through the physical aneurysm, my soul grew its own metaphorical one, a phantom presence regulating my days with an urgency to be alive, giving me life instead of claiming it from me, giving Captain Graceful a new understanding of the importance of ice rinks and rivers, starting blocks and finish lines.

Nearly ten years later, my symbolic aneurysm wraps itself around my mind, squeezing gently, reminding me that I am very much alive. I cherish its presence as it moves the blood rhythmically through my body, each pulse giving life to my goals and rhythm to my dreams as it whispers, *Do not miss a thing. You are alive. Live like it.* And I do. I have. I will.

Every now and then, my quiet aneurysm likes to give Captain Graceful a pop quiz, always the same question, just in different settings. *True or false: You are getting the most out of life.* This is the only inquiry on the test, and the aneurysm not only asks the question but provides the tutoring, making sure no dream is ever deferred. All impulses to quit must first pass through the aneurysm, and receive judgment there. This unknown pulse of what may or may never be tells me to go running in the rain, to hike through canyons, to bike over mountains. It lifts my body into the air when I skate. Do not miss a thing, it warns me. *Do not miss a thing.*

"Your mom made it, eh? I'm sure mine will, too," Lenny surmised, making the decision not to go home to visit his mother in Canada and leaving me to wonder if he had missed the point entirely or had just spent enough time with Hollywood on Ice that it had completely warped his sense of reality, life, and death. But who was I to judge? Little Miss Do Not Miss a Thing was missing everything from meals and periods to the entire point of it all. My own imaginary aneurysm had either exploded or disappeared, and I couldn't even tell the difference.

The truth was that if Len left the tour, surely one of the other male skaters would take his place and there was no guarantee the Canadian would ever get his solo spot back, especially with the steady expansion of his abdominal region compared with the twiggy Russian men. A future without skating was not something Len cared to consider. Such was the world of Hollywood on Ice that this fear of replacement could overpower that of a mother's death.

Death was the paradox that moved Hollywood on Ice from place to place, the death of ticket sales. Whereas most shows schedule their performances for a few select days or a week at most, Hollywood on Ice stayed until the tickets stopped selling and the townspeople grew tired of having our tent parked on the outskirts of their village. There was also the unspoken likelihood that the owner of Hollywood on Ice, Ernesto the octogenarian Mexican, could pass on at any moment and thus the tour would cease to function.

Spontaneity was not my strongest attribute. The volatility of Hollywood's performance schedule took a bit of getting used to, forcing my type A personality to retract a little further down the alphabet. Ever since Captain Graceful was born, there had not been a moment when I did not have an agenda. Ever since I had diagnosed myself with an honorary aneurysm, there was not a moment left to waste. Grown-ups called me driven, my peers believed I had a few screws loose, and I think the truth was somewhere in the middle. Time was kept by competitions, ice shows, track meets, regattas, and anything else that might bring me one step closer to my goals. To greatness. I knew where I wanted to go, how to get there, what it was going to take, and then programmed my days accordingly so that I could see through to the end of a calendar year knowing exactly where I'd be every day. This, of course, was a bit easier as a teenager growing up in an affluent suburb when I did not have to be responsible for small details like food, clothing, and shelter.

The Ice Capades contract packet (which I indelibly committed to memory) listed its show dates and travel departures by the hour, but Hollywood on Ice could barely see to the end of one week. We stayed for one unending month in Mar del Plata and two short days in the Chilean border town of La Calera, though the time spent in most venues fell somewhere in between. On the days when there was nothing of interest to talk about in the trailer, the subject of relocation could get the dialogue flowing in a heartbeat. Lenny was the great rumor starter, bounding into the trailer to spread the latest gossip; no country was too far-off or too far-fetched as a possible site for the greatness of Hollywood on Ice. In the months before I arrived on tour, the show had rambled through Colombia, Venezuela, and Peru—not a bad pilgrimage for a fleet of decaying trailers.

"Word's out, we're packing up on Thursday," Lenny confided one day, leaving us to trace the hearsay's validity back through the absurd lineages of Hollywood on Ice employees. Lora's sister's third husband's psychic kitten and its crystal hairball was in the office at the time the next city was selected, so, yeah, of course we're heading out this Thursday. Right.

"Really? Where are we headed? *¿Adónde? ¿Kuda?*"

"Nigeria."

"What?! How the hell are we getting to Nigeria, Lenny?"

"We're driving up . . . should take about three or four days."

"Um, Len . . . "

"Yo!"

"Nigeria is in Africa."

"Right on!"

"Africa is on the other side of the ocean. Do these trailers float or something?" I would not have been surprised if Lora tied the entirety of Hollywood on Ice to the backs of her Mexican workers and instructed them to dog-paddle their way from Argentina to Nigeria.

"No, no, no! We're going to the one upstate, next to Mexico." With this, a few brows furrowed, calling forth long-lost geography skills and Len-ese code breaking. Nigeria, driving, up*state?*

"Do you mean *Nicaragua?* We're going to drive up to Nicaragua? From Argentina?"

"Hellooo! That's what I've been trying to tell you."

The psychic cat was wrong, we never did make it to Nicaragua (either one of them) during my time with the tour. There was speculation about heading to Bolivia, Peru again, and even to Mexico's resort towns, but the skaters were always the last to find out where the show was ultimately destined, as ideas came and went faster than we could complete a quick change. The best part about the rumors was that they were exactly that, mysterious little fragments of half-truth and hints of possibility that change was on the way. In a setting that relied on the repetition and routine of unchanging choreography, sometimes the only way to feel as though life was moving forward was to experience the literal movement of travel, the impetus of onwardness.

When we moved from city to city, time expanded past curtain cues and dress rehearsals and sometimes we were given a full day off, as the complicated ice tent often needed a few extra hours of assembly. For me it was as though each new place was a new chance, a new beginning to an old dream. Maybe this city would be different, maybe this town will be better than the last, maybe here I could be a soloist, maybe now I could respect my body. And maybe cows could skate, dinosaurs could benefit from AA, and my grasp on reality might someday surpass the preschool level. When the management decided that we had exhausted all of northern and eastern Argentina, we boarded the fluorescent Hollywood on Ice bus and headed west for Chile, crossing the great plains of South America in a circus-style caravan.

꧁꧂

Chapter Seventeen

Finishing the Moment

¡"A la derecha!" the bus driver called. *"¡Ahora!"*

Everyone sitting on the left of the Hollywood on Ice bus grumpily moved over to the right-hand side as the oversize vehicle began to execute a hairpin turn down the narrow Chilean highway lurching its way through the west side of the Andes. Ruslan grumbled incoherent Russian, annoyed at the constant interruption of his hangover nap. Bella groaned in protest, her nail-polish application disturbed once again by the wavy driving. I no longer looked out the window, my hollow stomach twisting into queasy knots. We had passed the Chilean port of entry twenty minutes earlier, and our bus had begun its lunging and braking descent down the Andes mountain range toward Santiago, the next destination of Hollywood on Ice. The view was incredible at first, a celestial cluster of jagged snowcapped crests situated sharply against the backdrop of a sky so blue that its realness seemed questionable. Aconcagua, the highest mountain in the Americas, at 23,000 feet, appeared the same height as the rest of the surrounding summits, but as we began to creep deeper into the Andes, it remained enormous as the other peaks dwindled down to rolling hills and mediocre precipices.

"¡A la izquierda! ¡Ahora!"

The skaters sighed and shifted from the right of the bus over to the left again, hoping to create an even amount of weight distribution against the forces of gravity. Actively participating in the bus driver's goal of driving down the mountain instead of flying off it, the skaters pooled their weight together as the driver maneuvered the monstrous tour bus around yet another nauseous bend in the steep road. This would be the first and only instance of team bonding I experienced over the course of the tour, and the only moment when weight was genuinely appreciated. The fear of death by tour bus was strong enough to make all the skaters feel closer than family for forty-five minutes.

On one side of the bus were drop-offs leading to even more downhill switchbacks. Across the aisle, sheer walls of mountain were within reach on the other side of the glass. There were about sixteen hairpin turns to be made until any of us felt safe again. My contract with Hollywood on Ice mentioned nothing about crossing the Andes by way of a bus with feeble brakes underneath, a leaking roof overhead, and a bunch of vodka-guzzling, shower-shunning, sex-crazed male figure skaters occupying the seats across from me. Yet I had signed that wretched piece of paper, excited and willingly, on a dotted line that seemed so important at the time.

"Eeeeeeeeerrrrrrrrrrr . . . kaBOOM!!" Ruslan yelled at the crook of each turn, doing his best impersonation of failed bus brakes and the fate of its passengers.

La Calera was an impoverished village, midway between Santiago and the beach towns to the north, set inland and away from the Pacific. Hollywood decided at the last minute to camp on its outskirts en route to the capital. The roads were dusty and quiet, the shops homely and small, the inhabitants shocked to see Hollywood on Ice roll in with all its glittery grandeur. We stayed there only a week, but it was long enough to see that my fixation with starvation did not stay behind in Argentina, where I had attempted to abandon it. No longer was my mind just experimenting to see how much weight I could lose. Now it was an all-encompassing frenzied focus. The athlete inside me that once set goals of being the best skater she could now tried to form new goals, but everything seemed impossible and beyond my control. *Go for two days without looking at the scale, come on—you can do it!*

A strange thing happens when the body is denied food—it loses itself, in more ways than pounds and inches. Aside from being hungry, the physical symptoms of deprivation were showing up. My menstrual cycle had ceased. *Good,* I justified, giving no thought to its biological necessity. *It was a pain in the neck anyway.* My skin grew sallow and fuzzy with lanugo, a furlike coating of baby-fine hair that the body grows to keep from getting cold. *Barely noticeable,* I thought, *especially with a tan.* The hair on my head, now in its ridiculous shade of blond, was coming out in clumps in my brush. *Must be the dye job,* I lied to myself.

Deep inside my body, when I lay still and quiet in my bed and waited for sleep to rescue me from my thoughts, my heart would skip beats, or add a few to throw off the pattern of its regular double Dutch jump rope rhythm. Instead of *ba*-bum, *ba*-bum, *ba*-bum, the timing of my heart ba-*ba*-bumped or ba . . . . *bumped. I'm just tired* was the easiest dismissal. Sure as my legs and arms and buttocks slimmed down, so too did other places. Places that I never considered fat-carrying body parts. The skin around the knee, the flesh near the spine of the lower back, the front of the shin . . . all of it grew smaller. My hands grew bony and old-looking, my neck became frail and bobbleheadish, my breasts lost a cup size, as everything from armpits to earlobes began to vanish. Never before did it occur to me that when we lose weight, we lose ourselves. Only in my body's diminished state did I realize just how much there was to lose, how much there was to miss.

And, of course, there was the weakness. Every physical movement felt slow and lethargic, from smiling and waving to sit-ups and triceps dips in the trailer. Yet surprisingly, the desire to run did not fade with my energy supply. Running was caught in the purgatory of caloric duties and athletic prowess. *I'm still an athlete,* my mind attempted to fool my body as I laced my sneakers and ran through South American towns for hours.

I ran through the Chilean city streets of La Calera, out toward the winding roads that led to unknown places. If there was fear in venturing too far away, there was a stronger sense of dread in turning back too early and not burning all the calories I had consumed all day. There were rules to this starvation game, numbers to follow, ounces to account for. My mind picked out numbers to burn the same way Lora picked out our target weights: randomly and illogically. I ran for the food I would consume and then ran again to rid myself of it, lost more in my own thoughts than among the streets of an unfamiliar town. Chile might have been a beautiful country if I had stopped to look where I was going instead of letting it all pass by as a backdrop for anorexia.

The idea of leaving Hollywood on Ice and quitting this soured dream of professional skating ran through my mind as the endorphins created various scenarios of escape. *Just let go, just get out, wherever, however . . . get Captain Graceful ready to run for the suitcase on my command.* Yet while part of me yearned to quit the show, the other part — the athletic instinct — reminded me that throwing in the towel was intolerable, the worst sign of weakness an athlete could portray, a fracturing of mental toughness. My rational side was having a terrible time trying to persuade the rest of me that this show was not about athleticism and never would be, that this was not about throwing in the towel. How could it be? There was no towel, only makeup-removal Handi Wipes designed for easy disposal. Perhaps if I just kept on running, I could escape all the questions chasing after me.

There is a high school cross-country course in Wappingers Falls, New York, known for its undulating terrain and fierce weather conditions. In the fall, cold temperatures and cloudy skies lend to the seriousness of this place where young, high-strung runners arrive already buckling under the pressures of expectation, filing nervously out of the stumpy yellow school buses used for weekend meets. I loved the place. *Wappingers* was almost as fun to say as *Yonkers*.

Somewhere around the end of the second mile in the 5k race course, an abrupt decline results from a ramplike hill that drops steeply for about five or six feet before leveling out again. This hill is not a happy obstacle for runners. Because of its sudden grade and momentary angle, it is hard to take it in stride. Some racers shorten and slow their pace while others with longer legs stumble over their footing. I knew only one way to take the ledge: jump the damn thing. *Get back on it!* When the other runners slowed up for the insidious slope, I revved my pace and launched my body from the small cliff as if it were a sheet of ice and I had blades on the soles of my sneakers, craving the sweet pause of hang time before my stomach plummeted and my feet landed far from where they had last touched ground. I knew this airborne feeling well, it was just like launching into an axel or a death drop spin, save the contortion of twisting —-and the fact that in running, it helped to land both feet forward and not backward on one. That transitory pause, that serene moment of weightlessness, that brief but permanent comprehension of flight, is something a body will do anything for once it knows how to get there. This small topographical blemish on a racecourse in the northern boonies of Westchester County made me fall in love with running. Never once did calories or body weight enter my mind, never did I run to get away from something, it was all about moving forward, all about getting beyond my own limits. It was a release, not a confinement; a passion, not a hindrance; a beginning, not an ultimatum. Running was one foot in front of the other: simple, pure, and tough as hell.

I was not very fast when I started running in junior high, but I wanted to be because of all the attention the winners received. Everyone won ribbons at these meets, but the winners' always looked bluer, their trophies always had that extra little wrung of achievement glued beneath the feet of the golden, androgynous, minimannequin posed in eternal athleticism. Gangly, graceless, and forever at the crossroads of hormones and Oxy pads, I was gawky enough just trying to stand still, let alone attempting to run. I had arms like javelins, a wobbly pogo stick of a neck, feet the length of skis, and a torso quite unsure of its connective purpose. Set in motion, I looked like the closet sport shelf came tumbling down. But running felt good, and before long we grew into each other.

Running brought out my competitive fire differently than the determination I brought to skating competitions. In skating, winning a competition meant one's marks had to surpass another's. Judges come into play and decree winners and losers by subjective measurements. In cross-country, it was the body's job to surpass, physically moving beyond runner after runner until it decided what place to settle for. Even the sweat was different when racing, unlike the sticky film of rinkbound perspiration that either freezes or evaporates quickly in the cold, dense air. Running lets it all pour out — all that muscular toxicity, spiritual adrenaline, and mental gunk floods out of pores like some sort of physical baptism. Once converted, there is no turning back to the days of sedentary worship — which is wonderful and pure if you're not simultaneously trying to survive on Tic Tacs.

* * *

When the tour arrived in big cities such as Santiago, each skater was assigned publicity work on a rotating basis. The task of promoting Hollywood on Ice was never very difficult, sometimes it only involved filming one of our on-ice routines for a local *tele* commercial or handing out brochures and balloons in *el centro* of a bustling city. Of course, we were required to stand around in our skimpy outfits complete with skates while doing so, usually publicizing a lot more than we wanted. Other times we were taxied by Fernando in his yellow Mustang to radio stations and interviewed on the air by jovial disc jockeys who found the concept of figure skating in South America bizarre and amusing. Except for the confusion of verb tenses and not knowing the translation for *pizza dough* and *orange juice concentrate,* I had a pretty good grasp on the language from all the years of high school Spanish and was often chosen by Lora for radio duty. Apparently I wasn't too fat for that.

I spoke of the basics, giving my name, age, hometown of Nueva York, and how much I loved being a professional figure skater with Hollywood on Ice, figuring that bald-faced lies were perfectly acceptable when told in a foreign language. Sometimes I altered my bio just for the hell of it, my little fibs making me feel rebellious against Hollywood on Ice as I claimed various nationalities to obscure countries, doing my best to persuade the radio personnel that of course there were skating rinks in central Ethiopia or that growing up in an Afghani orphanage had not been so bad at all.

On the rare occasion that I mentioned my actual hometown suburb, the disc jockeys drew back in fear at the word *Bronx,* paid no attention to the *ville* and asked, *"¿Tienes pistola?"* Of course I carried a gun, I embellished, while pretending to search through my handbag, furthering the myth that everyone in New York totes around lethal artillery. Just like all Americans personally know Mitch, the lifeguard on *Baywatch,* another funny yet perplexing stereotype. *No tengo aquí.* I apologized for not having my pistol with me. I must have lent it to David Hasselhoff at my last lifeguard shindig.

After the gun situation was cleared up, the next question almost always involved Tonya and Nancy and whether I knew them personally or had any inside knowledge on the infamous bashing. Figure skaters generally shy away from this topic in disgust, as neither Olympian is re-

garded as the most positive ambassador of the sport. In the trailer Grígor
and a few of the other Russian skaters asked the same thing from time to
time.

"Keeaatrin from New York. You know Tonyanancy?"

"No, not personally."

"Friends, yes?"

"No, see, the U.S. is a pretty big—"

"Tonya bad girl."

"Yeah."

"Why she do that, hit Nancy?"

"Well, Grígor, you see—"

"Grígor like bad girl."

"Right. I'll let her know."

Grouping us into pairs, the management sent the female skaters
out for publicity dressed as Betty or Wilma or as a sassy little Bedrock
showgirl. Usually my Flintstone bikini was the assigned outfit for a parade, but now and again I would don the pebbly pearls, primitive pouf,
and white frock of Mrs. Flintstone. The dress was like most of the
Hollywood outfits—unflattering, uncomfortable, and sporting a
pornorific hemline—while one of the guys donned the purple Dino
costume and chased kids around whatever plaza we occupied. Felicia
and I, after heated arguments as to whose turn it was to be Betty, waited
outside the hotel for our ride. Fernando never drove the Flintstone
women in his sporty car. No, our means of transportation was
Hollywood's own Flintmobile—a golf cart with a prehistoric makeover
and cutouts in the floor from which to dangle our feet just like Fred and
Barney—which drove us down the traffic-infested city streets of South
American capitals.

The cart was driven by the malevolent little Rosario, who left
Felicia and me *(Gordita)* white-knuckled and breathless as he wove the
little plastic electric buggy between cars made of actual metal and trucks
that didn't have awnings made of fake saber-tooth-tiger pelts. Past el
Cerro San Lucía, el Correo Central, la Casa Colorada, la Plaza de Armas,
and la Iglesia de San Francisco, Santiago whirred the golf cart through a
blur of hurried tourists and steady panic while our fate lay at the mercy

of the apparent death wish of our hobbit-size chauffeur. There were no seat belts in the deathmobile, but the fear of flying through the windshield was slightly dulled by the fact that there wasn't one. We arrived windblown and insect-smattered and began the process of debugging each other before handing out flyers, grooming each other's poufy bouffants like a couple of grub-hungry orangutans in figure skates.

We posed for pictures with children, endured endless remarks of dull wit by goofy parents, tolerated the men who were a little too excited to see cartoon women in person, and waved at the elderly people who never realized we were dressed up. Publicity was something I enjoyed because it gave a purpose to my day and proved a temporary distraction from my hunger. Certainly there were worse ways to occupy one's time than making children smile and handing them balloons. The only downside to publicity duty was the occasional parade, whereby the entire cast dressed up in show regalia and drove through the city on flatbed trucks with music, posters, and amped-up loudspeakers screaming show times and ticket prices. Hitched to one of the trucks was a flat, skinny trailer bed with a vertical billboard ten feet high and thirty feet long. There was little room for anything else beside the billboard, like a place to stand, but Hollywood on Ice figured that was our problem, so they stacked as many skaters as they could on the little lip of leftover platform. We were instructed to hang on to the billboard with one hand and wave to the public with the other. I was not well versed in the subject of how to grip a smooth piece of vertical wall, but it did not surprise me in the least that Hollywood on Ice expected us to possess this superhero skill. *Able to drop thirty pounds in five weeks and suction herself to rapidly moving billboards . . . come see the amazing Spiderwaif! Twice nightly at seven and ten!*

When the parade truck's ignition snorted to life, we ambled onto the ledge of the billboard and clutched whatever rut, fingerhold, or other person's limb we could find, uttering Hail Marys at every turn. Sometimes forming a human chain with muscle-bound Ruslan anchored to one end of the truck and his counterpart Olga #3 at the other, we linked ourselves across the billboard ledge, looking more like protesters of Hollywood on Ice than supportive employees.

*   *   *

Santiago was the last city in which I was assigned publicity duty, but not because the management caught on to the discrepancies between my fictitious radio show bios and my real life story. Integrity was not one of the show's many requirements. There would be no more public endorsements because there would be no more Hollywood on Ice. At least not for me. After six months of Hollywood and two months of Holiday, things were coming to a boiling point in my tolerance level of the professional skating world. I was physically and mentally ill with weight loss, my expectations of figure skating had flown out the trailer curtain, and my boundaries of normalcy were finally pushed to their limits. I could handle the skating mammals and the rowing Russians and even the possibility that Nigeria had relocated to Central America, but it was beyond my comprehension how long I was supposed to stay on this ride. The contract with Hollywood was for a year, and I was at the halfway point. A year at Murray's flew by in a blink, college had lasted maybe a millisecond, but going to the trailer each day was like trudging through a soggy quagmire of wasted time, my body shackled to the dead weight of broken dreams.

Time and its obscure passage became an obsession. On the calendar in my suitcase I crossed off the days with sprawling X's like a prisoner raking her daily chalk lines down cell walls. Some days I drew one half of the X in the morning and saved the opposing slash for later in the day. Time had never passed this way before, slow and lethargic, as though tired of its own keeping. "To fill the hour," Emerson once called out to me from a textbook, "that is happiness. To finish the moment . . . to live the greatest number of good hours, to live on even terms with Time." Time and I were wasting each other away. With the unfilled hours, unfinished moments, and uneven terms, my disdain for the daily passage of time was the first of three epiphanies I had in Santiago.

The second inspiration for a quick getaway from the Hollywood lifestyle was slightly more concrete. In our Santiago hotel, Felicia and I neighbored Grígor the untiring oarsman and his girlfriend, Olga #2. Olga was a striking woman in her early twenties, with wavy strawberry blond hair and the high, symmetrical cheekbones of a fashion model; her face was equally chiseled by genetics and starvation. Small and thin, somewhere around five-three, Olga never smiled unless it was a residual effect of sarcasm. Other than that, she was quiet and kept to herself, the cold, withdrawn counterpart of her outgoing twin sister, Talia. She smoked outside the trailer, more so than most of the skaters, and avoided eye contact with most of the women.

My only connection with Olga was that we entered the "At the Hop!" number of the Flintstones routine together. Backstage, we waited in silence for our cue, rarely making eye contact and when we did we flattened our lips into the half-hearted effort of a civil grin. During one show an unexpected weather shift caught us all by surprise as the temperature hovered at fifty degrees, forty less than the daytime high of a South American summer. Olga and I waited, shivering, my hands cross-rubbing my upper arms for warmth while Olga ran her palms over her goose-bumped legs. When her hand brushed past her skating skirt, I noticed a lumpish bruise on her left hip. It was dark and round, the size of a softball at least, and had begun to turn from purple to green in places. There were other contusions, too, which I had not seen at first. Smaller marks the size of fingerprints smoldered in cooled colors upon her upper arm. Another streak of violet hovered near her neck. The rumor was that the markings were compliments of Grígor.

"Can't someone say something? Does Talia know about her sister?" I whispered once to Jody in the trailer.

"Everyone knows," Jody answered, shaking her head but offering nothing else. What everyone also knew was that Grígor rowed his boat to the witchy Olga #1's room on a regular basis and probably docked in other foreign ports as well before going back to the room he shared with Olga #2.

In our room in Santiago, Felicia and I fell into the habit of watching dubbed reruns of *T. J. Hooker* and the earliest *X-Files* late at night until the last bit of the Hollywood on Ice performance adrenaline drained from our nervous systems and sleep's lethargic cloud finally rolled in. There was little that could wake me from my depressive desire for sleep, but at three in the morning the sounds of one body being struck by another in the next room was enough to wake the dead. The displacement of furniture and breaking glass was a soft and gentle din in comparison to the throaty screams and the shockingly loud impact of skin on skin. Grígor's voice was deep and angry, slurred Russian words coming out in short bursts between the violent blows. Olga #2's screams were hardened by what I can only imagine was habit. We listened for what felt like hours, understanding both nothing and everything about what was going on next door. Various thoughts circled through my mind like bumper cars, crashing into one another without clear direction. The need to do something bounced off the fact that I had no idea what to do and collided with helplessness, guilt, and fear.

"We should tell Pam, she'll know how to handle this," Felicia suggested. I crept down the hall, passing the brutality of our neighbors' room, and took the stairs up to our line captain's quarters. Pam, not a three-thirty-in-the-morning person, came to the door pale and disheveled.

"Grígor is beating Olga again."

"Umhumm."

"What do we do?"

"If it's not on the ice, it's not our problem, Kathryn. Hollywood on Ice has nothing to do with that. Besides, that happens all the time with them."

"Pam, he's beating the shit out of her. You should hear it."

"Olga's tough, she can handle him. I've roomed next to them before."

"Could you at least tell Lora about this?" I knew she wouldn't. Even if she did tell, Lora would not have cared. I was grasping at straws.

"Yeah. Sure. I'll tell Lora tomorrow. G'night."

"But—"

"Good night, Kathryn."

"Fine. What room is Lenny in?"

Pam gestured to the door at the end of the hall and closed her own. At least Lenny could physically match Grígor and might be able to do something. But the Canadian was not home, as three was still early for him. Back downstairs the clamor continued, and Felicia and I turned on the television, upping the volume on a Spanish translation of *Baywatch* until the waves of one Hollywood overlapped the reality of another.

To work for a company that didn't like my body was one thing, but to be in a setting that would not even attempt to protect my body in a dangerous situation put a whole new spin on things. The level of

Hollywood's corruption had reached its limit, surpassing my notions of personal safety. Grígor and Olga might have had their problems, but they were far from isolated incidents. There were other men in the cast who came home late from their vampire outings and entered the rooms of unsuspecting skaters, looking for satisfactions that the vodka alone could not give them. Captain Graceful's shiny red cape was not enough to fight off the voracity of sexual and physical assaults. The vast majority of my common sense disappeared long ago, and I could not afford to lose any more. What if I forgot to lock my door? Screaming for help, I now realized, would be a pointless endeavor. Along with my desire to skate professionally, my peace of mind was gone completely.

May was a beautiful time in South America, as the season of autumn turned everything a bit cooler in central Chile. We wore sweatshirts and wool socks in the trailer between shows, the temperature falling off dramatically when the sun went down. I was cold not only from the weather but from the core of my body, where warmth was a luxury placed last on the list of what calories were needed for. First was the necessity of keeping my organs going, the second was running. Whatever energy remained went straight into obsessing about food, so there was just no more mental or physical power left for generating warmth. My eating was at an all-time low, some days surviving on as little as 361½ calories, the equivalent of four plums (with pits) and eighteen orange Tic Tacs (without the plastic case). Like warmth, there was no room for happiness, either. My body and brain were diminishing day by day, and even my sleep was not spared from the havoc of weight loss.

My third and final wake-up call came in its own time in the middle of the night, like the ghost of Christmas future, pointing its bony finger in the direction of my probable demise. My literal nightmare did not include a shrouded apparition of Dickensian magnitude but rather a plain-looking lady with an orderly bun and a sturdy clipboard whose presence sought to end my eating disorder.

The nightmare came to me in Santiago, on a Saturday night before a scheduled Sunday weigh-in, and was powerful enough to actually knock a small amount of sense into my goo-infused head, a little nubbin of logic for the psychoplankton to chew on. The dream took place on a flight of stairs, outdoors, that rose switchback-style to somewhere I could not see. I walked up the stairs and there were other people around, but no one spoke, we just all continued upward. Then on the opposite side of the stairwell, a few people floated down, and as they passed I noticed wings sprouting from the space between their shoulder blades. *Shit,* I thought to myself, *people with wings—not a good sign. This is not where I want to be headed right now.* Just as I turned to walk back, the stairs turned into an escalator and zoomed me right up to the top. A middle-aged lady with a clipboard approached me in my panicked state and said, *"Looks like you don't want to be here just yet."* I told her she had that right, sister. *"Problem is, your heart stopped beating."* Uh-oh, that seemed bad. She stared at me for a few seconds to let me know she was one serious angel, then scribbled something on her clipboard and said, *"It's your call. Want one more chance?"* I then flew back down the stairs, which had returned to immobile form, woke up from the dream, and sprang out of bed faster than Ebenezer Scrooge on Christmas morning. I ran across the room and made myself a tuna fish sandwich (complete with two pieces of bread and tuna fish in the middle).

I was unsure whether I believed in God, but this nondescript lady with the clipboard had sure managed to put the fear of something into me. Until that moment, I had not really considered that this starvation thing was strong enough to kill me, and I had no immediate access to the stats that said the cause of death for most anorexics is cardiac arrest. I forced down the tuna fish sandwich and kept an eye out for the spontaneous materialization of stairways and wings. I thought again of leaving the trailer, of rowing, of getting away from that place of ice and skeletons, angels and tuna fish.

What became clear that dream-ridden night was not that my eating disorder was instantly obliterated (that would take a bit of work) but that my goal of skating professionally no longer had its former value. All the strange scenarios of ice-show life, the politics, the waste of talent, the starvation of bodies — none of these factors had shown themselves to the little kid sitting in the audience of the Ice Capades. Somewhere the realization took root that I was not failing my dream but that it was failing me. What was this world of ice and skaters but so far removed from figure skating? This was the place of a dream deferred, a place where dreams literally turned into nightmares, a place where Sundays were anything but peaceful—yet I had insisted on living here.

Letting go of my expectations was not an easy matter. They had been around for thirteen years, and the thought of leaving skating was like deciding to cut a large hole through Captain Graceful's cape in midflight. Athleticism taught me mental and physical toughness. I knew what it took to endure pain and push onward, but to *let go?* This was something new, mentally excruciating and physically exhausting, something I had not trained for. Something Fix-it Woman carried no tools for. Never did it cross my mind that sometimes it takes courage to quit, to walk away from a dream come untrue, to leave behind the what-ifs and the what-should-be's, and to finally face up to what actually is. With my body falling apart and the realization that another six months on tour would do me serious harm, I began planning my escape.

✦

Chapter Eighteen

Operation Sunday

"Look," I said to Felicia, pointing at the map of South America in my Fodor's travel guide, "we can either bust out and head over to the airport in Santiago or flee through Peru when the show heads north in a few weeks." The last time I used words like *bust* and *flee* was in the early eighties, when my stuffed animals were held captive by the dark forces of my imaginary playmates. I bust and fled all over the backyard back then, but in our little Chilean hotel room, Peru was harder to map out than Bronxville. The only thing more terrifying than escaping was the prospect of staying put with Hollywood on Ice.

My roommate was tired and disappointed with the show as well, and still mourned that Holiday on Ice had not re-signed her after the Christmas tour. Felicia wanted to tour with Holiday's Blue Division, the one that traveled through England. That was her Ice Capades. Since the day we arrived in South America she wrote letters and made phone calls to Christa back in Switzerland, constantly asking if any openings with Holiday on Ice were available. Christa's answer was always the same: Felicia was on their mysterious list of people to call if any spots opened up, but there were no vacancies right now. Even Jody, our Canadian comrade, was ready to end her stint with Hollywood but was determined to hang on two more months, till her contract was up in July. She wanted to skate for Disney next, and I helped her make an audition videotape of her skating after sneaking into the tent to use Hollywood's ice rink. Disney would like Jody: she was a strong skater with a tiny body. After her contract ended with Hollywood, they signed her immediately.

For months Felicia and I had kept our spirits up by plotting imaginary escape routes all over the continent, daydreaming of visits to the Galápagos Islands in Ecuador and catching a ski weekend in Patagonia. We inventively scheduled trips visiting Iguazú Falls in Brazil, sightseeing in Buenos Aires, and relaxing on the beaches of Venezuela's Margarita Island before heading back home to our respective continents. But now, the idea of fleeing the trailer lost the fantasy element and came to life as a pragmatic scheme. Yet simply walking out and slamming the trailer's curtain behind us was easier said than done.

Our contracts with Hollywood on Ice were for one year and could not be terminated upon the mere request of the skater, although Lora had the right to pull our employment plug at any time. Escaping basically came down to quitting without notice, fleeing into the night or busting our way home somehow, abandoning the reimbursed plane ticket and final "paycheck" that awaited us at the end of our contract. Having survived on ten dollars a week for food for six months, I had saved enough to charter the Concorde. During the weeks when we didn't get IOU slips, Hollywood on Ice paid us in the currency of whatever country we were visiting, most of which I sent home via traveler's checks every few weeks as payday robberies occurred now and then. Having hidden some bills in instant-soup boxes and secret luggage pockets, I had just enough cash on hand to ensure a safe escape, but money alone was not the main obstacle.

There were no locked doors or armed Flintstone characters barring our physical passage from Hollywood on Ice to Freedom on Land, but there was one obstruction that kept our liberation at the mercy of Lora. Our passports were held hostage in Lora's office. Although it is illegal to detain another person's passport, Hollywood on Ice did not exactly tremble with nervousness about their wrongdoings. Other skaters had escaped Hollywood on Ice successfully. Jody told us of one woman who suffered a terrible fall in the poorly lit backstage clutter; she had stepped backward off a six-foot ledge and seriously injured her back. Hollywood on Ice refused to pay for a doctor or to release the skater from her contract, and after a week or two of constant pain, a few members of the cast put the ailing skater in a midnight taxi and got her to the airport in Lima, Peru, from where she flew home to Canada. "They're always looking for new skaters," Alexei had said back in the dressing room of Holiday on Ice. Now I understood why.

As for getting ahold of my passport, it did not bother me to lie to people who were already corrupt. I would simply explain to Lora that I needed to make a copy of it for business reasons back home. If she did not let me have access to it, I would invoke my MacGyver powers and break into the office using an eyelash curler and a ballpoint pen, then disable the alarm with a stick of gum and a skate lace. Or just steal the key.

The last thing on my mind was that Hollywood on Ice might be displeased with me. I finally summoned the courage to be displeased with them, to take a little blame off my shoulders and put some on theirs. Sometimes it takes courage to find fault in something other than ourselves, to give back the burdens that others place upon us. To bear the weight of my world was one thing, but to take on the immensity of another's was something that had begun to sap every drop of strength from my soul. *So you're not the Ice Capades, fine, I was willing to adapt . . . but who the hell do you think you are to judge my body, call me fat, dye me blond, and break my spirit?*

I entered the angry stage, the screw-you stage, the stage of emotion most necessary in bringing about change. I was through with spending my days as a mannequin, my nights as a sequin, and every moment in between as anything but the athlete that I used to know and missed so very much. *Kiss my ass, Lora, if you can find it.*

The plan, Operation Sunday, was formulated in three steps over three days and was to be executed after the chosen weekend's final show. Sundays brought paychecks as well as scales, and it was worth coordinating the escape accordingly. On the approaching Thursday at 0900 hours, my humongous wheelie suitcase would be shipped home via FedEx, leaving me with only a backpack, skates, and a wallet. The trick was getting the suitcase out of the hotel before any other skaters might see it and get suspicious, but we figured 0900 was fine because no one ever got up before noon. We still needed our skates for the two shows directly before the escape, but they could be mailed home later. On

Friday I would buy a train ticket for Chile's southern Lake District, where the first leg of my South American exploration would begin. There was still a month until the rowing camps started up in the United States, and the question of what to do in the interim was answered by the Fodor's guide. Going back to Bronxville was not an option just yet; there were things I had to think about first.

Physically craving a return to the athletic life I knew before professional skating, I assumed that the mental part would follow my body's lead but might need a little time off to aid the transition. Traveling through South America for a short while might be just the thing to help remedy my plankton-riddled mind and body. Finally, on Saturday, I would get the passport during the hustle and bustle of a three-show day, when the office was sporadically left unattended. Adding to the general chaos of the weekend shows was the fact that this was Hollywood on Ice's final Santiago performance before packing up and heading north to Colombia. The days prior to switching performance venues were always hectic for management, as everyone was caught up in the details of travel planning. The office door was usually open and Lora gone from behind the desk that held *los pasaportes.* All that was left was waiting for Sunday to come, to fill the hour, finish the moment, and begin to live on even terms with time.

Felicia was down with Operation Sunday but only as far as escaping to southern Chile. From there she would hop on a flight back to England and attempt to persuade Christa that she was committed to getting a spot with good old Holiday on Ice. My roommate's faith in pro skating still lived on in the possibility that Holiday might want her for one of their future world tours, and I was not sure if I admired Felicia's determination or thought she was crazier than I was. My family knew nothing of Operation Sunday; as far as they could tell, everything was peachy. I told my father in letters and phone calls that I was having some problems with food, and he was supportive but unclear as to what problems with food one could possibly have. I mentioned nothing of the weight loss to my mother, as something inside feared her reaction. She might think that weight loss was a good thing, but I did not want to believe that, so I kept it to myself. I could just say that the skating had not worked out, and I was going to do a little sight-seeing before coming back to New York. That was true enough.

With our suitcases shipped home and the train tickets purchased, Felicia and I awaited the final act of our escape as we twitched with nervous excitement in the trailer, just before our last night of back-to-back shows.

In front of my large, cracked trailer mirror I applied my makeup for the last time, quietly dropping the ultra-red lipstick into the trash instead of putting it back in my cosmetics pouch. The same fate followed for the concealer, the eyeliner, and the eyelashes, each falling into the bucket with a muffled *thump* so as not to draw suspicion from the other skaters. Then again, my neighbor Bella wouldn't catch on to the elements of escape if I had sat down and told her point-blank what I was doing.

Farewell, Bella, Felicia and I are fleeing the country tonight.

Yes, okay. See you tomorrow, Keeatrin.

From my mirror I untaped the pictures of my rowing team, the motivational quotes, the drawings from Cathi and Stefanie, and sandwiched them into my blue journal while I replaced their space on the mirror with generic cut-out photos from magazines so that it did not seem as if I was packing up for good. I gave my stash of books to Jody. *Sons and Lovers, Dracula, Lolita*—I had read them in the downtime of the trailer, finding great comfort in the characters who seemed to be in stranger places than I was, as the rest of the dressing room spun around me. *Dino, quit humping the sewing machine! Has anyone seen my Styrofoam head? Okay, ladies, who threw the scale at the air conditioner?*

From my drawer beneath the costume rack I took only what I needed—some hair elastics, contact lens solution, a pair of socks, and, in a moment of weakness, the laxatives and diet pills. The rest was disposable. For a moment my eyes fell upon Pam's soloist costume, a beautiful black halter-top skating dress that shone with the brilliance of five hundred rhinestones. Under the spotlight, it gleamed in a thousand directions, creating small galaxies that quivered all over the ceiling of the tent. I wanted that dress. Heavy for something made of spandex—maybe two pounds—it was weighed down by a multitude of glass beads and metal fasteners. I wanted to lift the dress into my bag and take it with me, take the one thing I never got to wear. Fingering the material, I slipped it off the hanger and held the costume close, letting the urge of theft run its course and return to morality on its own time. I pocketed only the memory of its shine and the feel of its almostness. It was such a breathtaking dress.

I looked around for what else I might have forgotten, but there was nothing left of mine. Only cold chairs and hot lightbulbs. Thick Styrofoam heads and thin human bodies. Outfits that were too small and mirrors that were too big. Pam walked into the trailer then, appearing as though she was about to call for weigh-ins but surprised us instead.

"Meeting tonight, between the shows," she said, looking right at me as she spoke.

There was a bit of trepidation over Pam's announcement, but it only added to my desire to get as far as possible from Hollywood on Ice. She couldn't have known about the passports; we hadn't taken them yet. The office had been occupied all day and we were waiting until the intermission to do the deed. Had she gained knowledge of Operation Sunday? Had Pam overheard Felicia and me whispering? Possibly. I had an undesired knack for speak-of-the-devil situations. Still, there was little sense in worrying about the post-show meeting, it was probably just another weigh-in anyway.

As the cast sat huddled in one of the trailers during the break between shows, the multilingual din died down when Pam entered with a stern look on her face. This seemed bad, but like all my other predictions about Hollywood on Ice since the day I had walked into the trailer, this too was wrong.

"The management has run into some financial difficulties and needs to make a few cutbacks. We are looking to release two skaters from their contracts. Return tickets home will be paid for. Any volunteers?"

Felicia and I looked at each other, her expression joyous and mine rather steamed. *Release?!* Foiled! My entire escape was foiled! Here I had worked so hard to explode my dream deferred into a thousand pieces to blow away all brokenheartedness, dramatically and symbolically breaking free from all plankton and goo as I fled to better things,

and now Hollywood on Ice was just letting me walk out of the tent, trying to pacify me with a measly plane ticket? The nerve of these people,
thinking they could just waltz in and climb up to the control panel of
Operation Sunday. Hell if I was just going to sit back and let them . . .

"We could cash in our tickets; they'd be about nine hundred dollars apiece," Felicia whispered.

I raised my hand. Felicia lifted hers. Our arms lingered in the air
above our head, graceful as the reach of a layback spin, awaiting Pam's
affirming nod and forever severing our ties with Hollywood on Ice and
their scales of injustice.

Five minutes before Sunday's last curtain rose, Rosario called,
"¡Cinco!" into the trailers and for the final time Felicia and I began the
ritual of perfection, double-checking our makeup, adjusting our fishnets,
running our fingers over our skate blades for stowaway sequins or other
tiny villains. When the opening music changed from lounge-style croon-
ing to quick rhythmic pulses of bass, we took our places behind the curtain on the wooden stage at the far end of the ice, waiting for the
houselights to dim and the strobe lights to deliver their hype.

"Swing, Kathryn," Oksana said, holding out her pinkie.

"Swing, Oksana," I replied, the Hollywood on Ice equivalent of
"break a leg," hooking pinkie fingers with the shiest but most pleasant
Russian on tour. Whispers of "swing" circulated up and down the set,
where we positioned ourselves according to height on the opening prop,
a flight of stairs that led to nowhere. The six tall showgirls took their
places on the steps above the skater-dancers. We wore the glistening
pink, purple, gold, and white costumes, spreading our bedizened skirts
open and capelike behind us, with turbans of flashy feathers strapped
onto our heads. Together, we were like a giant psychedelic peacock,
waiting in the dark to be released from our curtained cage.

I swung with Krystal, who hated the tradition and yanked people's
pinkies to let them know it. Olga #2 could not have cared less about swing,
too, presenting her pinkie like a lifeless hook, to be shook or not, whatever. Jody sang, "Swing," with bubbly excitement at every show, every
day, with her perfect-posture pinkie awaiting validation. We hooked
fingers for the last time, both our pinkies perky that night. Olga #1

wouldn't swing with me since I had told her to shut up the week before over something neither of us could remember but that probably had to do with Olga's voice volume. Felicia and I waited until the last possible moment to hook fingers, seeing how close we could swing before the curtain went up, before making a mad dash to our places at opposite ends of the stage. Sometimes we didn't make it and the curtain opened with twenty-two statuesque skaters and one or two scampering dorks.

In the downtime before the curtain's unveiling, I decided who was coming to see me perform for the final time that night. In the back row, barely visible in the wake of the stage lights and popcorn vendors, the dark shapes of foreign strangers became everyone I knew. Friends from Colgate, teammates from rowing, boys from old heartaches, skaters from Murray's, coaches from everywhere, Dick and Peggy, Hamilton and Wylie, my father, and even Emerson, Hughes, and Thoreau all showed up that night, filling seats and hours alike. Just minutes before the show, I pretended they were there to help me say good-bye. Just minutes before the show, even the hunger disappeared.

Finally, the hiss of the fog machine and the rumble of the escalating techno music came to a theatrical boil as the curtain separated through the swirling clouds of mechanical vapor, and the deep voice bellowed through the strobe-intruding darkness, *"Buenas noches, señoras y señores . . ."*

And so the tour went on its merry way, and neither Hollywood on Ice nor I wept for each other's loss. Only a few good-byes were said: Jody, Lenny, Pam, a couple of the nicer Russians, the seamstresses and the children, Cathi and Stefanie. If there was anything about the tour to be missed or recollected fondly, it wasn't coming to mind just yet. Maybe something would spring to mind while I was heading down the coast of Chile, but all I could think about at that moment was getting on the train.

In my little blue diary, the one designed to convey that I was not a head case who feared any food more caloric than an apple stem, I wrote of volcanic excursions, village explorations, and travel adventures all over South America. Since I was traveling around a continent often stereotyped as undeveloped and primitive, friends and family constantly inquired about cannibal activity and wild animals and wondered if men dragged their women around by the hair with one hand while holding a half-gnawed dinosaur limb in the other. I assured them that those phenomena existed only in the trailer and that the rest of South America was a fascinating place with historic, labyrinthine cities, breathtaking jungles, countryside charm, and beaches so pristine that somehow the water seems to be a different substance simply because the shores it rolls up on are unfamiliar.

Traveling proved to be both a therapeutic and harrowing experience, for it got me out and about but not far enough away from my problems. I was naive in believing I could outrun anorexia instead of confronting it. This became abundantly clear when Felicia and I passed by a souvenir vendor selling necklaces where on a single grain of rice, the man inscribed names with a fine-tipped pen and shellacked the tiny carbohydrate into wearable form.

"Jewelry!" Felicia marveled.

"Dinner!" I equated.

Felicia left for England a few days after we had tooled around the Lake District. I thought she was nuts for wanting to go back to the warehouse in Bern, to rehearse once again with Evelyn and David and subject her sanity to Jalena-like skaters with stables full of quirky qualities. Then again, for her, living with a roommate who counted out her daily Cheerios and removed her earrings and ponytail holder before weigh-ins was only so tolerable. Felicia loved me like a sister, but my problems were driving her bananas. Whole ones, peel and all. When I spoke of rowing and returning to healthy activities, she offered her full support but grew frustrated when I tried to persuade her that I could be an elite athlete while subsiding on biweekly cans of peas.

I was envious of Felicia, just as I had been jealous of all the skinny Russians. Holiday on Ice had been my roommate's dream tour since she was a child, while mine, the Ice Capades, was no longer available. She could keep trying and I could not, and this tore me up inside. Yet deep down I knew it was for the best that my days of pro skating were over and that there were other issues that needed dealing with. I could be alone with my thoughts as I traveled, so Felicia and I parted ways. I promised to take better care of myself, she promised not to fall off the ice, and we both promised to write frequently.

After exploring Argentina, Chile, Uruguay, Paraguay, a small blip of southeastern Brazil, and finally Venezuela by myself, it was time to go home. My head, however, was still in the trailer. It was time do something about the problem: time to get help. Time to make up with Captain Graceful, who had stopped speaking to me when I started starving myself. I knew I needed to eat more, but the plankton was still chomping away and I was producing goo at an alarming rate. Counseling seemed a good option, as my relationship with food was out of control and someone else might know how to deplanktonize me. Returning to amateur skating was something I could no longer imagine, for the tour left my feelings about skating confused and painful and it would take years until I felt the confidence to lace my skates again. No matter how hard I wanted to be an athlete, the tour still held tight to my mind, harping on the irrational mantra that being thin was better. What I still struggled with was the question, Better for whom? No amount of travel was going to uncover that answer.

❧

Chapter Nineteen

Stunning Revelations

My flight was booked from Margarita Island to New York City on a Sunday afternoon in June, and my parents arranged to meet me at the airport. While on tour, I had told them that I was sick, that my body wasn't right and my mind was having a rough time with eating, but I had kept to myself that more than thirty pounds had fallen from my once athletic body, and it wasn't stopping there. Surely they would see the loss for themselves and recognize the severity of the problem. But just to make sure, I dressed myself in a cry for help. Well, part cry/part twisted pride. There was a part of my brain that was weirdly proud and wanted to shout out, *See what I can do? Yeah, that's right, I'm the best damn weight loser this world has ever seen. Go ahead, pick a number of pounds, any number, I'll have it gone by five P.M. on Sunday!"*

In the bathroom of the plane I changed out of my grungy sweatpants and baggy flannel and into something that displayed my new body. Wearing a black sundress and a pair of sandals that easily showed my bony shoulders, my withered calves, my frail neck, my veiny feet and hands, and my dyed blond hair, of which more strands clung to the back of my clothes than to my head, I imagined my mother's expression of shock and my father's troubled concern. As it turned out, I should have flushed the dress instead of worn it.

My mother's expression was indeed one of shock, but not quite the kind I was expecting. I knew we had vastly different opinions of the ideal female body, but I did not understand how opposite until that moment, when she looked me up and down before uttering, "You're stunning. Absolutely stunning."

"I'm sick."

"But you look *fantastic*."

My father looked puzzled but said it was great to see me. Why I did not turn around, walk back into the airport, and get myself on a one-way flight to Antarctica that very moment was a question I dealt with for a very long time, but I figured there would not be much rowing in that part of the world. Whale blubber wasn't on my list of safe foods, and the chances of finding an eating-disorders therapist (which I'd promised myself while traveling South America) might be slim to none, so I braced myself for a long, hard journey, got in the station wagon, and headed toward Bronxville.

"Jesus, didn't they feed you down there?" Vinny Ventura complained when I walked into the NYAC boathouse that summer. Here was a man who understood my strength and was the first to show concern for all that had been lost from my body. "You're not rowing lightweight for me until you put on at least ten pounds," he continued, shaking his head.

A day or two in Bronxville was all it took to realize that home was not a good place for me to be, at least not with the way my mind was working. Or not working. My mother was so happy with my new appearance that for her, the tour was a miracle worker instead of a concentration camp. My muscular body was long gone, and my skinniness was much more feminine in her eyes. *Now,* she would tell her friends on the telephone, *now my daughter is beautiful.* Yet instead of sticking up for myself, I found her opinions difficult to bear and was barely able to recognize that her ideals of body image were not exactly helpful. Just painful. Beautiful *now?* My body was at the mercy of my mind, and my mind was split in two. One half saying, *You're sick, get help, then we can think about rowing,* while the other half—where the plankton thrived— said, *You're fine, get your butt in the boat, but don't put on any of that dreadful muscle, Gordita. You don't want to go through losing that again, especially since you just finally got yourself beautiful!* At home on the coffee table, my father's rowing magazines and my mother's *Vanity Fair*s towered next to each other. When I flipped through their pages, both called out, *You're one of us now, you're beautiful,* while the plankton and I argued about whom they were talking to.

Grocery stores became something overwhelming, and I avoided them at all cost because my physical cravings for food and my mental prohibition of it was enough to make me spontaneously combust in the frozen-food aisle. When my mother asked what I wanted from the store, I glared and said Slim-Fast with the twisted truthfulness of sarcasm, hoping somewhere in the back of my mind that she would sit me down with tears in her eyes and say, *No, honey, you need* food. *How about a nice big turkey and a few dozen pounds of stuffing with a mountain of mashed potatoes and a reservoir of gravy?* Instead, she asked what flavor. A day after being home, I took my stunning and beautiful self into the family room, sat my mother down, and told her I had a problem with food.

"Well, do you eat?"

"Yeah." Of course I eat, silly. I had a whole damn cracker six hours ago!

"Do you throw up?"

"No." I've tried that, but I prefer a good starving.

"Then what's the problem?"

My father knew something was wrong but could not understand the complexity of the situation surrounding my starvation. We went out for a walk and I tried to explain this force that held me back from eating. His brow furrowed and his eyes grew sad, but he did not understand the plankton.

"What is it that stops you from putting food in your mouth and eating it?" he asked gently and with soft concern. I sat down on the closest Miracle-Gro lawn and wrapped my arms around my balled-up knees.

"I dunno, Dad. Trying to figure that out." Not only did he have a healthy, normal approach to eating, but food was something we used to bond over when I was a little girl. Unlike Crouches With Radar, my father and I had celebrated food. When I was little, we went on BR trips, walking a mile or so from our house to the main street of our little suburb's local Baskin-Robbins. I loved our walks into town more than the ice cream itself, as my father and I talked about whatever was on our mind. Later on, when I needed to talk about important teenage issues, I'd call for a BR trip and Dad understood the code. Of course, my mother never went on BR trips, though she was invited to come along. Life and ice cream fused together as my dad and I walked down Hemlock Road, past our neighbors' well-dressed houses, across the high school football field at the bottom of our street, along the twisting sidewalk of Tanglewylde Avenue up to the shops, drugstores, newsstands, and boutiques filled with elegant superfluity that ran along Pondfield Road, where Baskin-Robbins sat between the Christian Science Reading Room and Raven's, a tired little pub frequented by retired little businessmen.

Things were so simple then. If I was hungry, I got two scoops. If I wasn't, I had one scoop. There was no panic of weight gain, not a thought of anxiety about fat grams. I was completely in tune with my body, and whatever it wanted me to eat, I ate. Now that all seemed so long ago and so far away. The Baskin-Robbins had gone out of business a few years back, my parents moved to a different house, and BR trips were a memory as distant as the comfort of food in general.

My father offered to help me sort out my issues by paying for counseling, but going to therapy and coming home to diet powder shakes felt a bit irrational. What I needed was a fresh start, a place where no one knew me from before the tour or could make corporeal comparisons to how I looked post–pro skating. A place where no one could drop by to keep tabs on my muscle development and buy me Slim-Fast and tell me I was *finally* pretty. It seemed that the NYAC was not going to be far enough away from the domestic pressures of being thin. I needed to go somewhere far enough to see myself.

A fellow NYAC rower got me into a national lightweight development camp in Boston, at the Riverside Boat Club. Greg and I had rowed together the previous fall, and he made some phone calls to a friend of his who was coaching the prestigious camp, promising that I was a talented rower. "She can pull a seven-nineteen on the erg," Greg told the head coach. That had been true thirty or forty pounds ago, but I assured him blindly that I could still row just as fast at my new weight. Faster even, if I needed to. My denial had a field day with that one.

In the meantime, I was admitted into the camp on the basis of the good recommendation and because another rower had just dropped out—not unlike my circumstances for getting into Hollywood on Ice. And so I moved to Boston to begin anew as an athlete and to forget the skating tour, discover counseling, kill the plankton, heal my body, and rest my mind. All good intentions and all doomed to fail, as the ideas were built upon the rubble of a former goal that I could not bring myself to raze but only remodel.

I did not take the time to properly set myself up for the new goal of rowing—I couldn't have. I never gave myself the chance to wake up from the nightmare of my skating disaster. Instead, I only yawned, rolled over, and found myself in a boathouse with a scale in one corner and calorie-counting ergometers in the other as I went head-to-head with another round of spandex outfits and weekly Sunday weigh-ins. Whatever notions of sport and athleticism lived in the boathouse, I was unable to see clearly as I warped the essence of rowing into a continuation of my festering dream.

✺

Chapter Twenty

Rowing with the Predator

"The most valuable thing we can do for the human psyche," writer Eudora Welty once crooned, "is to let it occasionally rest, wander, and live in the changing light of a room." This is good advice and works best when you let the psyche out if its straitjacket and slip food through the crack under the door a few times a day and maybe include a napkin with which to wipe away the spindles of drool. Other than that, the room idea is good and the changing light works wonders. After a few days of the displaced serenity that comes with being in a new place, my psyche was ready for another round of eating disorders.

Height did not work to my advantage in skating, as factors such as gravity and Evelyn, the Holiday on Ice choreographer, decided that shorter people were easier to work with. In rowing, height sets up the preliminary promise that those who are tall are proportionately strong. The women on the U.S. rowing development team seemed very happy to see me at first, as I walked into the boathouse at five-nine and visibly under the 125-pound international race weight requirement, clearly an asset-to-be for the program. Tall, thin, and strong was a powerful combination in rowing, and my first impression fooled my boatmates into thinking I possessed all three characteristics. Everyone else was a bit shorter and able to pack more muscle weight into their physical frames. Someone weighing less than 125 pounds meant that someone else in the boat could weigh enough to make up the difference, as the boat *average* was set at 125. In college, I rowed in the open-weight division because Colgate did not have a lightweight team (in collegiate/national racing, women have to weigh under 130) and because my skating had given me enough muscle power to land a seat in the varsity boat. Realistically, my height and natural weight left me in the lurch of elite rowing — too small to be a top-notch open weight, too tall to be a healthy lightweight.

Sadly, lightweight rowing does not take height and muscle mass into consideration, so the discrepancy between a five-five rower and one five-ten makes staying at 125 pounds easier for some than for others. There was no reason for my teammates to assume that I was anything but strong and healthy, since I had made it into the camp, and I had no intention of introducing them to my psychoplankton. Everything was finally going to be fine, I thought.

But it was not fine. Far from it. My first row did little to inspire the coach. My stroke timing was completely off — the blade of my oar entered the water late, came out even later. My swirling puddles of effort left in the wake of the boat were visibly smaller than everyone else's, and my posture was crinkly and slumped. Rowing had never felt like that before, heavy and tiring. The practice session would have been a perfect commercial shoot for Frosted Flakes, where Tony the Tiger, famous for rescuing bonking athletes, swooped down from who knows where and handed kids a bowl of his famous, sugary flakes. The slacking athlete, instantly fortified with nine essential vitamins and chemicals, always jumped back in her game and trumped her cereal-deficient competitors. There was no cartoon Tony around to save me on my first day back in a boat, only Coach Nelson, who shook his head and offered me a hearty bowl of disappointment.

The chance to prove my worth as an athlete presented itself twice more before the coach all but gave up on me for the remainder of the season. First, there was the erg test. All I had to do was sit down and pull the same score I had a little over a year ago. The only difference was that now I was physically and mentally a completely different person. The three baby bites of a banana-flavored PowerBar stored up in my pathetic energy vault were spent within the first minute, and for the remainder of the 2,000-meter timed test, I pulled slower and slower, as if I had dropped anchor somewhere along the way. My time was nearly a minute off, a large discrepancy in rowing, like an Olympic marathoner churning out 20-minute miles. A premature infant might have pulled a better erg test, and neither Nelson nor I were impressed with my efforts. Still, I assuaged myself with the belief that if all the other girls had eaten only a third of an energy bar since the day before, my erg score would have kicked their asses.

But it was not the Anorexia Olympics, and Nelson was not about to hand me a medal for an eight-minute erg test at an elite camp, no matter how much my logic thought it deserved one. *I am totally and mentally well! Not only did I ingest three whole bites of the banana PowerBar but I threw away the wrapper instead of eating it!* These women were serious about rowing and no matter how much I wanted to be, too, I was unable to let go of my disorder. Every day I showed up at the boathouse with the fullest notion of giving 110 percent, only to find that the plankton had whittled it down to about 2.78 percent by the time we shoved off from the dock. I rowed with my body and fought with my mind and kept my hunger-happy schizophrenia quiet in the locker room so no one else could see.

Not long after the erg test, one of our practices was a stair-running session at Harvard's football field. Stadium steps had been one of my favorite workouts while in college, as my skating muscles enabled me to take Colgate's stairs two at a time with ease and power, and the rush of passing my teammates mid-flight only spurred my desire to speed up and go harder. Again, I had failed to assess the situation of my present-day stair-climbing abilities. I took one step for their three, and by the third step I was huffing and puffing as though I had never engaged in athletics in my life.

My teammates probably liked me now more than ever, as none of them found me a threat to her position in the boat. Despite the "all for one" unity of rowing, development camps leave a margin of individual competitiveness, as everyone is striving for national recognition, competing both with and against their fellow oarsmen. I was out of the running in all senses.

With the erg test from hell and the stadium steps higher than heaven, Nelson saw all he needed to, and for the rest of the summer I was something akin to the spare oar of the team. Poor coach. He was promised a firecracker of a rower and wound up with a complete dud, to the sad surprise of us both. Yet he never addressed the situation of my strength and instead almost ignored me altogether, leaving me to wonder if that summer might have been different had he showed concern instead of annoyance. He did not cut me from the program, which I thought he might, but instead kept me on as a backup, just as I had once thought of rowing as a backup for my failed skating plans. In an unspoken, subconscious way, this was my comeuppance.

Eerily enough, weigh-ins came on Sundays in the boathouse just as they had on tour. Only now it was an old bar scale we stood on, and the process of moving the balance into place took a lot longer than Hollywood on Ice's instant red-arrow foot scale. Coach Nelson did not have us strip down and there were no monetary fines assessed, but it was clear in this sport that if we were over our target weight, our positions in the boat would be in jeopardy. Stepping on the scale still proved a harrowing experience, even though I knew being weighed was for athletic measures, not for Lora. I clenched my fingers into fists to keep from shaking, as one of the assistant coaches slid the bar weight into place, measuring what I still believed was my worth as a human being.

I was sentenced to "the gig" nearly every practice, a single-scull boat from the Paleozoic Era of rowing that looked like a warped canoe hastily made from a giant tree that had rotted to the core. Tom Hanks built a sturdier boat from his four-year collection of washed-ashore twigs in *Cast Away*. The gig was heavy and cumbersome, like a wooden dunce cap I had to row instead of wear. Perched in this boat, which was only slightly more narrow than my old Holiday elephant costume but still looked like an ice show prop, I row, row, rowed the gig weakly up the Charles day in and day out, watching as my healthy teammates swooshed by in the strength and unity of eights, fours, pairs, and doubles. I kept watch for ducks (that might have been wearing skates or carrying rifles) and beginner scullers who navigated their boats with novice movements and Grígor-style strokes, weaving through the Charles to the beat of their own rhythmically challenged drummer. What good came out of my solo expeditions was that I had time to think about the therapy sessions I had recently begun, letting my mind focus on what my counselor and I had discussed in a small office not far from the boathouse.

Mary Anne was a good therapist with bad furniture. The problem was the couch, a wicker ensemble with a cushion so comfortable that during our close-your-eyes-and-visualize segments, I fell asleep sitting straight up. The plankton did not care to wake me.

"Breathe in," Mary Anne invited. I did. "And exhale." I rarely made it to that part consciously. Something snorelike gurgled forth sooner or later. Two practices a day were taking a toll on my energy-deficient body, and when the opportunity to sleep presented itself, I obliged.

Mary Anne was the only therapist I could find who based her fees on a sliding scale, and because I needed to see her more than once a week, expenses had to be considered. My father offered to fund my therapy sessions, but I felt extremely guilty about having someone else pay to repair the psychological damage I had brought upon myself. We split it down the middle, my half coming from the savings of my tour experience. My mother did not think that therapy in general was a healthy thing. Therapy meant admitting one's baggage, issues, problems, and that was not appropriate for one's image, darling. Even from far away, she began to do and say some strange things that summer regarding my weight. A couple of college friends whom I saw often in Boston began to receive phone calls from my mother, in which she asked them to join forces with Crouches With Radar and make sure that I did not gain any weight back. *But please don't tell her that I've called you.* Tara, my former Colgate rowing teammate, told Crouches straight out that I needed to eat more and get healthy, to which my mother replied, *She doesn't need food, she just needs to take vitamins.* Yes, that was exactly what I needed. More Flintstones. When my friends told me of the phone calls, I knew that therapy was precisely where I needed to be.

Mary Anne liked worksheets and drawings and relaxation methods, and I went with the flow because just plain talking about the plankton was difficult and it was nice to have other venues of expression, even if they were a little out of the ordinary. She was a soft-spoken woman in her mid-forties with trace elements of hippieness in her free-flowing clothes and long, dark hair. Her office was on the second story of her home, a few miles from the apartment I rented halfway between Boston College and Boston University. I walked to and from our sessions, of course, making the wicker couch all the more inviting. In an upstairs study with plush cushions and philosophical bookcases, the afternoon shadows and changing light filtered in from nearby tree branches and danced slow waltzes on the wall behind my therapist as I began to talk about my body and let my psyche wander around the room.

I told Mary Anne the basics: I was a figure skater whose amateur and professional careers clashed in morals, leaving me confused enough to seek comfort in deranged eating patterns. I watched her eyebrows raise with delight and her face morph into the "Oooh! A figure skater! How lovely!" expression that too often comes with the immediate disclosure of such information. I told her that I was aware of my problem with food, but felt like Jekyll and Hyde when it came to deciding what to do about it. Some days I was in dire straits about my weight; other days I was convinced I was just fine. I wanted to be an athlete again, a very good one, great even, but the disorder was holding me back. There seemed to be so much beneath the surface. I couldn't figure out how to break the cycle. Could she? Could she help me find Captain Graceful again? Could she help me find greatness? Could she tell me why my mind put butter and olive oil in the same category as murder and the death penalty? But as much as I wanted answers, my flip side was skeptical. Couldn't Captain Graceful and I save the world all by ourselves? Couldn't I put in a call to Fix-it Woman and get this mess cleaned up?

Mary Anne gave me assignments, worksheets designed to make me reflect on my fears, hopes, needs, and responsibilities. They were semi-helpful but felt too much like homework. I began them with bold statements like "I am angry about . . ." or "What I am really hungry for is . . . ," but my answers surprised me, digging up family scenarios and feelings of inadequacy that dated much further back than the skating tour. Mary Anne called my plankton a "Predator with a capital *P*" and explained that it liked to prey on my thoughts and dreams. I could have told her that, but it felt good to hear someone else say it aloud. We sifted through a lot of interesting debris, mining my mind for nuggets of emotion. Some days all we unearthed were crumbly pebbles of remembrance, but other sessions brought little lumps of coal, diamonds in the rough that Mary Anne coaxed out with colorful, striking, albeit goofy methods.

She asked me to draw pictures of the Predator Plankton—*don't forget the capital* P, *Kathryn*—and what came out were stick-figure sketches of people and places and voices whose opinions I had stored up over the years and now swam through my gooey mind, looking for a way to get out. I drew them all yelling at me, and there I was, the stick figure with the big, sad face getting reamed out by the Plankton. The bittersweet duplicity of my solid memory had caught up with me in a negative manner. The management of Hollywood on Ice and my mother might have been large influences, but the list of Plankton grew lengthy: high school friends, college buddies, coaches, judges, skaters, rowers, runners, dancers, dieters, athletes, actresses, singers, writers, the media, skinny people, larger people, fathers, brothers, boyfriends, old people, little kids, people I knew, strangers I didn't. Somehow their fleeting yet enduring comments on weight had entered my head and lain dormant until ignited by the fuse of the tour. All the defensive voices, the ones that should have argued against these illogical thoughts, were missing. The thought of destroying all the Plankton was nice but overwhelming. It seemed a larger and longer task than just the summer months allowed (before I moved away from Boston in September), so Mary Anne and I agreed on taking baby steps.

My immediate concern was my athleticism and how to go about stopping the Plankton from taking away my strength completely. My therapist did not think it was a good idea for me to put my not-quite-stable mind and quite unstable body through such rigorous physical demands, but she acquiesced when I promised to eat more. My promise was not false, but it was meager. I made efforts and lived to tell about it, eating two-thirds of whatever I usually only ate half of. Baby steps, but steps nevertheless.

The time spent with Mary Anne was helpful not only from a therapeutic standpoint. Awkward in the presence of others, I was uneasy about my constant state of food-induced panic, which often caused me to say weird things. Talking to Mary Anne was good practice for conversation in general, something I was terribly lonely for. I became close with a few of the women on the rowing team but was still unable to open up and unleash my Planktonian burdens on them. I put on my happy face for them, which was good for everyone but made me feel like a victim of multiple personality disorder. *Dinner? No thanks, I'm not hungry. I ate earlier* (two days ago), *so I'll just grab a* (diet) *soda* (and watch you eat that chicken breast while I drool all over your sneakers), *okay?* And then there was the other kind of loneliness, the kind I knew from the trailer, the one that came with considering myself untouchable and yet left me hungering for touch.

That summer in Boston I dated a rower I had known briefly before the skating tour began. Brian was a tall, chiseled specimen of athleticism with a physique and a smile that battled for the title of most impressive feature. If the overused description of Greek god could be taken away from all other nominees and restored to its rightful owner, then Brian was deserving of the deistic designation. Steven was no longer in the picture, although I had seen him one last time before his wedding to give him a hug and a handshake and wish him luck with his fiancée.

Despite our physical attraction, Brian and I had other lovers who diverted our attention. Mine was insatiable hunger; his was elite athletics. It seemed a step up for me, as this time I was the "other woman" to something other than a human girlfriend. Trampy, it appeared, was lost along with all my weight that year, and as far as I was concerned, it was something I didn't need to regain. Back to straight-arrow city. My head was too messed-up for intimacy anyway. *No sex, Brian. Rolling around naked? Yeah, okay.*

Focused, determined, and dedicated in his quest to be the best, Brian concentrated all his energies on rowing. This I understood, admired, and did not mind being second to because I was engrossed in my own goals. While he planned out his training regimens, practice schedules, and race strategies with precise detail, I rigorously lined up which oatmeal packets could be eaten in what order over the course of the summer. Figuring out if Tuesdays should be apple cinnamon or plain, and whether or not to save maple sugar for the weekend, well, it was easy to see that Brian and I were both extremely goal-oriented people.

Our bodies shared a bed, but our minds lay in the embrace of ambitions so powerful that we mistook their asphyxiating squeeze for love, not love for each other but for the goals themselves. Born from two individual passions of sport, the dreams we chased for so long had somehow turned around and started chasing us, and we were too caught up in the movement to notice any shift of direction. His quest for the national (open-weight) team was nothing short of driven, but whatever inner pressures he felt about reaching it were secret and heavy. When he spoke of rowing, if he spoke of it at all, his words were monotone and his eyes were a vacant collection of parts, retinas and irises long retired from dancing.

Brian loved rowing about as much as I loved eating my canned carrots, but we were so distracted by our daily dedication that for all we knew, this fixation was what love, commitment, and being goal-oriented was all about. Neither of us spoke much of our obsessions, and though Brian might have caught a few glimpses of my Plankton, I kept my eating habits and my counseling appointments to myself. We spoke of things like the weather and the surface aspects of our families and friends, hiding from each other all the fears and fantasies we might have had in common, such details remaining buried beneath timing and location, oatmeal and oarlocks.

And so my days in Boston followed a consistent pattern of lively activities: mornings were spent rowing my special piece of driftwood, followed by nomadically roaming the streets of the city all afternoon until my therapy appointment, then running to the boathouse for the second round of dinghy fun, and then itinerantly navigating the city again till Brian got back from practice. I headed over to his place after I was sure that he had already eaten, then fell into bed to repeat the process the next day. For all the miles I covered walking in Boston, I did not see very much on my exploratory jaunts, only the ghosts of South America hovering overhead, as if to tell me I had not really gotten far away at all.

Sleep came either in heavy doses or in sporadic increments. Exhausted as I was from lack of nourishment, nighttime in my head was like a twelve-hour rave for the Plankton. As much as I enjoyed the feeling of a Greek god beside me, my self-esteem was far from comfortable with the situation. Confidence slipped away with the muscles that once put it there, and the thought that anyone could find me attractive was inconceivable. The catch-22 was that being alone was no picnic, either. There was a comfort I found with Brian, a combination of anonymity and physicality that worked only because both of us were at a similar stage in our lives. We spent our days looking for greatness and our nights in a mutual distraction that let us rest from the monsters of mediocrity that chased us through our dreams.

❧

Chapter Twenty-one

Detonation

Rowing, walking, counseling, tour memories . . . the summer passed by in glimpses of disconnected thought. Other than the repetitive pattern, I remember very little about rowing in Boston because one of the major side effects of starvation is stupidity. Biochemistry offers a better insight to the hows and whys of starvation-related brain dysfunction, citing such things as low serotonin levels, iron deficiencies, and all their attendant dangers. Unfortunately, my shallow surface knowledge of science and my self-righteous denial didn't work well together. Under the anorexia diagnosis and definitions, there was always a list of health risks I was generally aware of but usually dismissive about. It was easy to deny any psychological or internal-organ damage, since I couldn't actually *see* inside my mind and body. Anemia was only part of my problem, as I ate very few iron-fortified foods, but anemia didn't sound like such a bad thing. It even had a goddesslike ring to it, too pretty to be destructive. *Anemia, great ruler of all things sickly.* Then there was the threat of the female athlete triad, a triple play of disordered eating, amenorrhea, and osteoporosis. I had the first two covered, but osteoporosis? Why worry about that in my early twenties? A few holey bones would make me lighter! And besides, if the female athlete triad was really so serious, then doctors would have chosen a better acronym than FAT.

Scientific jargon aside, there is simply not enough energy for the brain to function clearly when deprived of food, so even my basic thought processes began to wilt. I was slow catching on to conversations, and even slower responding. A gnat's attention span was longer than mine if the subject at hand was not food-related. I feared talking to people, afraid I might slip up and show them the Plankton by mistake.

Hello, how are you?

Great! And you?

Fine, thanks, and you? By the way, do you know the caloric composition of dog biscuits because I just had three and really need to know. So, how are you?

I was certain that I was losing my mind as well as my body when things other than weight began to disappear from me. I began to notice a strange habit in Boston, something that I did not do while in South America. As I wandered the streets of Boston in between practices, I began to forget things. Sunglasses in stores, my wallet in the boathouse, sweatshirts in the locker room, car keys in coffee shops. I drove to practice and walked home, forgetting the car. I walked to the car and forgot where I wanted to go. I went places and forgot why. Some people misplace things every day or are genuinely absentminded, but I was not normally one of them. Pre-plankton, I was a busy little bee with more "to do" lists than I knew what to do with, so losing car keys and being unable to direct my thoughts were not natural occurences.

In some ways, my mind was struggling to be more active than it had been on tour. Rowing necessitated some concentration, whereas my days on tour had been spent blankly contemplating skinniness. Now, at the rowing camp, consistently having to assess my power when pulling on the oar and keeping in sync with the other rowers did require me to be mentally present and actively concentrating. Still, the physical repetition of rowing was ingrained enough in my memory vault so that I did not really have to think about when to pull on the oar and when to push off the foot stretchers. Forgetting that pattern would have been a whole different kind of stupid.

Mary Anne and I worked together on overcoming my stupidity (my word, not hers). One of the neatest breakthroughs we made was figuring out my addiction to eating the outsides of things, like wrappers and banana peels. Wrappers were simply the outer layers, the things that caught a person's eye, the aesthetic component of whatever lay inside. With all the pent-up emotions that came along with being told my appearance was not up to snuff by either skating or family officials, no wonder my mind wanted to consume—*internalize*—the one thing it felt it was lacking. The perfect wrapper. Whoa. Therapy was kinda cool! The counseling, combined with the general atmosphere of athleticism, was enough to persuade some of the Plankton to ease up on the constant brain chewing. The wrapper fetish fell by the wayside almost immediately, after I understood its cause. The regular food took a while longer.

Slowly I began to recognize things that I had not been able to see before the tour. My mother had her own issues with food and body image, and like the aneurysm, they went straight to dust-bunny city beneath the carpet of all things mentally buried. She habitually drank tea—a diuretic—between cigarettes—an appetite suppressant—and ate halves, thirds, and other fractions of meal portions. When I was growing up, she asked me to split everything from ham sandwiches to a can of Dr Pepper for lunch. She pushed plates away, half eaten, and called herself piggy when she took three bites of any dessert. Now it seemed as clear as day: I was not the first person in my family to struggle with my body. But I would make sure I was the last.

In addition to concentration exercises, while Mary Anne and I crayoned, chanted, and imagined happy things together, I picked up on a few more positive aspects about my lightweight rowing surroundings. Even though I was not ready to admit that rowing at under 125 pounds was not good for my body, I was constantly surrounded by women who were mentally stable and serious about their athleticism. Whereas I dribbled out one frail chin-up, they did multiple pull-ups with a beautiful intensity that gave me something to shoot for. The ease in their stride looked so much better than my lethargically shuffling legs when we went on team runs, and I wanted to feel this forgotten swiftness again. In the locker room they pulled out PowerBars and studied the nutrition labels, equating calories with *energy* instead of *enemy*. Even though rowing isn't free of eating-disordered athletes, my teammates were focused on food in a much healthier way than I was.

Their preoccupation with staying thin was out of concern for their sport and their teammates, so they could be perfectly effective mental and physical machines, not because they had a negative body image.

They did not think themselves ugly or unworthy. These women stuck up for their muscles and were ready to go to bat in defense of their bodies. If Lora ever walked into our boathouse and dared say something deprecating about one of these rowers, she would have been beaten silly by a mob of women with heavy oars. Their confidence was beautiful and delicately contagious, for every now and then I caught the faintest glimpse of self-esteem working its way back into my thoughts. *Let's draw that!* Mary Anne would have said. I might have drawn a team of women with oar-size forks eating a boatful of grilled Plankton.

A week or two before the Canadian Henley, our final regatta — one that Coach Nelson actually promised I could row in — I went to hear a man speak about athleticism and nutrition. Jess, a fellow lightweight teammate, invited me to hear six-time Ironman world champion Dave Scott speak about endurance racing and optimal energy intake.

"Who?" I asked.

"Dave Scott . . . the triathlete," Jess said. "You know, *the* Dave Scott?"

"Oh, okay. Sure." Ironwhat? I had no idea whom she was talking about and could not figure out if I was just ignorant or if the anorexia was making me an idiot again. Maybe I knew *the* Dave Scott but had just forgotten. All I knew of triathlons was the event I had witnessed in Mar del Plata, the fit and soggy racers chasing glory while I was lost in my world of impermissible hunger. Ironman . . . was that the crazy race with the hundred-or-so-mile bike ride between a ridiculously long swim and a marathon run?

"Yeah, that's the one. This guy is, like, a legend," Jess crooned.

Jess and I sat in a small health-food store in Cambridge with a dozen other people and listened to *the* Dave Scott lecture about sport performance and nutrition, the very things my body craved but could not handle. Ever since observing the race in South America I had secretly wanted to try a triathlon, but time and place and goo had not offered the opportunity.

I was quickly transfixed by the famous triathlete, more focused on his legs than his speech. Thick protrusions of veins bulged from his ankles and ran up his shaved calves like miniature embossed rivers of a purplish green current. On his forearms the same phenomenon occurred, as if the muscles were so developed that the blood vessels had to relocate to the outermost reaches of the skin. Some veins were smooth; others were knotty, like little snakes with full bellies scurrying beneath his epidermis. Had triathlon done such sculpting to his body? Fascinating.

The audience members asked questions about triathlon training and nutritional advice while I sat silently staring at the wall of MetRx Bars, Clif Bars, and protein powder shakes just beyond Dave Scott's head, lost in my hunger as usual. I do not recall one word that the veiny guru spoke, until Jess raised her hand. She began with a simple question, something about effective protein sources and then just kept on talking, launching into an explosive complaint about the stresses of lightweight rowing. Apparently I wasn't the only hungry one in the boathouse. She explained that we were elite-level rowers, and did he have any advice on what foods would sustain the body but get us through weigh-ins without adding weight? He suggested we try small, multiple meals throughout the day to rev up our metabolism and keep us satiated. I grew horrified at the notion of eating as often as he suggested while Jess kept rambling about lightweight woes and predicaments. *The* Dave Scott listened patiently while I mentally arranged the background of Clif Bars into categories of forbidden preference: cookies and cream definitely came before apricot, but after peanut butter chocolate chip. The famous Ironman was sympathetic but clearly thought we were nuts. Mmmm, nuts. Almonds before macadamias, but definitely after cashews.

"Maybe," he said with gentle caution, "there is a different sport that might suit you better." Jess quietly shook her head as if to acknowledge but disagree. For some reason, the calm simplicity of his words reverberated through my head and momentarily stilled the Plankton. What if there *was* something else? Something athletic that had no use for scales and weigh-ins? Some sport that revolved around the benefits of eating more instead of less? Some place where vein-laden muscles were seen as attributes, no matter how heavy each powerful limb grew? But, like my long-coveted skating solo, the focused desire to prove myself as a rower had overruled all thoughts of quitting the sport. I would have to take Dave Scott's words with me and mull them over for a while. Maybe take them over to Mary Anne and draw them out with her Crayolas to see what lay hidden in the meanings.

The Canadian Henley was the last race slated for Riverside's elite lightweight camp, and I was scheduled to row in the double scull event with a teammate named Hanna. Instead, I was thrown headfirst into a river of reality that marked the turning point in my journey back to a life without Plankton and a future of good health.

Coach Nelson read the lineups for the race, and Hanna and I were to make up Riverside B, the second of two boats entered by our team. Riverside A was composed of the two strongest women on our squad, and Hanna and I were thrown into the mix as noncontenders, a boat to be beaten, a chew toy for the big dogs of lightweight glory. After paddling around in the bloated log all summer, I was ecstatic just to row a boat that did not resemble a dock, not to mention with another human being! I had forgotten that my old competitive self would never have settled for being a "B" boat athlete. Neither would Hanna, and she spoke up about it, switching on a permanent light in my dark and gooey little head.

"I don't want to row with you," she said flatly. "Don't take it personally, but you're weak."

Shazam! Out of nowhere, just like that: detonation of the dream deferred. All festering sores of failed skating and rowing dreams finally came to their point of necessary yet unexpected explosion. I was blown away. There it was, her words clanging in my ears, ringing out a painful truth I had not heard before: I had become the kid picked last in gym class, the one no one wanted around, the weak link in the chain, the person an athlete vows never to become, and although I knew that it was something I had brought on myself, I had not thought anyone else could see it. But they could. In my thinness I had become naked. See-through. Transparent. In that moment of truth, those words from one strong athlete to one who used to be, everything changed and I finally saw daylight at the end of my tunnel vision. For the first time since the goo brought forth the Plankton a year ago, an old friend took root in the marshes of my confusion, burrowing down, holding fast, sprouting in quiet immediacy. Strength.

I wished for strength right then with such longing that I felt it course through my body in faint but steady pulses. First, I wished for strength enough to pummel Hanna, then for the strength to win our race, and then to promise myself that the weakness was over. For good. Forever. Good-bye. I wished for skating, the kind I used to know. I wanted stadium steps of Harvard proportion. I wished for weight rooms and double axels, boathouses and bagel shops. I wanted veiny legs like *the* Dave Scott's and the graceful arms of my long lost Captain. I wished for my mother to bring on the encircled models, and I wanted Mary Anne's big old crayons to X them out. I wished for breakfast, lunch, and dinner all in the same day. I wanted Sundays without scales, Sundays the way they used to be, bringing athletic competition — my personal religion, my sacred church. I wished for the lady with the wings and the clipboard to pencil me in eighty years from today, I'll see you then but not before. I wished for a toolbox full of self-esteem, I wanted to be the fix-it woman who would redream, reconstruct, and hammer everything into place again. I wanted to see the pigtailed little tomboy kick that ball once more. I wanted Lora to implode, and time to go backward, and to slap that lid back on Pandora's trailer-size box. I wanted to unlearn all the nutrition labels tattooed in my memory, to come undone from their spell, to unbraid myself from their caustic trilogy of fat, calories, and self-worth. All the false promises I had made in the name of starvation, all the weak attempts at fooling myself, all the pecking at crumbs I thought were feasts of sustenance. This time it was different because this time, I finally knew what I was hungry for. Survival. Confidence. Victory.

I knew then and there that if I could survive myself, all the negativity I had put my poor mind through, if I could outlast all the trivial imperfections for which I scrutinized my soul and body, if I could be at peace with the quietness of a moment left untouched by thought, then and only then would I find my weightless freedom and athletic power in all the Sundays yet to come.

ᴪ

Reconstruction

The triathletes call the connecting space between the swim, bike, and run "the transition," and that is basically what it is. Usually rectangular in shape, about 100 by 60 yards, the transition area is somewhat like the dimensions of a midsize grocery store parking lot. The field (or expanse of pavement) used for the transition spreads out as the hub of race activity, and always ends up in the same place, just off the shore of the swim venue. In the far corner of the transition area, a prerace volunteer brands the racer's thighs, calves, and arms with permanent pen, inscribing personal race numbers onto the slickness of newly shaved limbs. *In case one falls off while racing,* someone always jokes, *we'll know who to return it to.* Despite the contingent of athletic shoes worn without socks and the mildew-accumulating wetsuits, there is only one specific odor of a triathlon: the mordant whiff of indelible markers that then dies away with equal immediacy. There is also the faint lingering of chlorine or seawater that passes through the air of the transition area, though this scent usually goes unnoticed by those who are about to race, lost in athletic concentration.

From swim to bike and then again from bike to run, the athletes spend a few moments grabbing the appropriate gear for each segment of the lengthy race. In the first transition, swimmers peel their wetsuits, rip off their goggles, put on their bike shoes, and head out to the cycling course. In yet another variation on Snow White and the Seven Dwarfs, the transition area is happy home to Very Tanned Triathlete and the Thousand Bicycles, as each athlete tries to locate his vehicle among the multitude of Treks (trustworthy), Cannondales (cool), Specialized (speedy), Litespeeds (liquidation of bank account), and all the other metallic members of the cycling family.

"T2" sees the removal of the bike shoes; the hurried donning of sneakers, sunglasses, and race belts; and a mad dash to the run path. From outside the transition area, the fans cheer and the cameras snap as bystanders capture the athletic metamorphosis on film. There is little nudity in the transition area, although in Ironman races, those who opt for the comfort of complete dryness are ushered into single-sex changing tents with no mirrors or lightbulbs, just rickety chairs and flimsy curtain doors.

Along the right side of the transition area, pipelike bars run the length of the field, under which the equipment is stored in chronological order of how it will be used in the race: bike shoes, jersey, bike, helmet, sunglasses, hat, sneakers, race number, fuel belt. The gear is all the same, but some have personalized their equipment. Stickers on bicycles read of product sponsors, national flags, silly cartoon figures, even inspirational quotes. On the handlebars, some men tape photographs of scantily clad women, or whatever inspires them to pedal faster. Power-Bars are stripped from their wrappers and bent over the top tubes of the bike, race-ready for when the stomach sends forth its motivational rumble, *Feed me.* No one here eats the wrappers. On my bike, a list of heart-rate target zones is taped between my aero bars, and a shower of sticky red drops covers the surface of my yellow Trek. *Blood,* I tell my non-triathlete friends, *I sweat blood.* My training partners know that it is only highly concentrated fruit punch Gatorade that I spilled days ago and neglected to wipe away.

Before each designated transition space, a triathlete's personal items are arranged on a small towel, a place marker mirroring the mindset of the racer, strewn with personal necessities. Some racers lay out easily digestible energy gels. Some, Clif Bars. Others, Coca-Cola. Most, water. Penalties are assessed to those who leave their equipment out in the open, dangerous and trip-overable. Other fines include unbuckled helmets, getting outside assistance from spectators, and drafting off the bikers ahead, whereby our penalty times increase if the distance between bikes does not. Quick changes see a flurry of hurried fingers snapping this and bucking that, attaching to our spandex outfits all that we may need in the coming miles. Sunscreen is slathered on, turning our faces white and ghostly, which looks normal from afar but up close, freakish and supernatural.

Along the other side of the transition area tables are set up, rows of Dixie cups, shimmering with doses of Gatorade or water, their reflections flickering in the early Sunday morning sun. Triathletes race by, stealing a moment for swift hydration before heading onto the course. The volunteers and officials pick up the fallen cups, easing the torment of the ecologically disgruntled fans.

At most of the larger races no one knows anyone's name, appearances are masked by the similar costumes, which vary in color but share the basic bathing-suit form. Other than body type and run stride, the athletes are indistinguishable. Except for a handful of pros whose surnames are emblazoned on the back of their race suits, everyone else just goes by number: racer #361, racer #808. Some participants become obsessed with checking out others' calves, where each athlete is further identified by age group.

Triathletes come in such a wide variety of body types — stocky, tall, lean, thick, wiry, short — and those participating send a valuable lesson of self-esteem to the onlookers and future generations of the sport: It doesn't matter what you look like. If you train your body wisely and pull off your transitions cleanly, you too can win any race you want.

The day before an Ironman triathlon, the athletes gather in a tent at the end of the transition area for weigh-ins. In a 140-mile race, dehydration and sickness can wreak havoc on an athlete, bringing on dangerous levels of weight loss. Weigh-ins let the medical staff know exactly how depleted an athlete is, a statistic that could save his life. The scales in the transition area are peaceful and friendly, and those who stand on them are confident and care nothing of the digits that appear, though they are sometimes disappointed if the numbers are too small.

Race meetings take place in the transition area, where final instructions, rules, warnings, and regulations are announced before a race. Questions are asked and answered. Are there volunteers stationed at the intersections? What if we get lost? Will there be traffic, when will it start, how long will it be there? How cold is the water? Will there be food handed out on the course? Emotions run high in the transition area, as prerace nerves and long bathroom lines sometimes lead us to question what the hell we're doing there in the first place, and isn't there someplace better to spend a Sunday morning? Such thoughts are quelled by the starter's gun, and we know deep inside that this is exactly where we want to be. Only now, in the heart of a transition area, where I find myself in a place of confidence so far removed from Hollywood on Ice, can I begin to describe the world I saw cooped up inside that oblong box.

*   *   *

From the shore, the waves are so enormous that they crash over the tops of the four-foot-high buoys, sending the inflatable globes into anchored whirls of dizziness. The roughness of this morning's Atlantic Ocean is the quiet topic of conversation among some of the triathletes on the beach, while others silently focus on their prerace thoughts.

"Buena suerte, Katarín," says a voice behind me. It belongs to the manager of the hotel where I am staying, just up the road from the swim start. Ricardo is a triathlete as well. I return the good-luck sentiments.

"Gracias, Ricardo. Suerte."

The two fluorescent orange buoys are placed about 500 meters out from the shore and 500 meters away from each other. *Dos vueltas,* we will swim two times around them in a triangular pattern—beach to buoy one, buoy one to buoy two, buoy two back into beach and then once again. The bright spheres designate the swim course of the Mar del Plata Half Ironman Triathlon, which consists of a 1.2-mile swim, 56-mile bike, and 13.1-mile run.

I have come to this Argentinean city again nearly five years after Hollywood on Ice first wound its way through these streets. I am here alone. It is March 3, Sunday, at seven o'clock in the morning. I am a triathlete now, not a showgirl skater with an eating disorder. I am here to do the very race I witnessed that day long ago, during one of my starvation walks down a path I was certain would never end. What on earth were they *doing*—those bathing-suit-clad bike riders whizzing past me in a blur of determination and power, a whole herd of Captain Gracefuls barreling by with beautiful speed? I have the answer now. They were getting the most out of their bodies and their lives. They were finding greatness.

The gun goes off, the athletes go in, the swim goes round and round, and I have no time for nostalgia or reflections on how far my mind and body have come since the tour. Maybe later. I can think of that stuff during the run, but at the moment all concentration must be focused on the gargantuan waves that try to push me back to shore. When I race, my body is the furthest thing from my mind and yet the closest thing to my soul. And whether or not I acknowledge it consciously, this race is different from the other triathlons I've done over the past three years. Today, every arm stroke pulls me through more than just water, every gearshift propels me further down literal roads and metaphorical ones, and every footfall seems more symbolic than the one before, as I carry myself toward a finish line that will finish many things when I cross it. This is a race of erasure, a farewell to all my fears of unobtainable strength. It is a tying of my loose ends and an end of untying my losses — no longer will any shortcoming or negativity roam freely through my thoughts, never again will my body be transformed into less of itself.

The swim is over, but the day is far from being done. I have swallowed half of the Atlantic as the waves fed themselves to me for half an hour, in thick, salty, unasked-for servings. We make our way up onto the beach, shiny in slick penguiny wetsuits, waddling our way out from the sea and up to the concrete platform of Transition 1. Peeling off my wetsuit in haste, I notice the vacant spaces of four bikes from the elite women's transition rack where my yellow Trek remains. I head out onto the bike course in fifth place.

Nueve vueltas, nine times around a 6.3-mile bike course that each racer is responsible for counting. Velcroed to the top tube of my bicycle is a food pouch in which I have nine small pretzel rods. At the end of each circuit, I either eat one or chuck it toward the gutter, and this method becomes my edible abacus of laps remaining. There is also a lemon-flavored nutrition bar, two apple-cinnamon Carb-BOOM! gel packets, and half a peanut butter and jelly sandwich to snack on at given intervals. The only reason for the fractioned sandwich is that I already ate the other half. For digestive comfort, I do not eat all of this food during the race, but I like options. The buffet concept no longer frightens me.

My two water bottles ride with me for a while and then embark on their own triathlon; jumping, flying, and rolling down the street after I hit a few rough potholes. Yet dehydration worries are pacified: there is a Gatorade station at the end of each lap, and I love the popular South American flavor they have on hand — Orange-Grapefruit Blast. At the beginning of each lap, the race announcer calls out the names of those who ride past and every time I circle the course I hear *"Numero veinte, Katarín Bertine, la chica norteamericana,"* number twenty, Kathryn Bertine, the North American girl. I am the only woman here from the United States, a long way to travel. The crowd yells for me with a roar that I understand the minute I hear it. In the wake of September 11, they are cheering more for my country than just for some American triathlete. My energy doubles each time I roll past this section of the course.

No one here or at home knows the personal symbolism this race holds for me, and I hold it to myself and savor the privacy of a reborn dream still in its infant stages. I love this sport, I want to take it as far as I can, and where that might be is something I'll let the future handle. When people ask how or why I became involved with triathlon, I offer up some casual remark about how interesting it looked. The true answer — that I felt like drop-kicking my eating disorder's emaciated posterior into the next millennium — opens up a whole can of worms that I usually don't like to serve to the general public. I would rather have people see me for what I can do, not what I once did. Near the end of each bike loop, a group of teenage Argentinean boys in the crowd take to calling me "Power Cookie." I have no idea what this means, but it sounds mostly positive. Since anything related to the word *cookie* no longer freaks me out, I enjoy the nickname tremendously. *¡Vamos, Power Cookie, fuerte, fuerte!*

The wind is vicious and grows in strength as the bike course travels the coastal road not even a hundred yards in from the sea. In some places, the waves send their spray over my bike and body. The cycling segment takes less than three hours to complete, and the mental concentration of the fifty-six miles is overwhelming. Hazards reach out to grab those racers who fail to pay attention at all times, as ditches, gravel, stray dogs, lost water bottles, unassuming cars, clueless pedestrians, and other cyclists lurk as unintentional terrorists. *It's okay if my mind wanders,* I think to myself, *as long as my eyes do not.*

While riding a section of the course the day before the race, getting a sense for the direction and geography of the triathlon, a feeling of slight disappointment came over me when I learned that the racecourse was set southward down the coast instead of north, past El Hotel Gatex and the old site of Hollywood on Ice. I mourned what I thought might have made a good metaphor—moving past, moving forward, moving beyond, all that stuff. Only during the race does it occur to me that symbolism works in mysterious ways, as I realize I am traveling in the opposite direction of my failed dreams. *I finally knew what I was hungry for. Survival. Confidence. Victory.*

I do not notice the poster until the midway point of the eighth lap, and even then it almost goes unseen. At the Gatorade station/bike turnaround that lies just on the outskirts of Mar del Plata, there is only a small traffic light, a warehousish structure and a field of tired grass. There are so many people handing out bottles of water and Orange-Grapefruit Blast that I do not think of anything more profound than whether I am thirsty. Yet by the eighth lap, the crowd is dissipating and the volunteers have thinned out, and because the road is smooth and friendly, I come out of my aero position and swivel my neck for a quick stretch. In the moment it takes me to turn my head from left to right, something catches my eye on the side of the abandoned warehouse. As I maneuver my bike around the orange cone of the turn point, the building disappears behind me and I will have to confirm my sighting on the final lap, but I know what I saw.

Three words in faded orange lettering upon a weak blue background that I know was once a brilliant midnight color, two skaters frozen in a split-jump position crisscrossing each other's path in midair. They have the bodies of athletic goddesses, their muscles dressed in sequins, their smiles painted wide, their ponytails flying in freedom and unison. Though worn and wrinkled, this poster was unmistakable even at a distance.

"*¿Conoces Hollywood on Ice?*" I had asked the taxi driver who shuttled me from the Mar del Plata airport earlier that week, wondering if he had ever heard of the show.

"*Sí, sí. El show visitó el año pasado, durante este tiempo.*" The show visited here about this time last year. He took me down Avenida Constitución, the street most familiar to me from the touring days. El Hotel Gatex was still on the corner, but the brown-and-white exterior had bloomed into bright pink and green paint. Emilita's beauty salon was, like my blond hair, no longer around. And in the field where Hollywood on Ice had set up its regal tent and beckoning lights, a sway-back horse and a preoccupied goat now munched on the dismal vegetation behind the FOR SALE sign that hung crookedly on a post where the ticket booth had once stood.

On the final bike lap, I look again in anticipation and verification of what I saw glued to the old warehouse. Next to two vivid posters announcing a Brazilian circus coming to town, there was the old advertisement of Hollywood on Ice worn thin by a year's exposure but still bright enough to catch the eye. My eye, anyway. I turn my bike around the cone for the final time and in doing so turn my back on the poster for good. As I do, I notice one more thing. In the overgrown lot next to the poster, a kickball field slowly begins to unfold. An invisible little girl with lopsided pigtails waves to me, smiling, a red rubber ball rolling toward her. The last few miles of the bike segment are usually tiresome and lethargic, but today there is a little more to give despite the wind that tries to take everything from me. Kick it, kick it, kick it . . .

Transition 2 finds me in seventh place, two women having passed me on the bike, but today my competitive fire takes a backseat to my purpose in being there. Today, seventh is okay. I'll try to hold my place on the run. Off come the bike shoes and the helmet, on go the Asics, and my body heads out onto the four-lap run course.

I breathe funny when I run. Loud and noisy, as though I'm about to hyperventilate and pass out, only I don't. The problem stems back to a deviated septum, a hereditary blockage of cartilage wedged inside the intricate passages of my nasal cavity. It is not visible from the outside, and the deviated septum just hides out up there like Casper in the attic of my nose. Only about 25 percent of my oxygen gets in through my nose, the rest coming in through my mouth, which also serves as the necessary exit door, thus creating a very busy respiratory system. When I race, I sound like an obscene crank caller and look like a gruesome Halloween mask with gooky plasma oozing from various facial orifices. I am not a pretty racer and I have the action photos to prove it: my hair a lump of sweaty dreadlocks, salt stains running down my leg from the urine that has dried there, snot covering my nose and lips with the crusty determination of burnt lasagna on an aluminum pan. Although getting an operation that would allow me to breathe easier and supply more oxygen to my lungs would be handy indeed, I like the way my body sounds when it is working hard.

I like the gulpy breaths and yarns of spindly saliva that sail over my cheeks and sometimes trail behind me like the handlebar streamers on my old pink Huffy. This is where triathlon differs from figure skating. Though strength, stamina, and power entwine in both sports with similar intensity, rarely do you see a skater pee in the middle of her long program, when the triple jumps get really demanding. Usually there is no snot on the ice (though at Murray's it flew out or swung down from our noses like glorious pendulums of dedication to cold, cold mornings), and never did we spit on the slick surface beneath our feet. Sweat is there in both skating and endurance sports, but makeup is not worn in the latter event and triathletes do not often worry about making sure their mascara is waterproof. What I wouldn't give to see Michelle Kwan pour that bottle of Evian over her head in the kiss-and-cry well at the next world championships. But judges usually don't go for the wet look.

Skaters' four-minute programs are like sprint triathlons with plyometric sessions every few seconds in lieu of transition areas. Spandex covers both types of competitors, though the sequins are left out of Ironman competitions and sometimes replaced by the rosy, crystalline droplets of road rash that sparkle over the skin like bad-ass jewels of physical fortitude. There is a similarity of grace as well as strength, as the beauty of a solid landing edge is like the shape of a solid runner's stride at the height of her momentum.

I breathed just as loud in skating as I do in triathlon, only in skating it was drowned out by Tchaikovsky or Broadway melodies. In triathlon, nothing drowns out the sound of a competitor's approaching

footsteps, the shift of an unseen chain ring, or the determined breath of
a deviated septum. Such are the sounds that become the symphony of
triathlon competition, as these notes play through the mind of an endurance athlete and give persistent rhythm to her grueling journey.

Out of T2, up the road, past the spectators . . . now my head can
rest, now my mind can think of why it is here, and my body can do what
it came to do here in Argentina. Make peace with a memory that once
said *you can't*. Usually I just run, but today thoughts flow through my
head of their own accord, racing wherever they choose, free from the
Plankton of the past.

The foreign language of cheering fans dies down, and as the course
stretches through a less-populated road, the endorphins come forth like
Thoreau, sauntering over the hills and valleys of my bloodstream. What
do I think about when I run? Love comes to mind. I love everything
when I race. I love the muscles that swimming has rippled through my
back, now strong enough to shrug off whatever burdens try to crawl on.
I love my calves, indented with determination and the repetition of
sport. I love my stomach, strong on the outside and now even stronger
within. I even love Hollywood on Ice, for showing me who I really am.

I think about the last three years of triathlon, about the finish lines
I've crossed and those that lie ahead in all the Sundays yet to come. Two
Ironman races, six Half Ironmans, one world duathlon championship,
two southwest collegiate championship titles as a graduate student at the
University of Arizona, and more than forty Olympic and sprint distance
races combined. How I love this sport in which calories are viewed as energy and the more we eat, the faster our bodies can go. I think about
Felicia's letters, always asking if I'm eating enough. Enough for four, I
tell her — swimming, biking, running, but most important, for myself. I
think about Ironman Lake Placid, where the transition area was set up
in the backyard of the very rink where I spent all my summers training
for figure skating. The race had a mandatory weigh-in, and I think about
the panicky nerves that wanted me to run away from that scale, as it had
been four years since I had stepped on one. Mount Everest seemed easier to summit than that small, tin platform. But I did it. In this sport, not
weighing enough is frowned upon, not applauded.

I think of my own crowd who came to watch me become an

Ironman: my parents (Dad took split times, Mom compared the bodies of spandexed athletes; both enjoyed the day immensely), two steadfast high school friends, my muscle-healing massage therapist, and the best surprise of all, my brother. Peter — who had once barely been able to sit through a two-minute skating program — and his amazing wife, Sarah, who came to cheer me on from start to finish in a 140-mile race that lasted over eleven hours. He even made a sign with posterboard and Magic Markers that spelled GO KATHERIN! I knew whom he meant. At mile eleven of the marathon, my father reached out to give me a high-five. His arch is perfect, the follow-through steady. *Good job,* we cheer to each other, *you can do it!*

I think about the USATriathlon newsletter that came in the mail a few weeks ago and the tingly feeling that washed over me when I saw *All-American* next to my name. I think about the local swim company, which asked me to model for its competitive swimsuit catalog because it wanted athletes to represent AgonSwim, not stick figures barely able to make it through a lap. Circle *that,* I think. I send my mother a catalog. And a pen. My father tells me she has dog-eared some pages in approval. A good start.

I think about my feet — that there is something beautiful about the fact that I have only six toenails, the others have fallen off from athletic perseverance. Toenails are all that I allow my body to lose these days. I think about Lisa, my eating-disorder therapist in Tucson who worked with me for two and a half years after the tour. She helped me to cry for the loss of old dreams, and then showed me how to feed the new ones. When food and hope were too difficult to swallow and the Plankton seemed too overwhelming, it was Lisa who looked me straight in the eye and asked with the sharpest gentleness, *Do you want to be an athlete or not?* This was my checkpoint question, my lifeline through any dark and gooey days, and I ate my meals in silent chants of *yes,* brushing away tears until the day came that none spilled down at all. I think about the steak I'll have tonight after the race.

I think about Captain Graceful, wearing her new cape of indestructibility and how lucky I am to have her at my side. I think about the kids I coach at the Tucson Figure Skating Club. Mondays through Fridays I am a choreographer; I move other people's bodies into the positions of grace I see in their music. On Tuesdays I coach power skating, thinking of something Emerson once said—"In skating over thin ice, our safety is in our speed." I show my athletes how to push their bodies and enhance their endurance, keeping quiet that what I'm actually trying to build is their confidence. They'll find that out on their own someday. I think of Murray's.

During the last few draining miles of the run, I think of the first time I saw this race, a lifetime ago. There was no energy or confidence in my body that afternoon, but today I have a surplus of both and I marvel at the glorious rewards of time, patience, and progress. What the human body can endure under the spell of a peaceable mind is almost as remarkable as the merciless pressures we so often put on ourselves. I think of that "happiness right here, right now" philosophy that Pam and I once discussed in the trailer, and how today—in the midst of seventy miles of sore muscles, stomach cramps, throbbing knees, and fiery temperatures—I have found my eudaemonia.

Finally, I think of the finish. Today's finish, anyway. This is far from my last triathlon. The mighty coastal wind has sapped my strength and everything about the Mar del Plata Half Ironman will feel best when it is done. The swim tossed me around like a piece of helpless kelp, the men's winner lapped me twice on the bike, and the run took me and my cranky intestines an hour longer than usual to complete. I think of the newest lesson learned, that my slowest time and my best race can actually occur on the same day. When I make it to the line, there are no open arms awaiting me, only ghosts. But I can feel their congratulatory embrace. *You did it,* they whisper, then vanish forever.

There are no shouts of personal glory or tears of emotion at the finish, just my own raspy exhales of completion. There is no flag waving or medal kissing; triathlon is beautifully humble. I take a moment to look around the race site, but not for anything in particular. Maybe just to make sure that I am really here. The sea is calming down. Some clouds are rolling in. A few athletes are wheeling their bikes and equipment out of the transition area. The air smells like approaching rain and leftover athleticism, and I can hear the *scrrch, scrrch* of a street sweeper cleaning away the race debris. I finish in seventh place. Today it feels like gold. It feels like Sunday. Like greatness.

Epilogue

One of skating's greatest gifts is that it never truly leaves its athletes. I can see this now, as I have peeled back the layers of the professional experience to let my other memories of skating breathe again. Recently, the urge to skate has presented itself quietly inside my body, showing up within my thoughts when I least expect it. The passion to skate hits hardest when I am away from the ice and the feeling comes to me through music. Sometimes it is a song on the radio, something that I skated to in the past, or an old mixed tape in the car stereo, when suddenly I notice that one of my hands has strayed from the steering wheel to roll its wrist and fingers along with the emotion of the music. I keep my eyes on the road, but my limbs become so moved that I let them do just that.

At home, I have done axels in my kitchen when no one else is looking, in the imaginary arena that appears between the sink and the fridge. I have unloaded the dishwasher in time to my old short program, spiraling plates into cupboards, waltz-jumping groceries onto shelves when music surrounds my senses. I have curtsied to the toaster oven, and in the chrome reflection of the teakettle tarnished with a thousand water spots, I have seen an audience roaring with applause. I go to watch the tours of current champions and past legends who sometimes skate their way into my city in southwestern Arizona, always bringing a friend along so that during laybacks and spread eagles and poses of grace I can lean over and whisper, *I could do that, once.* When the Olympians do their triples, I repeat my statement beginning with the word *wish.* Sometimes I say nothing at all and just watch the path of the spotlight's beam and the glow of the skater within until I am sure I can feel the memory of its warmth.

At the rink in Tucson, sometimes I sneak onto the ice in the early afternoon when the young figure skaters are still in school and the emptiness of the rink is all mine. My legs feel the tightness of the forty-mile bike ride from that morning, my arms are heavy with the loving ache of swim practice, and my feet know that a run is scheduled in the near evening, but for the next few minutes my triathlon future yields to my skating past. The feel of the ice in Tucson is the same as it once was long ago in another rink, and my blades find comfort in its consistency. I put on music and wait for the sound to move my body. I linger through each note, the past seeping out through quiet movements. Though so many years have gone by, grace comes back to me as though it has been waiting patiently all along. Or maybe I have come back to grace. Either way, it knows I am there. *I wished for skating, the kind I used to know.* We will always know where to find each other.

Acknowledgments

David Halpern, my amazingly gifted and angelically patient agent; Asya Muchnick, my champion editor (aka Captain Chopchop), whose kind manner and incredible style made cutting 155 pages so much easier; Steve Lamont, the great guru of copyediting; and Shannon Byrne, for her immeasurable promotion work: thank you for taking a chance on a twenty-five-year-old nobody whose biggest dream in life was to be somebody. You're my unmeltable Ice Capades. And special thanks to Michael Pietsch, Emily Takoudes, Lindsay Berra, Gary Hoenig, Ken Baker, Fred Busch, Leila Philip, and Emi Yamaya for giving me my writing start.

The following people have, knowingly or not, shaped my life far beyond the categories of writing and athleticism. "Thank you" hardly covers it.

Linda Kellett Belger, the Litz team, Bibi Zillmer, Michele Buragas, Fred Kohler, Robin Baldwin, Meredith Sweeney, Murray's Rink and the YFSC kids/coaches of 1985–93, Danielle Schade, Tara Shedlosky, Heather Dobbins, Lisa Peterson, and of course Valley Dreisbach 'n' The Sophomores. Gary Ross, Coleman Brown, Anthony Aveni, John Hubbard, Don Vaughn, and Jean, the angelic keeper of Colgate's Frank Dining Hall who always asked "And how is your skating going?" as well as Rich Mok, for designing my web site. Also Vinny Ventura, Bill Kruse, Alison Hawthorne Deming, Sarah Collum Bertine, Lisa King, the kids at the Tucson FSC, Jimmy Riccitello. My love and thanks to Tyler Van Pelt, and of course Felicia Hopkinson, whose steady, solid friendship saved me from being even more of a nutcase than I already am.

Finally, a big thank-you to my family. Especially my dad, who taught me to be proud of my strength, my writing, and whatever endeavor I ever attempted. Like the kid in the drug commercial used to say, "I learned it by watching you." Thank you for teaching by example. I love you. Whenever you need a ride to the boathouse, I'll be there.

Special thanks to my current triathlon sponsors: TriSports.com, CarbBOOM, and Active.com (Breathe Right, Egg Beaters, Road ID) as well as my past sponsors, Splashworks and Performance Footwear. And my coach, Siri Lindley, who is the best role model Captain Graceful could have ever hoped for.

About the Author

Kathryn Bertine is a former professional figure skater and currently competes as an elite triathlete. She graduated from Colgate University in 1997 and holds an MFA in nonfiction writing from the University of Arizona. Her essays have appeared in numerous publications, most recently in *ESPN: The Magazine, Triathlete, Inside Triathlon,* and *Us Weekly.* She grew up in Bronxville, New York, and now resides in Boulder, Colorado, with her two young houseplants and pet computer. *All the Sundays Yet to Come* is her first book. For more information, please visit the author's web site at www.kathrynbertine.com.